T0382944

Measuring and Improving Performance

Information Technology Applications
in Lean Systems

Measuring and Improving Performance

Information Technology Applications in Lean Systems

James William Martin

CRC Press
Taylor & Francis Group
Boca Raton   London   New York

CRC Press is an imprint of the
Taylor & Francis Group, an **informa** business

CRC Press
Taylor & Francis Group
6000 Broken Sound Parkway NW, Suite 300
Boca Raton, FL 33487-2742

Library of Congress Cataloging-in-Publication Data

Martin, James William.
    Measuring and improving performance : information technology applications in lean systems / James William Martin.
        p. cm.
    Includes bibliographical references and index.
    ISBN 978-1-4200-8418-4 (hardcover : alk. paper)
    1. Project management. 2. Information technology. I. Title.

HD69.P75M373 2010
658.4'01--dc22

2009024477

Visit the Taylor & Francis Web site at
http://www.taylorandfrancis.com

and the CRC Press Web site at
http://www.crcpress.com

Contents

SECTION 2 PROCESS IMPROVEMENT METHODS

Preface

In an era of globalization, in which supply-chain functions are scattered across the world, measuring operational performance can be difficult. In fact, in the absence of measurement baselines, process improvements are often difficult or impossible to implement. In many situations, an organization may have a great amount of data locked up within its information technology (IT) systems, but it is unable to synthesize or use the data to improve its process workflows. Also, in many organizations there is often little synergy between an organization's IT and operational systems. Our goal must be to make IT systems flexible by integrating them in ways to make them more responsive to external demand and the immediate capacity constraints of an operational system. In other words, IT can be intelligently and even elegantly employed to simplify, standardize, and integrate the components of disparate IT and operational systems to create processes that dynamically respond to changes of customer demand within the limits of internal and external capacity constraints.

Many books have been written to describe methods to develop and deploy IT systems. These include the creation and management of software and hardware systems, as well as their features and functions within the context of measuring and improving operational performance. This has been an evolving process within many organizations over the past several decades. In many applications, IT deployment efforts have been very successful in both manufacturing and service systems. This is a well-known fact that is evident to anyone using a personal computer, the Internet, or one of the many excellent workflow management tools to help manage the flow of information through operational systems. Some of these books have become classics within the IT community. They are also listed in the Suggested Reading sections of each chapter. Examples include Brooks's *The Mythical Man-Month*, DeMarco and Lister's *Peopleware: Productive Projects and Teams*, Schwaber's *Agile Project Management with Scrum*, Hunt and Thomas's *The Pragmatic Programmer: From Journeyman to Master*, and Fowler's *Refactoring: Improving the Design of Existing Code*. The authors provide practical advice for creating software, and managing its development and commercialization activities. A common goal is to reduce the development cycle time of software projects to improve the overall effectiveness and efficiency of managing, creating, deploying, and maintaining software code. In this context, effectiveness is defined as doing the right work, and efficiency is doing the right work the right way.

However, from another perspective, the basic concepts, tools, and methods of Lean systems are also relevant to improving process effectiveness and efficiency. A major focus of this book, therefore, is to discuss the synergy gained from using best-in-class software management design and project management methods within Lean systems. In Chapter 5 we will learn some basic Lean concepts and then show how they can be used within systems that are heavily dependent on IT. From a Lean perspective, some relevant sources of information include Goldratt and Cox's *The Goal: A Process of Ongoing Improvement,* Suri's *Quick Response Manufacturing: A Companywide Approach to Reducing Lead Times,* and Womack and Jones's *Lean Thinking: Banish Waste and Create Wealth in Your Organization.* These books are also listed in the Suggested Reading section of Chapter 5. Our approach will be to link these diverse initiatives and concepts using three perspectives: project management, the efficient development of software code, and the application of both to improve the effectiveness and efficiency of Lean systems using IT. The project management perspective will use the concepts, tools, and methods of Agile Project Management (APM) with scrum. Some key titles include Augustine's *Managing Agile Projects* and Schwaber's *Agile Project Management with Scrum.* The perspective related to the efficient design of software and how it relates to Lean concepts will be discussed within the context of Hunt and Thomas's *The Pragmatic Programmer,* Fowler's *Refactoring,* and similar sources. Finally, the third key perspective, improving the effectiveness and efficiency of Lean systems, will be discussed based on several key authors, including those mentioned earlier. Many of these books are listed as suggested reading in more than one chapter.

The goal is to discuss these perspectives and show how they can be used synergistically to integrate IT applications within the operational systems of Lean organizations. The discussion will focus on two major areas. First, IT applications should be deployed within organizations to increase their flexibility in responding to external demand within the constraints of available resources. In other words, IT applications should be deployed effectively and efficiently to help achieve the goals of a Lean enterprise. Agile Project Management with scrum and related project management methods will be integral to these discussions. Second, to the extent that IT systems currently exist within an organization, it may be possible to modify them to accelerate the deployment of Lean systems to improve operational performance. Modifications to current IT systems are often necessary to make them more useful in a Lean work environment. This is because they represent a heavy investment in infrastructure and cannot be easily replaced due to high capital costs, or they may be necessary for practical reasons. An example of the latter situation is the use of a manufacturing resource planning II (MRPII) system to manage and control the manufacturing of thousands of products. An MRPII system or module converts independent demand from a master production schedule (MPS) using bill of material (BOM), inventory file, and related information to calculate the quantities of dependent-demand items. These dependent demand items are then ordered from suppliers or manufactured by an organization's production facilities. However, an MRPII module can be decoupled at lower levels to make it more responsive to changes in external demand and available resources to mimic, to some degree, a pull production system at a work-cell level. At higher levels of a BOM, however, the MRPII module can still coordinate production activities throughout a supply chain. It is through this type of out-of-the-box thinking that leading-edge concepts can help to integrate IT applications to facilitate the deployment of Lean systems. I wrote this book because I believe it will be useful to show how IT can support Lean applications in both manufacturing and service systems to increase their productivity.

I thank my editor, the late Raymond O'Connell, for encouraging me to publish this book, as well as the reviewers of the book who made constructive comments that changed its direction to a more practical and hands-on approach. I also thank my son, Paul, a computer science student attending Johns Hopkins University (class of 2011) for reading several key chapters in this book for their technical content. I also thank my daughter, Krysta, a student at Emory University School of Law and my wife, Marsha, for their support as well as several of my professional friends. These people include Peri Kaae, Manager of Process Improvement, Florence Woo, Linc Markham, and William Johnson. I also want to thank Elaine Kowansky and Ram Josyula, formerly of General Electric and who are now owners of Gelrad Consulting. Finally, I thank my graduate students and clients, who have provided the inspiration for this book.

Introduction

> Once we rid ourselves of traditional thinking we can get on with creating the future.
>
> **—James Bertrand**

This book has been written for Lean and Six Sigma practitioners to help them understand some of the important concepts related to the creation or modification of software to support process management and improvement activities in Lean systems. In other words, it is not a reference for programmers but is intended instead as a source of information for Lean practitioners who have been assigned the responsibility of creating a new information technology (IT) application; improving the performance of an existing IT application; or integrating an IT application within an operational system to improve its performance relative to time, quality, or cost.

Many operational systems are now global and globalization has been evolving over the past several decades. This evolutionary process has been described by several authors and particularly in the books *Why Globalization Works* by Martin Wolf and *Adam Smith in Beijing: Lineages of the 21st Century* by Giovanni Arrighi. These authors describe the impact of globalization on business organizations as well as societies in general. In support of these globalization concepts and framework, I write from an operational perspective with a focus on increasing organizational productivity through the application of IT to improve Lean production systems. In the synthesis of the critical ideas put forth by these and other authors, my goal has been to develop a conceptual framework from which to move Lean systems to their next level across the various countries and cultures who are participants of global supply chains, which often consist of combinations of service and manufacturing processes. In other words, as the world has globalized and evolved into service economies, the need to develop and deploy IT to increase operational efficiency and, in turn, organizational productivity has become more critical. These topics are especially important in a world that has come to rely on increasingly higher levels of productivity to maintain its standard of living in an environment of increasing resource constraints.

However, although an organization's goal is to improve its overall operational efficiency, improvement activities must begin at lower levels to ensure that operational systems are designed to efficiently respond to changing customer requirements as well as customers' evolving value expectations. This work must be able to be done anywhere in the world. Therefore the operational systems that are supported by IT must also be designed to simultaneously service customers of many different countries, languages, and cultures. For example, every day and in a routine manner, service workers in the United States, India, China, and many other locations around the world interact through common workflow systems. These workflow systems consist of many diverse functions, and may also support several different languages in diverse cultural and political environments. For example, workflow systems routinely manage the operational systems that create and manufacture products and services. The ordering and shipment of computers, consumer electronics, and books are typical examples of global workflows that touch many diverse customers. Global workflows also help manage the internal day-to-day operations of numerous organizations. Examples include managing accounts payables, receivables, and similar financial functions of an organization.

In response to these types of organizational needs, diverse IT applications have been successfully deployed across global supply chains using a variety of project management methodologies. As an example, if a deployment's goal was to create a major software and hardware product, then classical project management methods such as the IBM® Rational Unified Process (RUP)®, which are designed to manage large and complex projects, might have been successfully used by an organization. However, if modifications to a current IT system were required or smaller IT project applications needed to be managed, then perhaps Agile Project Management (APM) with scrum methods were used to ensure that a project met its schedule, cost, and performance targets. Although management of IT projects can be complicated, overly complex project management methods need to be avoided in favor of choosing the best set of management methods to ensure a project's success. In this context, several excellent sources of information include *Peopleware: Productive Projects and Teams* by DeMarco and Lister and *The Mythical Man-Month* by Brooks. These classical references describe key elements of IT project management, including common fallacies related to team formation and resource management. They also show how to improve a project's effectiveness and efficiency using proven tools and methods. A major goal of this book is to improve IT management relative to its impact on Lean systems. Related goals are the efficient design and deployment of software as well as the application of these concepts to improve a Lean system. We will integrate these concepts with those discussed in other sources such as the suggested readings at the end of every chapter. A key vehicle to achieve the goal of effective project management will be an in-depth discussion of APM and scrum in the context of Lean IT project management, as well as Lean concepts and applications. *Managing Agile Projects* by Augustine and *Agile Project Management with Scrum* by Schwaber are excellent references that describe APM and scrum. Software

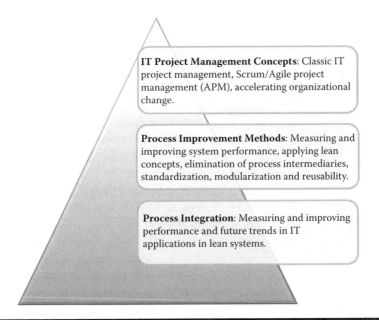

Figure I.1   Focus of the book.

design principles will also be discussed in the context of their Lean analogues. The discussion of Lean applications will build on these key concepts.

This book is divided into three major parts, as shown in Figure I.1, consisting of eight chapters. The first part consists of two chapters that discuss classic IT and APM project management methods. This information is important because IT applications in Lean systems can easily go off track, resulting in a longer project implementation cycle time and higher costs. We will discuss two project management methods that have been shown to be very successful in practice. These will include elements of classical project management as well as RUP, and then APM with scrum. Understanding the strengths of these approaches can make project management more effective. As an example, large-scale projects that create and deploy complex hardware and software systems usually require a higher degree of project structure because the team participants are numerous and are often scattered across geographically dispersed work locations. Also, there are many hardware and software subsystems that must be created, integrated, tested, and deployed in an integrated manner to ensure they will interface and function correctly in a final product. In contrast, the creation and deployment of small- to moderate-size IT system applications, or modifications to current systems, are usually best implemented using APM with scrum. APM methods require that a system's functionality be produced at frequent intervals using activity backlogs and scrum sprints. The expectation of customers and key stakeholders is that over weeks or months their requirements will be met. In some IT applications a combination of both project management methodologies may also be useful. In summary, APM with scrum can be used at a project work activity level either as a standalone project management strategy or within an RUP project management structure.

In the second part of this book, tools and methods useful for process improvement are discussed in Chapters 3, 4, 5, and 6. The topics include accelerating organizational change, translating customer requirements, applying Lean concepts, and creating and deploying software to support Lean systems. The major goal of these chapters is to move from the discussion of project management to an important discussion associated with the capture of customer needs and requirements, and to translate these requirements into specifications. The discussion of Lean topics in Chapter 5 is necessary to provide context for the various IT topics that are being discussed to show the similarities of each approach. The information contained within Chapter 6 is designed to provide Lean practitioners with some understanding of key topics important to the creation of software code. This information may be useful either when Lean practitioners assist IT teams or if they require the assistance of IT professionals to implement Lean systems within their process workflows.

Chapters 7 and 8 complete the third part of this book. Chapter 7 contains examples from manufacturing and service industries that integrate classical Lean tools and methods with various IT applications. Chapter 8 discusses the measurement and improvement of Lean systems within a Lean environment. The unifying concept of Chapter 8 is process integration. Process integration is discussed relative to sharing information using performance dashboards and the global integration of IT systems in support of operations.

Project Management Methods

Table I.1 describes several project management methods used to manage the creation, modification, and deployment of software. Several of these project management methods use, with some modifications, common tools and methods. Most people are familiar with classical project management, which is a set of formal tools and methods used to plan and manage resources to achieve goals and objectives within schedule and budget. These tools and methods include project charters, activity scheduling charts (Gantt charts), issue lists, and similar methods to capture customer requirements and manage project resources to achieve a project's schedule, cost, and performance targets. Additional tools and methods include work breakdown structure (WBS) charts as well as stakeholder and risk analysis tools. There are many other tools, methods, and templates used to manage projects in a classical sense, and several of these will be discussed in Chapter 1.

The Waterfall Model is the second project management method listed in Table I.1. This model has fallen into general disuse because it employs a sequential software development process in which client requirements and their translation

Table I.1 IT Project Management Methods

Method	Major Characteristics
Classical project management	A set of formal tools and methods used to plan and manage resources to achieve goals and objectives within schedule and budget. Typical tools and methods include project charters, Gantt charts, a work breakdown structure (WBS), and stakeholder and risk analyses.
Waterfall Model	A sequential software development process in which client requirements and their translation into software code is developed in sequence using seven phases: obtaining client requirements, software code design, construction, integration of software modules, testing and error correction, client installation, and subsequent maintenance of the software product. All activities are completed within their phase prior to moving to the next phase.
IBM® Rational Unified Process (RUP)	A software development process that emphasizes development of code in iterations, which balance stakeholder requirements through high collaboration across teams. The process is divided into four phases: inception, elaboration, construction, and transition. Major methods include requirements analysis, building and modeling software code through implementation, and testing. Related project management methods include managing risk and resources according to the project's schedule and cost targets. Key tools include an assessment at each software development milestone (iteration), project status metrics, a list of issues and problems, work orders to delegate work task activities, and periodic project reviews.
Lean project management	A set of formal tools and methods that translate customer value elements into a process to identify non-value-adding work tasks to simplify, standardize, and mistake-proof a process. The emphasis is on hands-on and highly visible data collection and analysis.
Agile Project Management (APM)	A set of methods that emphasize the rapid delivery of working software code to clients using small collocated and self-organizing teams that have daily contact with their clients and other key stakeholders.

continued

Table I.1 (continued)   IT Project Management Methods

Method	Major Characteristics
Agile Unified Process (AUP)	Uses agile project methods in the context of the Rational Unified Process with an emphasis on the use of a development release for quality assurance testing and a subsequent production release. Documentation that is not integrated within software code is kept simple and only used as necessary.
Scrum	A project management approach to running software projects using practices and predefined roles and responsibilities to conduct "sprints" having a duration of 15 to 20 days to complete useable software code. Activities include highly interactive client and other stakeholder involvement. Typical methods include scrum meetings, activity backlogs, and sprint backlogs.
Extreme Programming (EP)	A set of methods that attempt to create an initial solution to client requirements that is simple and testable. In fact, requirements are written directly in the form of automated tests, which must be passed at each integration of code development. Code is written and tested by the client and team, and additional product functionality is added only when necessary using an incremental approach. Typical methods include pair programming, test-driven code development, incremental releases of code, and adherence to standard coding standards.

into specifications and software code is sequentially developed using seven phases. These phases are obtaining client requirements, the design of software code, its construction, the integration of software algorithms and modules, software testing and error correction, client installation, and subsequent maintenance of the software product. Since all project activities must be completed within their current phase prior to moving to the next phase, project cycle times tend to be longer than if APM with scrum or other methods were used as a project management framework. Another way to think of the Waterfall methodology is that completed work activities are thrown "over the fence" to the next project team. In contrast, APM with scrum and several other project management methods facilitate working concurrently across teams to improve a project's coordination and communication to enable a higher degree of project management and control. Concurrent implies that project teams communicate in parallel to provide clear visibility of a project's status relative to its ongoing or completed work activities. A Waterfall project management approach also increases a project's cycle time and costs and results in lower quality levels, as opposed to using a concurrent approach that engages team members, customers, and suppliers on a frequent basis.

IBM developed the RUP to deploy complicated hardware and software systems as one answer to the many issues surrounding classic project management and Waterfall methods. RUP is designed for the project management of new hardware and software systems that create new features and functions. In this context, new user requirements are translated into hardware and software systems that span numerous project teams. In other words, RUP was created to support the creation of new and complex IT architecture. RUP is a software development process using a project management approach that emphasizes the development of software code in discrete iterations. This approach attempts to balance stakeholder requirements by promoting a high degree of collaboration across teams. Key stakeholders, including various organizational functions, suppliers, and customers, have an interest in a project's ongoing work activities, resource requirements, and goal achievement. Key characteristics of the RUP project management approach include the continuous adaptation of project management methodologies in response to customer needs, the balancing of key stakeholder priorities, a focus on the quality of written software code, team communication, concurrent collaboration, and proving that customer requirements (regarding new and useful features and algorithm functions) are met on a frequent basis. This is in contrast to waiting until close to the end of a project to conduct full system testing. Another useful characteristic of RUP methodology is its focus on elevating the abstraction level of software coding. It should also be noted that this is a common best-in-class practice of modern software design. An elevation of a system's abstraction level will be discussed within the context of APM and scrum in Chapter 6, because this is one of many ways to improve the efficiency of creating standardized and flexible software code.

RUP is divided into four phases: product inception, elaboration, construction, and transition. In the inception phase of a project, the expected resources and their costs, which are based on estimated work activities, are compared to budgeted amounts to ensure that a project, as currently defined, will meet its financial objectives. If a project is over budget, then redesign of a product and its work activities may be necessary, or the project's budget may need to be increased prior to proceeding to its next phase. In the elaboration phase, a product's basic concept and requirements are created and developed as defined by its features and functions. This detail includes customer and stakeholder requirements, use cases, and examples of software architecture and prototypes, which show how the required product features and functions will be achieved within the constraints of a project's resources and with an acceptable level of risk. Prior to leaving the elaboration phase, a business plan for a project should be revised based on available information regarding product testing and other performance requirements. In the construction phase of a project, software code is created and a product's features and functions are fully developed and tested. If a project is large and complex, then subteams will be testing their portions of the software code in a concurrent manner and then sharing testing information on an ongoing basis with other teams. In the final phase of a project, the completed product is deployed to the end user or customer (if external to an organization) and its performance is monitored over time to ensure it meets user requirements. Specific RUP project management methods include requirements analysis, building and modeling software code through its implementation, testing, and managing risk and resources according to a project's schedule and cost targets. Key tools include an assessment at each software development milestone (iteration), project status metrics, a list of issues and problems, work orders to delegate work task activities, and periodic project reviews. The RUP project management method will be discussed in more detail in Chapter 1.

Lean project management is a set of formal tools and methods that translate customer requirements into value-adding (VA) work tasks. This translation information is also used to identify non-value-adding (NVA) work tasks that are not aligned with customer requirements. A major goal of the Lean methodology is to eliminate NVA work activities from a process and then to simplify, standardize, and mistake-proof the remaining work tasks. The emphasis of a Lean project management approach includes hands-on and highly visible data collection and analysis activities, which are used to improve process workflows (including project management work activities) as applicable. With respect to the management of IT projects, Lean concepts have been either developed independently or extracted from commonly available Lean practices and then modified to make them more effective in the management and control of IT projects. APM with scrum is an excellent example of how Lean concepts are analogous to those developed and adapted for use in the management of IT projects. We will discuss Lean methods in Chapter 5 and then use this information in Chapters 6, 7, and 8 to provide a framework for the measurement and improvement of Lean systems using IT.

APM is a project management methodology that emphasizes linking all work activities via an activity backlog to customer requirements and then into a system's features and functions. An activity backlog is broken down into sets of work activities. These work activities are designed to create discrete components of functionality using scrum sprints. The goal of this work breakdown is a rapid delivery of working software code to clients. An advantage of using APM with scrum is that software code is reviewed and tested at frequent intervals. The project management portion of APM is managed using small self-organizing teams that have daily contact with their clients and other key stakeholders. We will discuss APM with scrum in Chapter 2.

The Agile Unified Process (AUP) uses APM methods and scrum in the context of RUP. The goal of AUP is the immediate and frequent use of newly designed software code for quality assurance testing and the subsequent production release of software. In AUP, documentation that is not integrated within software code is kept simple and only used as necessary. This approach helps to ensure that a project's management framework and associated work activities can be simplified to make them more flexible. In contrast to RUP, AUP uses a reduced set of project management methodologies and disciplines. These include obtaining customer requirements to build an accurate model, creating executable software code to make a model operational, and testing the software code at frequent intervals. In summary, the AUP project management methods use APM with scrum within an RUP framework.

Scrum is a project management approach to running software projects using agile management practices, including the use of predefined roles and responsibilities to conduct sprints. Sprints have a typical duration of 15 to 20 days and they are designed to produce useable software code. Scrum activities include highly interactive client and stakeholder involvement using scrum review meetings as well as activity and sprint backlogs. Lean practitioners will recognize that scrum methods embody several basic Lean concepts. It should be noted that scrum has also developed a culture of its own including acronyms used to describe its project management process and activities. For instance, a project manager on a scrum team is called a scrum master, and a project WBS is arranged as an activity backlog and executed using sprints. Scrum also divides people into two groups. The first group, or the project team that is doing the work, has a direct relationship to building software code versus the second group of stakeholders that reviews a project's status, and newly created and tested software code. An analogy is often used by scrum teams that names the people who are committed to writing software code as the "pigs" and other people such as stakeholders or support people as the "chickens." The pigs are committed to a project, but the chickens are not. Scrum project methods will be discussed further in Chapter 2.

Extreme Programming (EP) is a set of software development methods that create an initial solution to client requirements that is simple and testable. Client requirements are written directly in the form of automated tests, which must be successfully completed as key components of software code are developed. In this project management methodology, software code is written by a team and tested by the client. Additional product functionality is added only when necessary, using an incremental approach. Typical methods used in EP include pair programming, test-driven code development, incremental releases of code, and adherence to standard coding standards. In this way, EP shares many of the features of APM and scrum project management methods. EP also recommends starting with the simplest possible software design and then only adding additional features and functions when they are necessary to meet customer requirements. In summary, EP represents a set of software design principles used to design and test software code. However, one disadvantage of using EP methodology in isolation rather than using a more holistic project management and control methodology is that project documentation is not reinforced in EP. In complicated projects this may result in inaccurate or imprecise software requirements.

The goal of this book is to integrate key features of these diverse project management methods and apply them to accelerate the creation and deployment of software and hardware to support Lean systems. This goal is illustrated in Figure I.2.

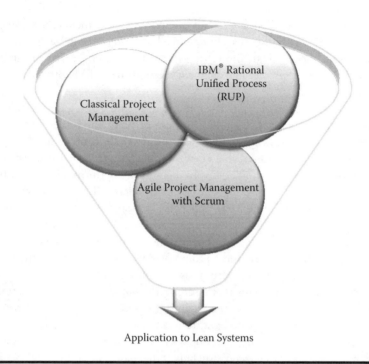

Application to Lean Systems

Figure I.2   Integration of successful project management methods.

In the subsequent chapters of this book, the emphasis will be on the modification of IT systems to improve operational productivity. Specifically, we will focus on an integration of classical, RUP, and APM with scrum methods within Lean environments. In addition to our discussion of IT applications within Lean environments, we will review common IT applications at several hierarchal levels within a business organization from both a manufacturing and service system perspective. These hierarchal levels are shown in Table I.2 as a collection of one or more IT systems that integrate several functions across one or more organizations to create an enterprisewide system. At the next lower organizational level, a system integrates one or several process workflows. Examples of these systems include purchase-to-pay processes that span several organizations, finance and accounting systems, procurement systems, materials planning systems, distribution requirements systems, and forecasting systems. At the third level are process workflows. A process workflow is an integrated set of operational work tasks that are coordinated to produce one type of work product. Examples include account payables, account receivables, procurement, customer support, and other focused business functions. Milestone activities are a combination of operations that when completed produce a measurable unit of system functionality. These milestones may include process workflows such as invoicing clients, managing invoices, and receiving and recording payment of an invoice within an accounts payable system. Each of these milestones consists of one or several work

Table I.2   Hierarchal Levels of Process Analysis

Hierarchal Level	Description
Enterprise	A collection of one or more information technology (IT) systems that integrate several functions across one or more organizations. Examples include systems that manage purchase-to-pay across several businesses and their suppliers and customers.
System	An integrated process that manages one organizational function across one or more business units. Examples include finance and accounting, procurement, materials planning, distribution requirements, and forecasting.
Process workflow	A set of operational work tasks coordinated to produce one type of work product. Examples would be account payables, account receivables, procurement, customer support, and other business functions.
Milestone activity	A combination of operations that when completed produce a measurable unit of system functionality. Components include portions of a process workflow such as invoicing clients, managing invoices, and receiving and recording payment of an invoice. Each of these components consists of one or more operations.
Operation	A combination of several work tasks that provide similar work within a process workflow.
Work task	A combination of work elements that are organized to provide a single unit of work, such as completing a form, answering a request for information, and providing a report.
Work element	A component of a work task consisting of a single action, such as picking up a form, adding information to its data fields, or sending it to a subsequent operation.

operations. A work operation is a combination of several work tasks that provide a single unit of work or work object within a process workflow. Work tasks are a combination of work elements that are organized as an operation. Examples of a single unit of work or work object within an operation may include completing a form, answering a request for information, providing a report, or similar aggregated work tasks. Finally, a work element is a component of a work task consisting of a single action such as picking up a form, adding information to its data fields, or sending it to a subsequent operation for different work to be performed on the work object. IT can be used or modified to increase organizational productivity.

Value Integration

Our goal will be to discuss efficient project management methods to increase the productivity of global supply chains. The focus will be on using IT to increase the operational performance of Lean systems. The enhancement and integration of supply-chain value is characterized in part by a high degree of collaboration between its participants and efficient asset utilizations. In turn, participant collaboration is enhanced by effective team communication as well as the creation of value-adding business relationships. These relationships include organizational frameworks such as joint ventures, partnerships, outsourcing noncore work, and licensing of assets as well as the contracting and disposal of assets as necessary. These activities and their structural frameworks are useful in focusing an organization on its core competencies and reducing risks associated with technology, cost, schedules, customers, laws and regulations, culture, and supply.

Customer value expectations change relative to timeliness, cost, perceived usefulness, performance expectations, and relative importance. To increase the value content of a supply chain, an organization must align its strategies and operations to create products and services that reflect the voice of its customers (VOC) and stakeholders. As a result, an organization's strategy, at an operational level, should reflect several specific activities. These activities include increasing available capacity in a cost-efficient or smart manner to make production operations more flexible. This does not necessarily imply the purchasing of additional facilities, new equipment, and hiring new employees. For example, capacity can be increased and made available as needed through contractual or other business arrangements such as asset sharing. This may be especially true in work environments heavily integrated within IT systems. A common example is call center networks, which are typically geographically dispersed. In these networks, capacity can be easily ramped up or down depending on the external demand placed on a system. IT is also very useful in simplifying and standardizing work through other supply chains by eliminating nonessential functional intermediaries that inhibit the flow of materials and information and NVA work tasks within the remaining activities. An adherence to global standards is also necessary to improve communication and help simplify product and process designs. This is true in today's global supply chains, which consist of organizations containing a high degree of diversity that reflects local employee, supplier, and customer demographics. IT systems can help integrate these diverse supply-chain resources and participants through common process workflows around the world to lower cost and cycle times, and improve quality.

Measuring and improving operational performance within a Lean system can be accelerated by effectively and efficiently deploying IT applications. It will also increase the value content of a supply chain versus its competitors. As a result, its productivity and asset utilizations will become higher. Typical characteristics of high value-adding supply chains include a high degree of product availability through the deployment of effective demand management strategies; a low per-unit transaction cost to drive low costs at all supply-chain levels; and supply chain participants through improved quality, reduced cycle time, and more efficient product and process designs. IT is an important enabler in process design as well as subsequent improvement activities. This is because it helps to eliminate organizational intermediaries as well as NVA work activities. These types of improvements increase asset availability, flexibility, utilization, and efficiency between all participants within a supply chain. In this context, a major focus of this book will be to increase value integration within Lean systems to reduce lead times and costs, and improve quality. In summary, the goal will be to show how IT applications can augment Lean methods to facilitate the consistent delivery of high quality and differentiated products and services.

Suggested Readings

Arrighi, Giovanni. 2007. *Adam Smith in Beijing: Lineages of the Twenty-First Century*. London: Verson.

Augustine, Sanjiv. 2005. *Managing Agile Projects*. Upper Saddle River, NJ: Prentice Hall.

Bossidy, Larry, and Ram Charan (with Charles Burck). 2002. *Execution: The Discipline of Getting Things Done*. New York: Crown Business.

Brooks, Frederick P. Jr. 1995. *The Mythical Man-Month*. Boston: Addison-Wesley.

Davis, Stan, and Christopher Meyer. 1998. *Blur: The Speed of Change in the Connected Economy*. Boston: Addison-Wesley.

DeMarco, Tom, and Timothy Lister. 1999. *Peopleware: Productive Projects and Teams*. New York: Dorset House.

Friedman, Thomas L. 2006. *The World Is Flat*. New York: Farrar, Strauss and Giroux.

Kotter, John P. 1996. *Leading Change*. Boston: Harvard Business School Press.

Martin, James William. 2008. *Operational Excellence: Using Lean Six Sigma to Translate Customer Value through Global Supply Chains*. Boca Raton, FL: Auerbach.

Schwaber, Ken. 2004. *Agile Project Management with Scrum*. Redmond, WA: Microsoft Press.

Wolfe, Martin. 2004. *Why Globalization Works*. New Haven, CT: Yale University Press.

The Author

James W. Martin is president of Six Sigma Integration, Inc., a Lean Six Sigma consulting firm in Rehoboth, Massachusetts, and is the author of *Lean Six Sigma for the Office*; *Operational Excellence: Using Lean Six Sigma to Translate Customer Value through Global Supply Chains*; and *Lean Six Sigma for Supply Chain Management: The 10-Step Solution Process*. As a Lean Six Sigma consultant and Master Black Belt for 15 years, Martin has trained and mentored more than 2,000 executives, deployment champions, Master Black Belts, Black Belts, Green Belts, and Lean practitioners in Lean Six Sigma methods including supply chain applications. As part of this consulting work, he led successful Lean Six Sigma assessments and deployments across Japan, China, Korea, Singapore, Malaysia, Thailand, Australia, North America, and Europe. This work included organizations in retail sales, residential and commercial service, banking, insurance, financial services, measurement systems, aerospace component manufacturing, electronic manufacturing, controls, building products, industrial equipment, and consumer products. He has also served as an instructor at Providence College's Graduate School of Business since 1988, where he teaches courses in operations research, operations management, and economic forecasting, as well as related quantitative subjects. He counsels MBA candidates from government organizations and leading corporations. Martin holds an MS in mechanical engineering, Northeastern University; an MBA, Providence College; and a BS in industrial engineering, University of Rhode Island. He also holds several patents and has written numerous articles on quality and process improvement.

IT PROJECT MANAGEMENT CONCEPTS

1

Chapter 1

Highly Structured Project Management

We build too many walls and not enough bridges.

—Isaac Newton

Overview

In this chapter we will discuss project management methods that are useful in managing highly complicated information technology (IT) projects. In this context, one well-known project management method is the IBM® Rational Unified Process (RUP). In Chapter 2 we will discuss Agile Project Management (APM) with scrum and Extreme Programming (EP). These project management methods can be applied to effectively manage any software project. They are useful in smaller projects, and within more structured projects they facilitate the deployment of project management methods such as RUP. IT project management and software design have also greatly benefited from the application of APM. For example, APM uses Lean principles such as a strong customer focus, small and highly trained work groups, and frequent feedback between the design group and key stakeholders. These management practices result in higher quality software products and reduced cycle time from product concept to market deployment and commercialization. As we move through this book, we will focus on the three perspectives that were discussed in the preface: management of software projects, the efficient design and deployment of software, and their synergistic application to improve the effectiveness and efficiency of Lean systems using IT.

IT can be deployed either as completely new applications or modifications of current IT applications within operational systems including those managed using Lean principles. Also, different approaches to project management can also be taken depending on the level of project complexity within hardware and software deployments. For example, for many large and complex projects, a structured project management methodology such as RUP would be preferable than using the more simplified APM with scrum methodology. This recommendation is especially true if a project was impacted by numerous stakeholders from diverse organizational functions and had many complicated and interrelated subsystems. However, this does not imply that APM should not be effectively applied within portions of a larger RUP-managed project to simplify its work activities and reduce the development cycle time of its various subsystems relative to their features and functions. On the other hand, deployments in which current IT systems are either being upgraded or consist of off-the-shelf hardware and software components, might benefit directly from using an APM with scrum approach. In this context, APM methods may be the best project management strategy for Lean IT projects having well-defined deliverables and tight completion schedules. However, regardless of the specific software project management approach used, major goals of RUP, APM, or one of several other software project management methods are used to create, modify, and deploy IT systems to automate, simplify, standardize, and mistake-proof an organization's manual work tasks and other work. In this automated work, various degrees of technical sophistication may be required to improve the operational performance of a Lean system.

Capability Maturity Models

As an introduction to IT project management, we will discuss some key characteristics of the Capability Maturity Models. In this context, a generic version of a maturity model is shown in Figure 1.1. It is characterized by five levels of maturity through which an IT system evolves. These maturity levels are baseline, well defined, standardized, effectively managed, and optimized. The concept is that as an organization's IT systems mature they become more standardized and proactive. The evolutionary path proceeds from an initial state in which IT roles and responsibilities have not been formalized to higher maturity states in which the activities comprising an IT project management framework become repeatable through standardization of requirements and their associated work methods. A maturity model then continues its evolution into an IT framework in which project management activities are proactively managed and continuously improved over time in a systematic and formal manner.

A Capability Maturity Model can also be classified by the several major functions that support the IT creation, development, and commercialization process. These functions include engineering, project management, support, and process

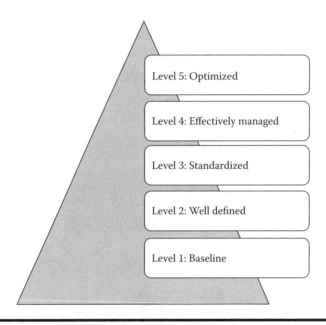

Figure 1.1   Information maturity models.

management (see Table 1.1). Application of a maturity model through these types of organizational functions will help to ensure that product requirements, such as schedule, performance, and cost, are met when a product is released to either external or internal users. For example, important engineering activities include managing and translating customer and stakeholder requirements, product integration relative to hardware and software features and functions through the creation of software code as well as the development of required technical solutions to known issues, and product validation through testing and performance verification. Typical maturity model project management activities include managing customer, key stakeholder, and supplier relationships; monitoring and controlling project activities, managing team priorities and resources; and providing related project support. Risk management and reporting is also critical. Supporting functions include configuration management, measurement and analysis, quality assurance, decision analysis and resolution as well as causal analysis and resolution. Process management activities include creating and managing process definitions, training employees and users, and measuring and analyzing hardware and software performance. These activities also include the release and commercialization of software products. In summary, a Capability Maturity Model provides a framework from which to measure the evolution and maturity levels of IT systems within an organization and provides useful comparative benchmarking information. In this regard, the Capability Maturity Model Integration (CMMI)® approach developed by the Software Engineering Institute (SEI) at Carnegie Mellon University is highly recommended.

Table 1.1   Key Attributes of an IT Maturity Model

• Engineering	• Requirements management and development
	• Product integration
	• Required technical solutions
	• Product validation and verification
• Project management	• Project planning
	• Supplier relationships
	• Project monitoring and control
	• Team management
	• Risk management and reporting
• Support	• Configuration management
	• Configuration measurement and analysis
	• Quality assurance
	• Decision analysis and resolution
	• Causal analysis and resolution
• Process management	• Process definitions
	• Training
	• Performance measurement and analysis
	• System deployment

Highly Structured Project Management

A highly structured project management method such as RUP is often used to manage complicated hardware and software projects. However, if its project management activities are simplified, then this method can also be used to manage smaller projects. However, APM with scrum will most likely be a more useful project management approach for smaller projects unless there are significant complexities regarding the location of supporting teams or the final integration of hardware and software systems. APM is also more useful in situations when customer and key stakeholder requirements are either not fully developed or understood, or a project's scope is limited or changes. An example of key elements of a structured project management methodology is shown in Figure 1.2. This example includes four phases: conceptualization or inception, design creation and evaluation or elaboration, building or construction, and commercialization or transition. These are executed by a project team relative to requirements related to change management and project management as well as customers and

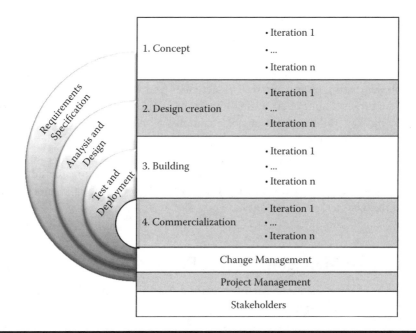

Figure 1.2 provides the following phases and elements:

1. Concept	• Iteration 1
	• ...
	• Iteration n
2. Design creation	• Iteration 1
	• ...
	• Iteration n
3. Building	• Iteration 1
	• ...
	• Iteration n
4. Commercialization	• Iteration 1
	• ...
	• Iteration n
Change Management	
Project Management	
Stakeholders	

Requirements Specification / Analysis and Design / Test and Deployment

Figure 1.2   IT project management for complicated projects.

key stakeholders. In this context, customer and key stakeholder requirements are specified, analyzed, designed, tested, and deployed to a larger user community.

In the concept phase of a project, its expected resources and their costs, which are based on estimated work activities, are compared to budgeted amounts to ensure that the project, as currently defined, will meet its financial objectives. If a project is over budget at this point, then a redesign of a software product and its associated work activities is necessary, or the project's budget must be increased prior to its next phase. In the design phase, a project's work activities become better defined as the requirements of a software product become firm. However, product requirements and hence project activities are defined initially only at a high level using use cases, descriptions of software architecture, and prototypes, which show basic product features and functions. Prior to leaving the design phase, the business plan for a project will be revised based on any new information regarding product evaluations. In the building phase of a project, software code is created and a product's features and functions are fully developed and tested. Also, if a project is large and complex, then teams may be testing discrete components of software code, but in a concurrent manner and sharing this testing information with other teams. In the final phase of a project, the completed product, including hardware, software, and associated documentation, is deployed to the end user or customer (if external to an organization) and its performance is monitored over time to ensure it meets user requirements.

Specific project management methods include requirements analysis, building and modeling software code through its implementation and testing, and managing project risks and resources according to the project's schedule and financial targets. In this context, important project management tools require creating a time-phased listing of sequential work activities and their lower-level work tasks to build a project Gantt chart. Other important project management tools include identifying key milestones at major iterations of the newly created software code, creating management reports of project status metrics, deploying a list of project issues and problems, creating work orders to complete the remaining work activities, and holding periodic project reviews between a project team and its key stakeholders and perhaps customers. These tools will be discussed in more detail later in this chapter.

Factors for Managing Project Risk

Regardless of the project management method that is chosen by a Lean IT team, project risk must be carefully evaluated and managed to ensure its success. Several major project risks are listed in Figure 1.3. We will also continue this discussion in Chapter 3 using Table 3.4, which describes several other project risks in the context of managing change issues associated when deploying projects within an organization. The risks listed in Figure 1.3 include those associated with customer and key stakeholder requirements, regulatory requirements, technology issues, the availability of supply, and product performance issues. It should be noted that there may be additional types of risks that are dependent on a particular industry and project application. Customer or client risks may include changes to a project's scope and requirements, the cancellation of a project, or other factors that impact a project's original schedule, its cost, or other objectives. Some client risks can be

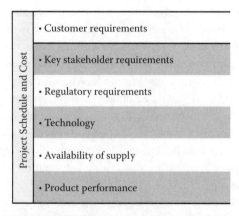

Figure 1.3 Factors for managing project risk.

mitigated by working closely with major clients to understand their requirements. However, despite working closely with a client, there may be situations in which a project is canceled or its original scope has been modified to such a large extent that it becomes in effect a completely new project. In these situations a Lean IT team should have contingency plans to manage the impact of the changes. Key stakeholder risks may be associated with resources necessary to support a project's work activities. Resources may include materials, information, or the people necessary to support a project team in its work activities. Stakeholder risk may be exacerbated by poor communication between a team and its key stakeholders. Regulatory risks may include changes in laws and regulations that obsolete a product or require that it be significantly modified. Regulatory risks may also differ by country or a specific region within a country. However, this type of risk can be mitigated by ensuring that a project team and its stakeholders have the necessary knowledge of local laws and regulations. Technology risks may include an obsolescence of technology that is integral to a new product or a reliance on new technology that is not commercially available. A project with a heavy reliance on a new technology that has not been commercialized will generally have a high probability of not being delivered on schedule or meeting its cost and performance targets. One solution to this type of risk is to develop new technology prior to using it in commercial projects. Supply risks impact a product's cost or the availability of a product's materials and subcomponents, or other critical resources such as people, equipment, and facilities. Supplier risks can be managed by identifying alternative suppliers and creating contingency plans. In summary, a project team must identify the risks that might adversely impact its project's schedule, cost, and other objectives.

Classic Project Management Activities

RUP and similar IT project management methods depend to varying degrees on a combination of classical project management methodologies, Lean concepts, and unique IT tools and methods. In this section we will discuss several additional project management tools and methods, which are listed in Table 1.2. This information has proven to be very useful to Lean IT teams using RUP or APM and scrum. The first project tool listed in Table 1.2 is the creation of a simple sequential listing of a project's work activities. This listing is also called a work breakdown structure (WBS). A WBS includes all work activities necessary to complete a project, their precedence relationships, their resource requirements, and the expected outputs when they are completed. Typical outputs include cost and schedule targets, which are realized when a work activity has been completed. In fact, projects are normally controlled by the activity duration on the critical path, and costs are continually evaluated relative to a project's budget or a reduction in cycle time. However, it should be noted that cycle-time reductions usually require the addition of resources to a project and incremental cost increases. Also, at a more advanced level of

Table 1.2   Classic Project Management Activities

Project Management Activity	Key Characteristics
1. Develop a list of project work activity.	List work activity, its resource inputs, its expected outputs, its time duration, and relationship to other work activities.
2. Identify critical work activity that must be done on schedule.	Identify the project's critical path and the work activities on the critical path.
3. Identify milestone activities that must be successfully executed to meet the project schedule and cost.	Divide the project into key groups of work activities and correlate the groups to their expected completion schedule.
4. Create responsibility matrix of resources to work activities and schedule.	Develop the project schedule using a Gantt chart and deploy resources to the work activities to execute the project schedule.
5. Track key project metrics.	1. Working days used versus allocated for the project. 2. Work activities that must be completed within 24 hours. 3. Currently overallocated resources by work activity. 4. Unscheduled activities that have been or must be completed including resource requirements and schedule. 5. Work activities starting within the next 10 days. 6. Work activities in progress including percentage complete. 7. Completed work activities including consumed resources, cost, and schedule adherence. 8. Work activities that have been started late. 9. Work activities that are not meeting schedule or cost targets. 10. Actual versus target resource usage. 11. Project cash flow projections.

Table 1.2 (continued)   Classic Project Management Activities

Project Management Activity	Key Characteristics
	12. Actual versus budgeted cost.
	13. Work activities that are over budget.
	14. Currently identified project risks, issues, and concerns.
	15. All other issues currently impacting the project schedule and cost.
	16. Work activities that can be "crashed" to reduce their expected completion time.
6. Communicate and report project status to key stakeholders.	Use communication plans, issues logs, and similar methods to communicate project status.

analysis, the duration of an activity can be represented by a probability distribution rather than a single expected or average time.

A WBS example is shown in Figure 1.4 for a hypothetical software development process. This example will also be discussed in the context of APM with scrum in Chapter 2 as well as several other chapters. The WBS shown in Figure 1.4 lists the project's work activities and shows both their relationships relative to predecessors as well as their expected duration. The expected duration in the example is measured in person days. In this example, "expected" means the average time to complete a work activity. The corresponding process map is also shown in the same figure. Using this WBS, a project manager can create an activity matrix that shows the relationships between each activity, its required resources, its cost, and time duration.

Another way to visualize a WBS is to create a Gantt chart. A Gantt chart shows a project's schedule as a series of interrelated work activities that are offset by their expected completion times. A Gantt chart based on the WBS example shown in Figure 1.4 is shown in Figure 1.5. In this example, the project's critical activities have been highlighted in Figures 1.5 and 1.6. Notice that the sequence of critical work activities implies the project will be completed in 120 days. However, it may be possible to complete some of the work activities on the critical path more quickly if additional resources are provided to one or more activities on the critical path. As an example, perhaps work activity 1a could be completed in 10 rather than 20 days if two people were added to the activity. However, this may not always be effective if an activity is always behind schedule. It has been shown that just throwing people at a project may actually lengthen the completion times of its work activities and its overall schedule. This situation may occur if the additional people must be trained by other team members or have a negative impact on a team's ability to do its work. This concept was discussed by DeMarco and Lister

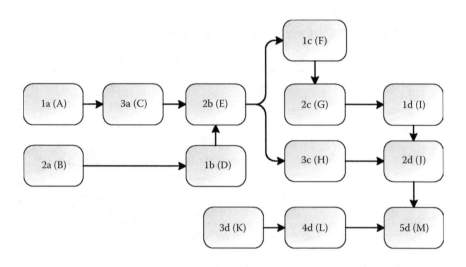

Discrete System Function	Work Activities	Person Days	Immediate Predecessors
A	1a	20	None
	2a	20	None
	3a	20	1a
B	1b	15	2a
	2b	15	3a, 1b
C	1c	10	2b
	2c	10	1c
	3c	10	2b
D	1d	10	2c
	2d	5	3c, 1d
	3d	5	None
	4d	10	3d
	5d	30	2d, 4d

Figure 1.4 Work breakdown structure (WBS).

in their book *Peopleware: Productive Projects and Teams* as well as by Brooks in his book *The Mythical Man-Month*.

Figure 1.6 uses the information of Figure 1.4 to demonstrate the critical path method (CPM), but without its calculations. The critical path is shown as the shaded activities. In practice, a critical path would be identified applying an algorithm that is used to determine activities that must be started and finished on schedule so a project is not delayed. In contrast, work activities not on a project's critical path have "slack" time. This implies they can be started at later times (but within a

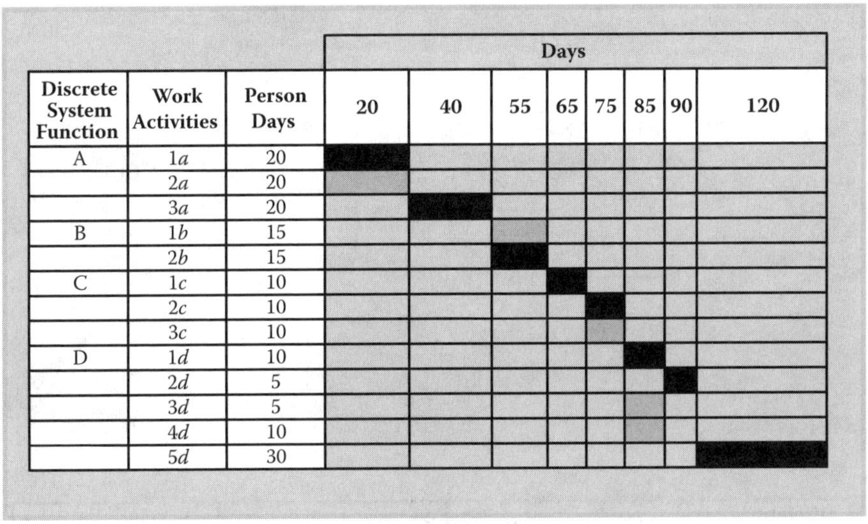

Discrete System Function	Work Activities	Person Days	Days							
			20	40	55	65	75	85	90	120
A	1a	20								
	2a	20								
	3a	20								
B	1b	15								
	2b	15								
C	1c	10								
	2c	10								
	3c	10								
D	1d	10								
	2d	5								
	3d	5								
	4d	10								
	5d	30								

Figure 1.5   Gantt chart.

specific range) and still be completed on time when they are needed by subsequent or downstream activities. In other words, they can be started later without having an impact on a project's overall schedule or cycle time. How is the critical path calculated in practice? Software algorithms calculate the earliest start (ES) and finish (EF) times for every work activity using a forward pass through a network. Then a backward pass is made through the network to calculate the latest start (LS) and latest finish (LF) times. The available slack time is calculated as either ES–LS or EF–LF. If the slack time is zero then this activity must be started and finished on time. Once work activities have been identified and prioritized relative to their criticality, milestone activities are identified. Milestone activities are aggregated work activities that must be successfully completed to meet a project's schedule, performance, and cost targets. A milestone is reached when a sequence of related work activities are completed by a project team. As a result, milestones are useful in managing a project's periodic design reviews because they include one or more critical activities as well as other aggregated work activities that represent completed features and functions.

As a project is deployed, project metrics are used to ensure its objectives are met in practice. Several common project metrics are shown in Table 1.2. We will discuss these metrics within the context of project management and continue to expand these discussions in subsequent chapters. For example, in Chapter 8, the topics will focus on measuring and improving performance from several perspectives. However, the 16 metrics listed in Table 1.2 are a good place to begin our discussion of Lean IT project management. These metrics focus on the measurement of a project's schedule, cost, and related objectives such as product performance.

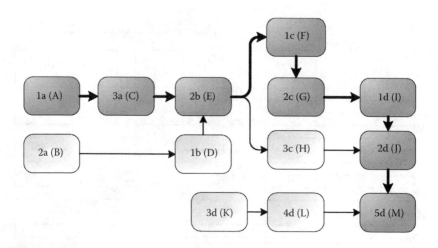

Discrete System Function	Work Activities	Person Days	Earliest Start	Latest Start	Earliest Finish	Latest Finish	Slack	Critical Path
A	1a	20	0	0	20	20	0	Yes
	2a	20	0	5	20	25	5	
	3a	20	20	20	40	40	0	Yes
B	1b	15	20	25	35	40	5	
	2b	15	40	40	55	55	0	Yes
C	1c	10	55	55	65	65	0	Yes
	2c	10	65	65	75	75	0	Yes
	3c	10	55	75	65	85	20	
D	1d	10	75	75	85	85	0	Yes
	2d	5	85	85	90	90	0	Yes
	3d	5	0	75	5	80	75	
	4d	10	5	80	15	90	75	
	5d	30	90	90	120	120	0	Yes

Figure 1.6 Critical path method (CPM).

Also, to a large extent, their focus is on the use of exception reports, measuring actual versus planned levels relative to time, cost, or performance, or monitoring the completion of work tasks.

As an example, measuring working days used versus allocated ensures that a project's resources remain aligned with their original estimates. Also, discrepancies between actual versus budgeted resources enables a project manager to take immediate action to manage a project issue when it occurs or create mitigation plans in advance. Abnormally high resource use, relative to originally planned levels, may be an indication that there have been inefficiencies executing one or more work activities or the original estimates of budgeted resources were incorrect. Working days also directly correlate to a project's labor costs as well as its schedule. The second metric, work activities that must be completed within 24 hours, is important to ensure that a project's work activities have the necessary resources to enable them to remain on schedule. Although 24 hours was used as a target in this metric, it should be noted that any other relevant time increment can be used in practice. The key concept is that a project manager should focus on those critical work activities that need to be completed immediately. The third metric, currently overallocated resources by work activity, measures excess resources by each work activity. An excess of resources may occur because of unexpected increases in efficiency relative to the use of materials or labor. Alternatively, predecessor work activities might not have been completed on schedule. This would prevent a work activity from being started as originally scheduled. Many projects also have unscheduled activities that must be completed prior to working on subsequent activities. These situations, although not common, require reallocations of resources. This might adversely impact a project's schedule and cost. In addition to having a high priority for immediate work activities, it is also a good idea to maintain visibility of work tasks that are scheduled to start within the next several days. In some projects, resources may have to be transported to where the work is located, which requires planning. The metric "work activities starting within the next 10 days" can be used to provide visibility to upcoming work activities in these situations.

Two additional project management metrics listed in Table 1.2 include work activities in progress including percentage complete; and work activities that have been completed including their consumed resources, actual to target cost, and percentage schedule adherence. These project management metrics enable a project manager to track how well a project is being executed relative to its original planned resource consumption, schedule, and cost. Additional metrics listed in Table 1.2 include work activities that have been started late, work activities not meeting schedule or cost targets, actual versus target resource usage, project cash flow projections, actual versus budgeted cost, and work activities that are over budget. The purpose of these metrics is to provide more effective project management and control by identifying exceptions to a project's plan. The last three metrics are currently identified project risks, issues, and concerns; all other issues currently impacting the project schedule and cost; and work activities that can be "crashed" to reduce their expected completion time, but at a higher cost. The first two of these metrics enable a project manager to capture information that might adversely impact a project, but which is not found in previous metrics. The last metric is useful in identifying ways to shorten a project's expected completion time by adding additional resources. These resources could be in the form of additional people, materials, or equipment.

The sixth project management activity listed in Table 1.2 is communicate and report project status to key stakeholders. Communication takes several forms and must be customized for its target audience as well as its intended message. Common communication tools and methods include creating status reports, issues logs, risks analyses, holding frequent team and stakeholder meetings, and similar methods that improve the quality of the information used to manage projects.

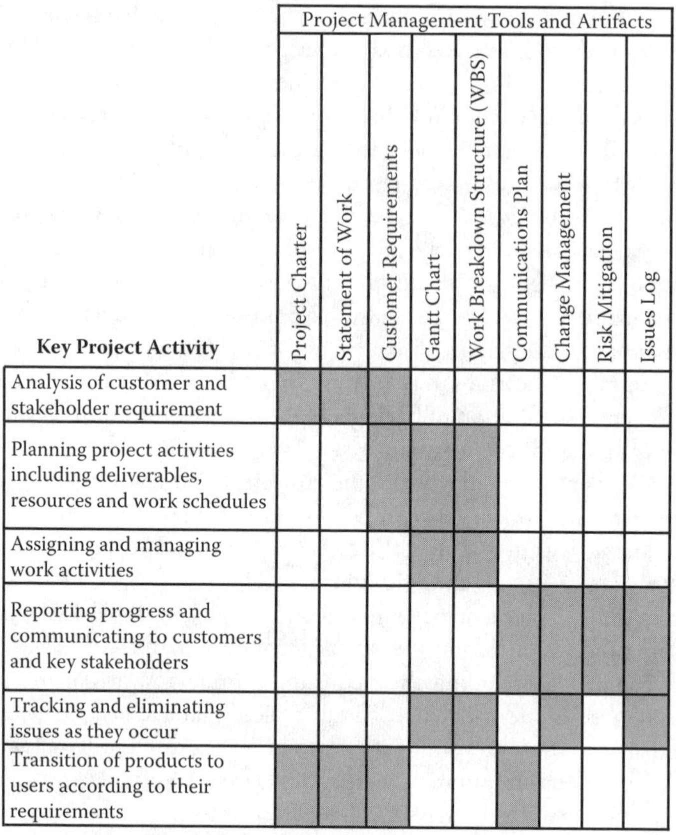

Key Project Activity	Project Management Tools and Artifacts								
	Project Charter	Statement of Work	Customer Requirements	Gantt Chart	Work Breakdown Structure (WBS)	Communications Plan	Change Management	Risk Mitigation	Issues Log
Analysis of customer and stakeholder requirement	■	■	■					■	
Planning project activities including deliverables, resources and work schedules			■	■	■				
Assigning and managing work activities				■	■				
Reporting progress and communicating to customers and key stakeholders						■	■	■	■
Tracking and eliminating issues as they occur				■			■	■	■
Transition of products to users according to their requirements	■	■	■		■	■			

Figure 1.7   Classic project management tools and work objects.

Communication tools and methods will be discussed in Chapter 3 in the context of accelerating organizational change through the use of project charters, clarifying team roles and responsibilities, conducting a key stakeholder analysis, analyzing various promoting and restraining factors that impact a project, analyzing organizational structures, identifying and managing project risks and issues, and creating effective project communications.

In addition to the six project management activities listed in Table 1.2, Figure 1.7 provides a cross-reference between high-level or aggregated project management objectives and the tools that are often used to obtain this information. These aggregated activities are analysis of client and stakeholder requirements, planning project activities including deliverables, resources, and work schedules, assigning and managing work activities; reporting progress and communicating to clients and key stakeholders, tracking and eliminating issues as they occur, and transition of products to users according to their requirements. Cross-referenced to these aggregated activities are typical project management tools, methods, and work objects. It should be noted that some of these tools and methods are used to promote more than one project objective. For instance, a project charter, statement of work, and the identification of customer requirements help identify and analyze customer and key stakeholder requirements. The balance of the tools shown in Figure 1.7 include a Gantt chart, a hierarchal organization of work activities using a WBS, a communications plan with supporting documentation, a risk analysis and mitigation plan, and finally an issues log. WBS and Gantt charts were discussed earlier in this chapter. Risk analysis was also discussed, but at a high level. The balance of these tools and methods will be discussed in Chapter 3.

Key Requirements Characteristics

It has been shown through many studies of different industries that if a product or service has not been properly designed to meet client requirements under all expected usage conditions, the cost increases from its design to deployment. For example, if a design issue is found earlier in its development cycle, then it can be more easily fixed as opposed to it being built into a product and shipped to a customer only to have it returned. In fact, there is a multiplier effect in that the overall standard cost of a product increases as it is being built and finally released to customers. This concept is shown in Figure 1.8. The concept of a multiplier is that if it costs $100 per unit to fix a problem when it is found during design work, it most

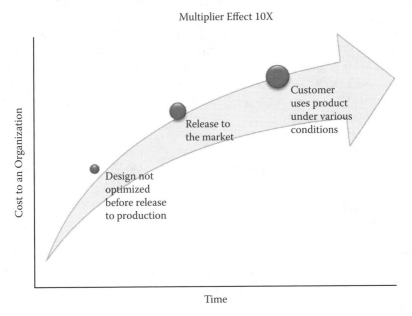

Figure 1.8   Correct requirements reduces failures.

Table 1.3 Key Requirements Characteristics

Key Characteristic	Explanation
1. Quantitative	Requirements can be efficiently analyzed using small sample sizes.
2. Measureable	Requirements can be collected accurately and precisely with proper resolution and they are stable over time. They can also be verified by others using standardized testing methods or analysis.
3. Consistent	Requirements do not contradict other system requirements.
4. Client focused	Requirements meet customer needs per contractual agreement.
5. Balanced	Requirements also meet other stakeholder requirements.
6. Simple	Requirements can be represented in a format that properly trained people can easily understand.

likely will cost $1,000 per unit during production and $10,000 per unit after it has been delivered to a customer. Failures only exacerbate cost issues because having to repair or replace a product at remote locations is more expensive than doing it internally. A large number of failures occur when a product or service does not reflect customer requirements under actual usage conditions. The result of failures is high warranty cost, which is reflected in higher labor and materials expenses to correct the problem. It has been found that increasing the resources upfront when designing a new product or service, and gathering and correctly translating the voice of the customer (VOC) into a new product and service design is an effective strategy to execute design activities.

An important first step in the design of any system, but especially software, is to correctly translate key customer requirements from design concepts through to features and functions of finished products and services. Table 1.3 classifies several common requirements into six characteristics relative to if a requirement is quantitative, measurable, consistent, client focused, balanced, or simple. A quantitative requirement, at least in this context, implies that a requirement can be represented as a number. Ideally, it can be measured along a scale and also be represented as a continuous probability distribution to facilitate statistical analyses. This approach facilitates data collection and analysis with relatively small sample sizes, rather than if a requirement has been classified into several discrete categories. An example of a continuous quantitative variable would be measuring the height of several people, as opposed to discretely classifying their heights as either over or under two meters. A measureable requirement also implies that a system's performance can be verified by others using standardized testing methods and analysis. Also, requirements should be consistent and not contradict other requirements. To ensure that contradictions do not occur in practice, performance testing must be carefully designed to evaluate the impact of requirements relative to one another using valid experimental designs as well as approved validation methods. Good requirements should fully conform to contractual agreements and be balanced to meet the needs of different stakeholders. Finally, requirements should be simple so that properly trained people can easily understand their meaning. These six characteristics are a minimum description of good design requirements for any system including software.

Common Design Issues

Issues related to the design of Lean IT software systems can be classified into the five categories shown in Table 1.4. They include issues related to project communication, system performance with respect to features and functions, design testing, supporting functions, and the distribution of a product and service. Project communication is in many respects the most important category since it forms the basis of all subsequent design activities including the translation of requirements into specifications. Poor project communication also adversely impacts how team members are organized and interact with one another during a project. Issues caused by poor project communication can be seen as poorly developed project plans and schedules, an inability to accurately measure a project's schedule, cost, and other objectives as well as the risks listed in Figure 1.3. These include poor team collaboration, poor coordination of work activities, and poor communication of a project's status to key stakeholders and team members through various project phases as the design process progresses.

Communication issues relative to developing an accurate project plan and schedule normally occur when a team is not diverse or properly affiliated. This may bias a team's estimates of how long it will take to complete its work activities. Also, in many situations a project's schedule and work plan may be inaccurate because the information provided by customers and key stakeholders is inaccurate or changes. A third common reason for inaccurate project plans is arbitrary project schedule or cost targets or unreasonable product performance targets that has been imposed on a team by its leadership. Unfortunately, these types of communication issues are very common. The best way to overcome them is to accurately obtain the voice of the customer (VOC) and voice of the business (VOB), create a realistic project plan, and hold frequent design reviews with customers and key stakeholders. People may not like what they hear, but at least they will know the consequence of not properly resourcing a team or forcing project completion targets by management edict. These types of communication issues are also discussed by DeMarco and Lister in their book *Peopleware*.

Table 1.4   Common Design Issues

Project Issue	Examples
1. Project communication	• Poorly developed project plan and schedule. • An inability to accurately assess project schedule, cost, performance, technological, and other risks. • Poor team collaboration. • Poor coordination of work tasks. • Poor communication of project status to key stakeholders and team members relative to the review of product design iterations.
2. System performance	• Requirements that are not aligned with customer or stakeholder needs in a formal manner. • Contradictory requirements that have not been detected during design reviews. • Design changes not made with the full concurrence of stakeholders. • Poorly integrated system objects. • A failure to create tools and templates to provide work object (artifact) support at various iterations of a design. • Poorly designed systems that do not function under actual field conditions.
3. Testing	• Systems not tested for all requirements nor for interactions between test objects that adversely impact functions. • System defects and other issues not properly identified, tracked, and eliminated prior to product release. • Not verifying that all customer and stakeholder requirements have been met per contract.
4. Support	• Product packaging and support procedures have not been fully reviewed and determined to be sufficient to meet all customer requirements.
5. Distribution	• Packaging has not been tested or confirmed to meet product distribution requirements. • Product is not available per sales and marketing plan or as scheduled if for internal use.

Poor performance issues are caused when features and functions have not been aligned with customer or stakeholder needs in a formal manner, upfront, prior to designing a product or service. This situation occurs either when contradictory requirements have not been found during formal design reviews or design changes have not been made with the full concurrence of all stakeholders. It may also occur if, from a technical perspective, there exist one or more poorly integrated system objects. In this context, a Lean IT team may fail to create the necessary tools, templates, or other relevant work objects (artifacts) to support their team. The result may be that components of a hardware or software system may not function under actual field conditions or fail to satisfy other customer and key stakeholder requirements.

Inadequate product testing creates other design issues. These occur when systems have not being fully tested or unknown interactions exist between test objects, which adversely impact the ability of a system to function. Other testing issues occur when system defects have not been properly identified, tracked, and eliminated prior to a product's release to production. As a result, customer requirements should be validated internally during the testing and evaluation process. The expense of failures, after receipt by a customer, is significantly higher than if they were identified and eliminated earlier. We will discuss these concepts in greater detail in Chapters 4 and 6.

The best designed software will not create high customer or client satisfaction if it cannot be installed correctly or if its supporting documentation is confusing. This implies that the effective distribution of a new product depends on its packaging design. In other words, if a product's packaging has not been properly tested to confirm that it meets basic distribution requirements, the result will be damaged products. In this context, instructions for use and training are also important considerations when distributing new software products. When distribution requirements are not considered, then customers will complain and return purchased products.

Summary

The management of IT projects depends, to varying degrees, on a combination of project management methodologies. These methodologies include highly structured methods such as IBM's RUP, APM with scrum, and classic project management tools and methods that emphasize Lean concepts. Other useful project management tools and methods discussed included WBS, Gantt charts, managing project risk, and the importance of obtaining correct customer requirements to reduce product and service failures. These topics will also be discussed in increasing detail in later chapters of this book.

Suggested Reading

Augustine, Sanjiv. 2005. *Managing Agile Projects*. Upper Saddle River, NJ: Prentice Hall.

Bustard, David, Peter Kawalek, and Mark Norris. 2000. *Systems Modeling for Business Process Improvement*. Boston: Artech House.

DeMarco, Tom, and Timothy Lister. 1999. *Peopleware: Productive Projects and Teams*. New York: Dorset House.

George, Michael L., James Works, and Kimberly Watson-Hemphill. 2005. *Fast Innovation*. New York: McGraw-Hill.

Martin, James William. 2008. *Operational Excellence: Using Lean Six Sigma to Translate Customer Value through Global Supply Chains*. Boca Raton, FL: Auerbach.

Martin, James William. 2009. *Lean Six Sigma for the Office*. Boca Raton, FL: CRC Press.

Schwaber, Ken. 2004. *Agile Project Management with Scrum*. Redmond, WA: Microsoft Press.

Suh, Nam Pyo. 2001. *Axiomatic Design: Advances and Applications*. New York: Oxford University Press.

Yang, Kai, and Basem El-Haik. 2003. *Design for Six Sigma: A Roadmap for Product Development*. New York: McGraw-Hill.

Chapter 2

Agile Project Management with Scrum

There's a way to do it better—find it.

—**Thomas Edison**

Overview

Prior to discussing ways to measure and improve performance in Lean IT systems, we need to discuss three basic concepts shown in Figure 2.1. The first concept was discussed in Chapter 1. This discussion included several classic project management methods as well as the IBM® Rational Unified Process (RUP). We will continue to expand on these concepts in subsequent chapters of this book. In this chapter we will discuss Agile Project Management (APM) with scrum and in Chapter 5 we will discuss Lean concepts and applications. The goal will be to arrive at Chapters 7 and 8 with sufficient knowledge of these three concepts to understand the critical components that support the measurement and improvement of Lean systems using information technology (IT).

Agile Project Management with scrum applies Lean concepts to the management of software design projects. APM is a proven methodology that helps reduce software development time and improve product quality. It also facilitates process improvement activities when work tasks are highly automated and must be modified to improve their efficiency. Several important characteristics of the APM methodology are described in Figure 2.2. These characteristics will be discussed

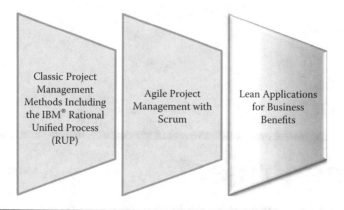

Figure 2.1   Information technology (IT) deployment in Lean systems.

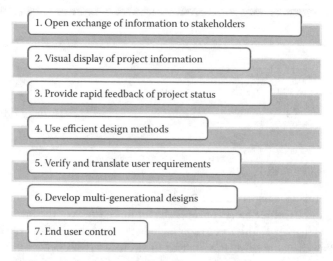

Figure 2.2   Key characteristics of Agile Project Management.

in this chapter as well as throughout the rest of this book examples will be provided to illustrate the important APM concepts. In many ways these concepts are similar to those used in Lean process improvement. As an example, the concept of open exchange of information to stakeholders correlates to obtaining the voice of the customer (VOC), which is a critical Lean concept since a process can only be simplified by identifying operational work tasks important to a customer. The visual display of project information is also used in Lean systems to enable local work teams to see process problems at a glance. Visual controls range from metric status reporting to marking off locations where materials, tools, and equipment should be placed every day. Lean systems are also characterized by their ability to provide rapid feedback of project status. Simple systems are easier to measure and manage than more complicated ones. Also, rapid feedback enables a team to change its project plan if necessary based on the feedback obtained from customers and key stakeholders. Using efficient design methods is always an important concept regardless of whether the system being designed is hardware, software, or processes work activities such as those commonly used in lean systems.

As a project proceeds, it is important to periodically obtain feedback from customers and key stakeholders. It is also important to verify user requirements, relative to the features and functions of a product or service. However, multi-generational designs are also useful. This is because they reinforce the concept that a new product or service will change over time in response to new user require-ments. This requires that a new design be flexible so it can evolve within the limits of current technology. Another key characteristic of APM is end-user control, which ensures a high degree of end-user control of a software design process using frequent feedback through scrum sprints. Finally, those Lean IT projects that are managed using APM with scrum have significantly reduced software development cycle times because work activities are "pulled" using an activity backlog, which is a simple work breakdown structure (WBS). An advantage of using an activity backlog is that it is highly visible to all team members and key stakeholders. This facilitates team interactions and communication as well as communication with customers and key project stakeholders. A useful feature of a higher-level activity backlog is that it is broken down into scrum sprints in which each sprint is designed to produce discrete components of a product's features and functions, which are immediately reviewed by all project stakeholders.

Another important APM concept is that a team initiates all its work using a project's charter in an aligned manner. However, a statement of work is sometimes created prior to developing a project charter. This is because a statement of work is a document that is usually broader than a single project charter. In fact, several smaller projects may be initiated from a single statement of work. In a project charter, a project's goals and objectives or deliverables should be well defined and accurately represent customer requirements. Key components of a project charter describe its expected business benefits, required resources, team members, its schedule, associ-ated risks and dependencies, and other relevant factors. It should also be noted that a project's business benefits may be either financial or nonfinancial. In other words, the objective of project charters varies. It could be very broad with a focus over an entire system or it could be focused on a very small portion of a system. However, the basis of a project charter should be the voice of the customer (VOC) and voice of the business (VOB). In software development projects, the VOC and VOB, as represented by product requirements, are translated into a product's specifications and then into the project's work activities using an activity backlog.

It should also be reiterated that many of the methods employed by APM practi-tioners are directly analogous to those used in Lean assessments and related process improvement activities. However, there are some differences between the two project management approaches because their applications are different. For example,

Lean assessments are normally applied to the analysis and improvement of process workflows, whereas APM methods are used to improve work activities with heavy IT content or where software products are being modified or created. In APM with scrum applications, a project's deliverables will be in the form of prioritized and highly detailed user specifications, which are based on customer requirements.

So far in this section we have discussed several analogies between Lean and APM. We will now provide specific examples of these analogies. First, basic Lean concepts include understanding customer value as defined by the VOC and VOB, ensuring that work activities are highly visible and using rapid improvement cycles to identify and execute improvement activities. In APM, execution of work in cycles using scrum sprints is analogous to Lean's "transfer batch" and "reduced" setup time methodologies, which are used to reduce cycle time. A transfer batch refers to the movement of objects from one operation to another as single units once work has been performed on them. This is in contrast to batching several work objects as a lot and then transferring them as a group to the next work operation. It has been shown that lead-time reductions of more than 60 percent are easily attainable using a transfer batch scheduling strategy. In this manner, APM's work activities are designed to create, modify, or eliminate and test software components using scrum sprints rather than waiting to the end of the design process. This project management approach quickly identifies design mistakes as they occur when customers and key stakeholders review discrete components of product features and functions. Additional Lean concepts such as work simplification, standardization, and modularization are also evident in the APM approach to project management and software design.

A software design team should clearly link design attributes with customer or user requirements as well as those of key stakeholders to ensure an alignment of business benefits. It should be noted that customer and user requirements are captured using VOC methods, whereas key stakeholder requirements are captured using VOB methods. There is a difference between the two methodologies. Customers are concerned with product and service cost, cycle time, and performance. In contrast, although key stakeholders are also concerned with these product and service criteria, profitability, resource requirements, and other business criteria are also important. In other words, there will always be a balance struck between VOC and VOB prioritization and design criteria, although achieving a balance between the two is not an easy task. However, templates and standardized procedures can be used to methodically identify and analyze customer and stakeholder requirements. These requirements can then be translated into a logical WBS and used to define a project's activity backlog.

Key aspects of VOC and VOB identification and translation will always include elements of effective communication, change management, a cultural assessment, and infrastructure analysis. Different customers and stakeholders will also have different views of which requirements are most important when designing a new product or service. As an example, effective team and stakeholder communication is important during the VOC and VOB translation process and is executed using different communication formats, which depend on the complexity of a message as well as its emotional impact. Highly complicated and emotional messages should be communicated in person as opposed to simple and standard messages that can be communicated via e-mail or in similar formats. In other words, complicated VOC and VOB information should also be gathered in person. But, routine status reports and similar information can be transmitted via e-mail since their format is highly standardized. Communication is also impacted by the diversity of an APM team, its customers, and key stakeholders. For instance, some cultures are open and casual, whereas others are hierarchal and formal. This fact makes it important to understand the cultural environment of an organization relative to the project being managed. Organizational infrastructure is also important because it impacts a project's available resources and similar supporting systems. Resource allocation is important because every project requires information, people, materials, and equipment to achieve it goals. In the remainder of this chapter we will discuss other key characteristics of APM.

Open Exchange of Information to Stakeholders

Open communication is a critical aspect of APM. Understanding what customers need and value and then creating products and services to satisfy those needs and values is the basis of product development. Open communication is important to ensure that an APM team focuses on the important features and functions of a software product. Failure to accurately capture this information could result in a situation in which a team inaccurately translates customer needs and values into product requirements and then into a product's specifications. This situation may result in either rework or a unsalable product. Recall that communication between an APM team, its customers, and stakeholders begins upfront when the team identifies and clarifies a project's goals. These goals include the design and testing of software features and functions. An APM team openly engages its customers and stakeholders in a two-way dialog to honestly report the status of its project's activities on a frequent basis at the end of each scrum sprint. This enables all participants to recommend improvements to the management of the project.

Most people would think that open communication is easy to achieve in practice. But, unfortunately it is not for a variety of reasons. Perhaps the most straightforward example is when an external consulting team is brought in to manage modifications to existing software and hardware systems. In these situations, a consulting team will have a project sponsor as well as a written statement of work that communicates to key stakeholders both the type and extent of the project work to be done as well as its cost, schedule, and other objectives. The project sponsor may have preconceived ideas of how a system should be modified. Other issues may be related to the resources, which are not under the control of a project's sponsor but are necessary to support a project. In other words, a project's key stakeholders may not fully support a project team due to competing priorities. In addition, stakeholders may have different work styles, which range from democratic to autocratic. Autocratic styles are prevalent within organizations and they adversely impact the ability of an APM team to complete its work activities. Finally, stakeholders may also have different work styles and preferred ways to receive a team's communication. These situations may create barriers to the smooth flow of project information both within and external to a project team. As a result, a project's cost and schedule targets might be adversely impacted and the software product being created or modified may not achieve its performance targets. These types of issues also occur when internal project teams are deployed within an organization. APM with scrum has proven to be a key solution to these types of project communication issues and other organizational barriers to a project's execution.

Visual Display of Project Information

Visual displays of project work tasks, activities, and milestones help to manage and communicate the project's status because everyone can easily see work activities that have been completed as well as those that are in progress. Visual displays are especially important in maintaining visibility to a project's milestone activities during a project. It also helps to keep a project on schedule and within its budget. Visual displays of project work activities also clearly link a team's work activities with specific project outcomes to align them with a project's goals and objectives.

APM with scrum is deployed and managed by visually displaying on a whiteboard a project's requirements and its associated work activities. These work activities create the necessary software features and functions. This project management approach also creates a highly visible and interactive work environment. As work activities are completed, the APM team updates the activity backlog information written on the whiteboard. This update is usually done daily. A whiteboard also enables an APM team to quickly update or change their projects' status as new information becomes available. This approach allows all participants including stakeholders to see a project's plan being executed as work activities are completed one by one. The project information written on whiteboards includes customer requirements, which have been broken down into lower-level work activities and tasks. They are listed in a hierarchal format, organized into scrum sprints, and prioritized for completion by one or more team members. Scrum sprints are structured so that at the end of a sprint, a portion of a system has been designed and tested to produce one or more software features or functions for either a newly designed or modified work product. A work product may include a product, service, or process improvement. Resources are applied to the scheduled activities that comprise each sprint. For example, in a software development project, programmers and support personnel are one type of resource that would be assigned to a sprint. But programmers also need access to other hardware and software systems to design and test software code and validate its features and functions to meet customer and stakeholder requirements.

Project visibility is also enhanced if supplemental information is available. Supplemental information includes information from a team's daily data collection and analyses activities, management reports, process maps, and similar sources of product and process information. These sources of information are placed near the whiteboard in a team's project room. A project room or war room is a dedicated room that is used to hold team meetings and to visibly display a project's work activities and analyses. This enables an APM team to facilitate daily team meetings at the beginning and end of each work day. For example, imagine a room in which a whiteboard contains information of an agile team's project's schedule or activity backlog, organized as scrum sprints, for the next several weeks. In this context, the scrum sprints also serve as milestone activities. Cross-referenced to an activity backlog would also be relevant project and product development metrics to enable an agile team to measure its success against a project's original VOC and VOB goals. In addition, management reports, data collection templates, and analyses would also be organized on the room's walls to provide detail to help customers and key stakeholders understand the activity backlog and its metrics. This supplementary information helps a team understand the many interrelated work tasks in progress. If the focus of a team's activities is process analysis and improvement, there will be a map of the process being investigated, which has been heavily quantified. On the other hand, if the team's focus is design of new software, then the information will include drawings of key systems, testing reports, and similar information. The purpose of daily meetings is to review a team's activity backlog. During a daily meeting, completed work activities are checked off and uncompleted work activities are either reviewed or reprioritized and assigned to the next scrum sprint. Team updates are also periodically held with key stakeholders and, if necessary, customers. The information these combined team and stakeholder meetings provide can also be updated at frequent intervals based on new information.

Provide Rapid Feedback of Project Status

APM with scrum uses sprints to create a rapid feedback system by using several incremental software development cycles to ensure a new or modified product design or process functions properly within a user's work environment and according to the performance requirements required by contract. In these evaluation activities, the tools and methods of Chapter 1 as well as feedback loops, checklists, functional testing, and frequent meetings with customers and stakeholders are used to manage projects. During a sprint, and as part of the project management process, team members communicate their work activities on a daily basis to ensure there is no redundancy between them and that work is being performed as scheduled by the activity backlog. Changes are also made to a project's original work plan as they become necessary. Then, at the end of a sprint, an agile team's completed work activities are reviewed with key customers and project stakeholders. In this context, a sprint can be considered as a milestone activity within a project, in the classical project management sense. An APM approach provides rapid feedback, which facilitates project management and the creation of useful products and services.

Use Efficient Design Methods

Different types of products and services require the use of common as well as specialized design methods. For example, the design of mechanical systems requires the use of specialized mechanical engineering tools such as computer-aided design (CAD), mechanical testing, and tolerance analysis of components. In contrast, industrial engineering methods such as work analysis and design, ergonomics, and similar industrial engineering methods are used to design manual work tasks. In software design, programmers create algorithms to provide useful features and system functions. However, although different and highly specialized tools and methods are used in software design to develop diverse products and services, there are common and proven design methods and principles that are applicable across different industries and design activities. One important common design principle requires accurately obtaining the VOC and VOB to create simple and standardized products and services. In this design approach, additional features and functions are only added if customers value them. Integral to these concepts is the use of modularized and standardized components. As an example, a common practice in software design is the use of off-the-shelf reusable software. Mistake proofing is another common design concept that should be used to prevent or immediately detect product and service failures. In this book, we will discuss these and other principles as they relate to project management and software design in Lean systems. We will discuss software design methods in Chapter 6.

Verify and Translate User Requirements

In Chapter 1, we discussed the six key software design characteristics shown in Table 1.3. In that discussion, it was mentioned that user requirements should be expressed in a format that is quantitative, measureable, consistent, client focused, balanced, and simple. APM has proven to be particularly useful in achieving these goals because it is highly focused on customer and stakeholder requirements and their continual feedback through various design iterations. It is important that a design team meets frequently with its customers and key stakeholders to ensure that these goals are met in practice. This will help to ensure an accurate translation of user requirements throughout the development of a product or service. In this context, scrum sprints are an important enabling methodology to provide

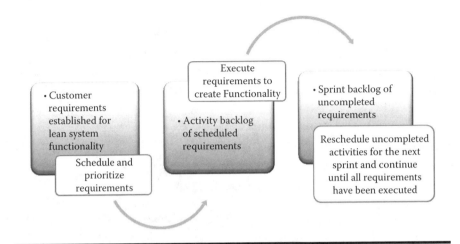

Figure 2.3   Scrum sprints.

this continual and rapid feedback of system features and functionality at frequent intervals. Figure 2.3 shows the basic concept behind a scrum sprint. First, the customer requirements of a new software product or process are identified and listed on a whiteboard as an activity backlog. Second, the work tasks necessary to meet requirements through the creation of software features are listed, prioritized, and scheduled, and team members pull their activities from the activity backlog. Recall that an activity backlog is a highly visible schedule drawn on a whiteboard and used by an APM team to check off completed work tasks during its scrum sprints.

A scrum sprint is designed to deliver discrete features or functions that can be tested, reviewed, and approved by customers and key stakeholders of a product. In other words, when all the work activities of a sprint have been completed, then an APM team has delivered a measurable output. This measurable output could be an algorithm, key product features, or functional requirements that are part of an overall product design. The duration of a sprint will usually vary between several days to weeks and a software project will usually consist of several sprints. Work activities that are not completed during an assigned sprint will be assigned to the next sprint and reprioritized. Alternatively, the duration of a sprint may be increased to accommodate a schedule miss. In some ways a sprint resembles a kaizen event in Lean manufacturing because team members are brought together to focus on a limited number of work activities to make process improvements in just a few days. Both scrum sprints and kaizen events depend on a firm set of objectives or deliverables that are focused on customer and stakeholder requirements. The execution of a sprint's work activities is also highly interactive and visible.

An example of an activity backlog is shown in Figure 2.4. Imagine that this information has been placed on a whiteboard and all key stakeholders can see the various work activities shown on the whiteboard. Then as the team reviews the activity backlog, each team member pulls or signs up for the work tasks on the

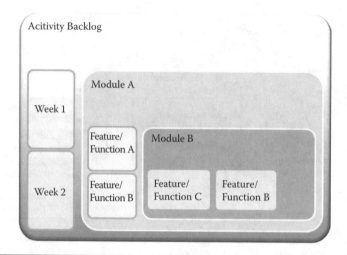

Figure 2.4 Managing an activity backlog.

list at the beginning of a sprint. In reviewing Figure 2.4, it should be noted that a sprint's work activities are organized to deliver predefined and discrete system features and functions or other measurable outputs. In addition, as discussed earlier, design analyses and other information relevant to the teams' design activities are distributed within an APM team's work area. Sprints are also useful when a Lean IT team is modifying software to enhance a software system's ability to integrate Lean concepts within a process workflow.

APM with scrum also helps to integrate and standardize software design activities. The concept of design integration is shown in Figure 2.5 as consisting of three steps. We have already discussed the importance of team communication as well as the use of APM scrum sprints, frequent meetings, and activity backlogs in the communication process. In this way, design consistency is maintained through visual displays of project work activities, and daily and end-of-sprint feedback sessions. However, best-in-class product design methodologies are also employed. This is a complicated set of activities that, as mentioned earlier, varies by industry. However, at its most basic level, the qualitative customer requirements must be translated into quantitative specifications that enable products and services to be built, tested, and confirmed as meeting customer and stakeholder requirements. This more complicated discussion must wait until Chapter 6. But generally speaking, an initial product design should be created using the minimum number of product features and functions that will satisfy its diverse stakeholder requirements. Additional product features and functions should only be added to this initial design if they are directly related to these requirements. In other words, keep a design simple. Second, standardized and modulized software should be used to the greatest extent possible. Ideally, this software will be off the shelf. Third, software should be fully tested and mistake-proofed. Ideally, this will be an automated process.

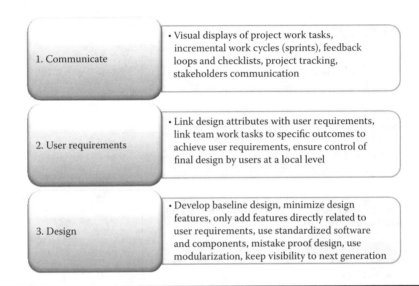

Figure 2.5   Integrating design activities using Agile Project Management.

Develop Multigenerational Designs

Multigenerational designs are a useful concept to manage a product design and its evolution over time to match changes in customer preferences. Using this design approach helps a team maintain design flexibility and standardization in the first generation of a new design. It may seem contrary to think of standardization and flexibility in the same context. However, when algorithms can be reused or swapped out of a product because they were first designed in a simple, standardized, or modular manner, then changes are easier to make in subsequent product designs. The key enabler in a multigenerational design approach is visibility to current and future customer and stakeholder requirements. Effective testing strategies are also important throughout a multigenerational design process.

Figure 2.6 shows an example of how some key elements of a multigenerational design for an e-commerce portal can be created in practice. However, this example contains only high-level customer or user requirements, whereas a complete multigenerational plan would include additional information such as specifications, costs, systems impacted, risks and issues, timing, and other relevant categories. The multigenerational planning starts with basic features and functions of the system and evolves into more sophisticated versions over time. For example, in the first generation basic features and functions include requirements such as the site code must be well documented, its capacity should provide acceptable response times, it should be Web based, it should link to other organizational sites, the site must be easily accessible through a few clicks of the computer mouse, it must be customizable by users, it must have excellent search capability, all organizational branding and logos

Generation 1	Generation 2	Generation 3
1. Site code must be well documented.	12. Should be multilingual (3 languages).	19. Expand languages to top 10 customers.
2. Its capacity should be correctly estimated to provide acceptable response times.	13. Handle currencies in approved languages.	20. Expand currencies to all countries.
3. It should be web based.	14. Be available 24 hours per day and 7 days per week.	21. Expand capacity to handle 100 times initial capacity.
4. It should link to other organizations.	15. Include all suppliers and products.	22. Integrate with financial functions.
5. Site must be easily accessible through a few clicks of the computer mouse.	16. Site available to all users anytime.	
6. Customizable by users.	17. Expand capacity to handle 10 times initial capacity.	
7. Have excellent search capability.	18. Expand to include distribution center order entry functions.	
8. Should be web based.		
9. All organizational branding and logos must be correctly displayed.		
10. All prices must be updated on-time.		
11. Information must be accurate.		

Figure 2.6 Multigenerational design: Creating an e-commerce portal.

must be correctly displayed, all prices must be updated on time, and its information must be accurate. When the second generation design is created, it will have enhanced features and functions to appeal to additional market segments and customers. These features and functions include a multilingual capability, increased currency handling options, be available 24 hours per day and seven days per week, include all suppliers and products that the organization services, its capacity should

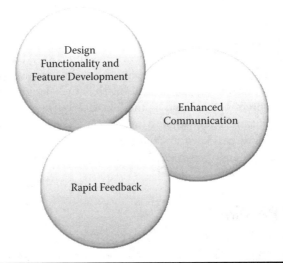

Figure 2.7   Sprint synergies.

be expanded to handle ten times its initial capacity, and an additional distribution center order entry function should be added to its available features. Finally, in the third generation, the e-commerce portal's features and functions are expanded to include additional languages and currencies as well as increased capacity and financial transaction capabilities. An advantage of using a multigenerational design approach is that even if all the features are not fully deployed, a design team can evaluate the advantages and disadvantages of pursuing different design options. We will expand this e-commerce discussion from various perspectives in subsequent chapters.

End-User Control

Over the past several decades, software design and commercialization activities have undergone a revolution in effectiveness and efficiency. The underlying bases for improvements in software project management have been to include end users or customers and key stakeholders in all phases of software design. APM using scrum sprints have helped greatly in this regard. This is true even in highly structured project management environments such as RUP. In summary, scrum sprints are a very useful software project management tool because they enhance communication between an agile team and its customers and key stakeholders through the rapid feedback of a product's features and functions. Scrum sprints also enable more effective control of the final product design by its users at a local level. These concepts are qualitatively shown in Figure 2.7 in which key characteristics of scrum sprints are positioned as a synergistic tool to execute APM.

Summary

APM with scrum sprints was a necessary invention to help mange software projects to increase quality, and reduce development time and cost. APM methodologies also embody several important Lean concepts. These include using agile teams to obtain the VOC; create software products using the VOC; design simple, standardized, and mistake-proofing tools and methods; and frequently review the status of product testing and similar validations with customers and key stakeholders. In the next chapter we will discuss key tools and methods used by agile teams to manage product and process change activities.

Suggested Reading

Augustine, Sanjiv. 2005. *Managing Agile Projects*. Upper Saddle River, NJ: Prentice Hall.

Martin, James William. 2008. *Operational Excellence: Using Lean Six Sigma to Translate Customer Value through Global Supply Chains*. Boca Raton, FL: Auerbach.

Martin, James William. 2009. *Lean Six Sigma for the Office*. Boca Raton, FL: CRC Press.

Schwaber, Ken. 2004. *Agile Project Management with Scrum*. Redmond, WA: Microsoft Press.

PROCESS IMPROVEMENT METHODS

2

Chapter 3

Accelerating Organizational Change

It is not necessary to change. Survival is not mandatory.

—W. Edwards Deming

Overview

Many external and internal factors impact organizations and make them change. Organizations need to change for many reasons. For example, external economic conditions may deteriorate causing a loss of major customers. The loss of one or more customers may require that changes be made in available capacity or new customers must be retained to replace those who have been lost. Also, technology may change how products and services are designed, produced, and delivered to customers. This type of organizational risk must be mitigated by monitoring changes in relevant technologies as well as industry trends. New competitors which may require change also enter an industry to change its competitive dynamics. Internal factors may include poor organizational strategy or poor execution of goals and objectives. Other issues may be related to resource scarcity where resources include labor, materials, equipment, and capital as well as similar sources. There are many other situations that may require an organization to change.

Regardless of the external and internal pressures on an organization, there are proven methods that can help its diverse stakeholders understand why various types of changes are required and how to successfully implement change using teams. In this chapter, we will discuss some of the important concepts, tools, and methods project teams can use to manage change activities within their projects. The discussion will be focused on how a team should be formed and its interactions with its customers and key stakeholders. This information is important because an Agile Project Management (APM) team helps to create or modify software products and services within dynamic work environments. In other words, sometimes software modifications are made to existing information technology (IT) systems. But, at other times, an entire IT system may need to be scrapped and a newer one created to meet operational needs within a Lean system. In this chapter, we will discuss the concepts, tools, and methods that have been shown to be useful in successfully changing an organization.

The goal of a change initiative is to move an organization from its current performance levels to a desired future state. This future state could be determined through strategic considerations, technology requirements, or an analysis of the best way that a product or service should be produced. Identifying a future state condition and actually creating and sustaining it over time may be very difficult. This is especially true if important elements of organizational change activities are ignored by an APM or Lean IT team. In other words, the creation of a future state is not simply a matter of making changes to a product or service and the various work processes that support them, and hoping for success. For example, Figure 3.1 suggests that to move from a current state through an intermediate and finally a future state, there are several required and sequential change activities that must be implemented. In this implementation process, the first step is to understand why

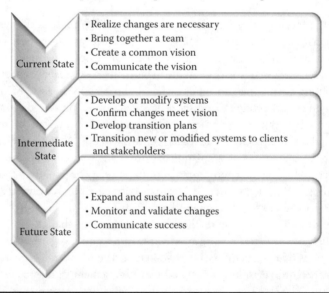

Current State
• Realize changes are necessary
• Bring together a team
• Create a common vision
• Communicate the vision

Intermediate State
• Develop or modify systems
• Confirm changes meet vision
• Develop transition plans
• Transition new or modified systems to clients and stakeholders

Future State
• Expand and sustain changes
• Monitor and validate changes
• Communicate success

Figure 3.1 Implementing organizational change.

a change is necessary, what it will be, how it will be done, who will be impacted, where and when it will take place, and the overall impact of the change on an organization. In this context, changes of various types may be required for a variety of reasons. Generally speaking, these reasons may be related to technology, the economy, suppliers, customers, regulations, or other factors.

There are several types of changes from a software design perspective that can be made. Some changes are necessary to create new products or modify older ones. Others are designed to improve process efficiency and increase productivity. However, once changes have been determined to be necessary, a project team should be brought together to complete the necessary work activities to implement the changes. In some situations, changes may only be understood at a local project level through a team's data collection and analysis activities. In other words, an organization may not know in advance which specific changes are required to improve its products or services, if they are process focused. In these situations, an organization's process improvement activities are often implemented at a local level and then expanded, from a strategic perspective, project by project.

Although change activities, which are the focus of process improvement activities, often occur at a local level within an organization, they should be aligned with an organization's goals and objectives using a formal project charter. A project charter describes why a project is important; its key stakeholders; its goals and objectives and the resources it requires to create, manage, and complete a project. An important second step of an effective change process is to bring a team together to create and communicate a common vision of why a project is necessary. It should be noted that there may be several types of communications a team may need to use throughout its project to communicate new information to its customers, key stakeholders, and the larger organization. As an example, in the beginning of a project, important information will include its goals and objectives, the expected business benefits, its area of focus or where the work will be performed, team members, the required resources, and its impact on people. In the early stages of a project, the focus should be to gain organizational support for a team's project activities. The support of a project's sponsors and champions is also important because they obtain scarce organizational resources for an improvement team and coordinate its work activities with customers and key stakeholders.

A team's work activities will vary depending if the work is focused on the creation of new products and services, modifications of current IT systems, or process improvements, which depend on software modifications. For example, work activities that are associated with the creation of new products are often industry specific. In other words, if an industry is software centric, then its project teams will create software. Also, depending on the complexity of the resultant hardware and software systems, a Lean IT team may be highly structured in a formal manner using methodologies such as the IBM® Rational Unified Process (RUP). However, if less project management structure is required then APM with scrum may be used to manage an IT project. In addition, combinations of the two project management approaches may be the best strategy. It should be noted that other industries may use different approaches in the design of their products. For example, in the automotive industry, the design and commercialization practices of the Automotive Industry Action Group (AIAG) are often used to manage the product development process from a design concept through to production and distribution using classical project management methodologies, but with a concurrent strategy to reduce a project's cycle time. In contrast, the work activities of a Lean project team, which is focused on modifying a current IT system and its processes, will most likely use an APM with scrum project management approach. It should be noted that APM with scrum, by its underlying nature, has several characteristics of effective change management that are continuously reinforced by their frequent usage. Examples include an activity backlog, scrum sprint, and frequent feedback to a project team from key stakeholders and customers as necessary.

As a project team begins its fact-finding activities, information is collected and analyzed to build models of how a new system should be created or its current systems modified to achieve its goals and objectives. The management of change activities is important during the creation of new and modified software systems. Transition planning of a project's solutions is also important because prior to the deployment of new products and services, transition plans must be developed with the support of key organizational stakeholders. This is because stakeholders will most likely either directly use the new or modified systems, or they will supply or receive information and resources from these systems. Changes should also be communicated in an easy-to-understand format. In summary, the management of a project team's change activities and communications is important to successful project execution.

Change Readiness

A project's success will be enhanced by understanding the perceptions of its customers and key stakeholders regarding the planned process improvements. Also, organizations differ in their ability to accept change both from within and without the organization. In fact, many organizations resist change and will only embrace it when they are under tremendous pressure due to poor sales, rising costs, regulatory issues, or other factors. These factors impede productivity as well as the long-term viability of an organization. In contrast, other organizations embrace change on a continuing basis. As a result, they have a greater ability to dynamically respond to the many internal and external processes that impact them. Formal change management tools and methods will increase the ability of a team to understand the many organizational issues and perceptions that impact the likelihood of their project's success.

Organizational barriers to change exist for a variety of reasons. Some of these reasons are well intentioned but misguided, whereas others are selfish and not in an organization's best interest. Barriers to change must also be identified and eliminated on a continuing basis, otherwise the change activities necessary to execute an organization's strategic goals and objectives will be inhibited. Although our discussion will be at the team and project level, it will be useful to also understand and discuss several characteristics of flexible organizations that embrace change. A major characteristic of successful change programs is the alignment of an organization's goals and objectives to support change activities. In other words, are its rewards and recognition systems aligned, at all levels, with its strategic goals and objectives? Reward and recognition systems include promotions, bonuses, pay increases, employee recognition, and other benefits that create incentives for employees to support an organization's strategies. Reward and recognition systems have an important impact on the ability of an organization to change its products, services, and processes. In summary, a reward and recognition infrastructure must be in place to promote organizational change.

A communication infrastructure should also be available to support change activities. This infrastructure should also be able to support communications at several organizational levels and use appropriate communication formats. As an example, when an important software project has been created and deployed, an organization's senior management should discuss why the project is important. This communication can be done through employee meetings, newsletters, and similar venues. From another perspective, perhaps a project's successes can also be communicated to the larger organization. In this context, communications associated with individual and team recognitions can also be used to promote a project. It should be noted that in these communication activities, it is very important that messages be consistent at every level within an organization and easy to understand by everyone. Finally, communications should also reflect the relative importance of the required change throughout an organization by describing its business benefits as well as how people can support it.

It is well known that organizational strategy should be executed through improvement projects in an integrated manner. Over time, solutions from many projects will slowly change an organization's products, services, and its process workflows, and create a culture that embraces the right types of changes. An important enabler of organizational changes is the creation and use of formal project charters that measure and validate a project's organizational impact and benefits. As part of the project chartering activities, team roles and responsibilities should also have been clearly defined and communicated to key organizational stakeholders. Key project supporting roles include deployment champions, financial analysts, and various functional support people. Another important project characteristic is the effective transition of projects to process owners and local work teams. An example of common transition activities includes training a local work team and process owner to use the appropriate tools and methods to support a team's improvements. Improvements are identified from a team's design activities or its root cause analysis. They are implemented to ensure that the necessary process changes will be sustained over time and fully integrated into an organization's formal performance management and control systems. In other words, processes, and in turn organizational change, requires that products and their processes be either created or modified in a formal manner. All improvement work should also be documented using a control plan that describes important characteristics of a product, service, or modified process. This description includes specification targets and reactions plans, which are executed if specifications are not met in practice. This methodological project approach will ensure organizational changes will be sustainable over time.

Key Change Tools and Methods

Many organizations use the tools and methods listed in Table 3.1 to capture, analyze, and communicate their key change objectives to stakeholders and the larger organization. We will discuss these tools and methods with an assumption that the higher-level strategic goals and objectives have been established and that an APM or Lean IT project team has been assigned to improve a process workflow by designing, deploying, or modifying a current IT system. The scope of an assigned project as well as its objectives, resources, and key stakeholders are some of the critical elements a team must consider prior to developing its project's schedule or engaging in substantive work activities with other people within the organization. In this context, project scoping activities are useful in clarifying a project's objectives and their critical performance measures, as these impact customers, stakeholders, and team members. Effective project scoping also helps a team to clarify its project's objectives and define the conditions that will make its project successful. A team's authority should also be clarified using a project charter so it is clearly understood by the people who are either impacted by a project's solutions or are required to provide resources and other assistance. These success criteria enable a team to confirm its project's objectives, its authority, how its project's success will be measured, and the roles and responsibilities of team members. Once these basic elements of team formation and project scoping have been clarified, a project team can begin to engage its key customers and stakeholders to analyze their requirements.

A formal stakeholder analysis helps to identify internal or external people who may be impacted by a project or whose support is required to complete it. Stakeholders represent diverse parts of an organization as well as suppliers, customers, industry groups, regulatory agencies, and similar interested groups. Once stakeholders have been identified and their goals clarified, a team conducts an analysis to identify potential sources of stakeholder resistance. Sources of resistance will often be associated with cultural differences, issues with sharing available resources, the potential loss of organizational power, and similar factors. A resistance analysis is used to develop strategies to influence key stakeholders to support a project. For example, different key stakeholders will provide their support to varying degrees depending on their perceived best interest. Stakeholders who will directly benefit

Table 3.1 Key Change Tools

Tool/Method	Description
1. Project scoping	Used to clarify project objectives, critical measures, customers, stakeholders, and team members. Helps team to clarify the project's objectives and define its success measurements.
2. Team authority and clarity	Helps team to confirm its objectives, perceived authority, how success will be measured, team roles, and responsibilities. Helps team to reach consensus on its goals, roles, and responsibilities.
3. Stakeholder analysis	Identifies internal and external organizations impacted by a project or whose support is required by a team.
4. Resistance analysis (force-field analysis)	Helps team to identify potential sources of stakeholder resistance relative to major factors related to culture, resources, power, and similar factors. Used to develop strategies to influence stakeholders to gain their support to varying degrees.
5. Infrastructure analysis	Helps a team to analyze organizational systems relative to their impact on change and the team's projects. Systems include rewards and recognition, training, personal development, information technology, and similar systems. Shows a team significant barriers to project activities including data collection, resource requirements, and eventual solutions. Once risk factors are identified, strategies can be developed to mitigate these risks.
6. Risk analysis	Different types of risks, including schedule, technical, cultural, and economic, can impact projects.
7. Communication planning	Clear and consistent messages to stakeholders and the larger organization relative to why changes are necessary, what they will look like, and the types of support required for the team's activities. Helps a team obtain project support and resources.

from a project's solutions will likely be highly supportive of a project. In contrast, those who will lose power or must provide resources may resist a project or want to modify its scope. A resistance analysis enables a team to identify these inhibiting factors and create strategies to eliminate or minimize their impact.

An infrastructure analysis is another change management tool that helps a team to identify and analyze diverse organizational systems and their impact on a project.

In this context, infrastructural systems include people, materials, facilities, and equipment that impact a project. Examples of these infrastructural systems include rewards and recognition systems, training systems, personal development systems, and the current level of IT as well as its availability and capability. Depending on the particular industry and organization there are other types of infrastructural systems that impact a project. The purpose of an infrastructure analysis is to show a team where significant barriers exist, which may impede the execution of a project. For example, barriers may adversely impact the ability of a team to collect and analyze data to create products and service or make process improvements.

At this point in a project, the information a Lean IT team has collected is combined into a formal benefit and risk analysis. Depending on the nature and extent of a project's risks, strategies are developed to mitigate them. A project can also be exposed to several different types of risk. This is why a risk analysis is useful. Typical project risks are related to schedule attainment, technical barriers, cultural and language differences, religion and political differences, and macro- and micro-economic issues. The final change management tool listed in Table 3.1 is project communications. Effective communication is integral to a team's success because it informs key stakeholders of vital aspects of a project. Communications to key stakeholders and the larger organization should be clear and consistent relative to what the changes will be, why they are necessary, and the support required to implement changes. Effective communication is important because it helps a team obtain resources and organizational support for its project activities.

Developing Project Charters

Project charters are formal documents describing why a project is necessary, its business benefits and risks, its completion schedule, key milestone activities, and the resources required to execute its work activities. In addition, a project charter describes where a project will be focused as well as its customers, stakeholders, team members, and support people. Charters exist in many forms, but they have the basic elements shown in Figure 3.2. Project charters are created to enable an improvement team to modify existing products and process, whereas a design team is formed to create specifications and documentation for new products and processes. It is always important that a team agrees with its project's goals and objectives, the expected business benefits, and the schedule of work activities necessary to complete its project. In this context, a project charter is always a good communication tool to facilitate the creation and execution of any project.

The first major section of a project charter describes its business problem including its extent, frequency, location, and negative impact on a business. This impact could be stated as either an actual or future impact to an organization. This section of a project charter is called its problem statement. Incorporated into a problem statement as well as several other sections within a project charter is the project's business

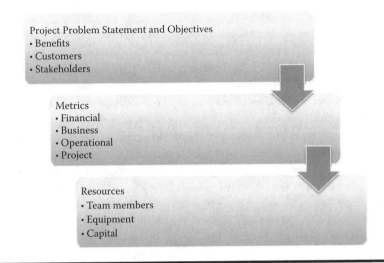

Figure 3.2 Developing project charters.

benefits, which should be described using quantitative metrics. Metrics can be classified as financial, business, operational, and project related. It should also be noted that depending on the specific organization and project application, there may be other metric classifications. An example would be metrics related to health and safety.

Financial metrics are represented in monetary units which include currencies such as dollars, cash flow, and revenue and asset investment amounts. These metrics are found within financial statements and similar reports. Common financial statements include profit and loss (PL) statements, balance sheets, and cash flow analyses. A profit and loss statement shows revenues and their adjustments minus expenses. A balance sheet shows the valuation of assets such as plants and facilities, equipment, inventory, accounts receivables, and similar assets minus liabilities. Liabilities include account classifications such as short- and long-term debt, which appear as accounts payables and loans outstanding. Cash flow statements show the relative liquidity or availability of cash by time period. Financial metrics are important in estimating project benefits and cost which include increased revenue, reduced costs, or accelerated cash flows. The other major metric classifications should be directly linked with financial benefits. As an example, if a project is focused on improving the response time of an information system to a customer request, then its financial benefits as well as its customer requirements should be calculated to determine the feasibility of providing a reduced response time to customers. The benefits must be balanced against the cost of choosing a team to make the necessary hardware and software changes.

Business metrics are usually represented as percentages or in forms that can be disaggregated and aggregated across an organization at various levels. Examples include time, numbers of incidents, monetary units, floor space, and similar metrics that can be represented in a format, which is either quantitative or a percentage. These types of metrics are also useful when comparing one project or business unit to another. This makes them useful in quantifying project benefits. For example, accounts receivable aging can be compared across several business units if they purchase similar products or services. Alternatively, the performance of a single business unit can be compared with its own performance over time. This type of information also helps a project team to identify business issues and create projects to solve them.

Operational metrics should always be linked to higher-level financial and business metrics. There are hundreds or perhaps thousands of operational metrics specific to different industries and organizations. At a very high level, operational metrics can be categorized into basic classifications of time, quality, performance, and similar categories. A project team is usually provided with information describing the performance of higher-level metrics, which indicate process issues. Examples include issues related to long cycle times or quality problems such as not meeting software testing specifications. These higher-level metrics may need to be disaggregated if they are process related to create project charters that can be focused to a specific business unit's process workflows.

Project metrics describe the specific goals and objectives a project team has been assigned to investigate and improve. One common example is the time a customer waits for service. Once a team identifies its higher-level project metric, it may also find through its investigations that one or more lower-level metrics contribute to the average level and variation of the higher-level project metric. As a result, as a team works through its data collection and analysis activities, there may be several related metrics that need to be investigated and improved. However, all metrics must be linked in an easy to understand manner in a way that financial metrics link to business metrics and business metrics link to operational metrics, which finally link to project metrics. In other words, the important concept is that all the metrics used to describe a project must be tied together. Then when lower-level project metrics are improved, these improvements will also be seen in a project's higher-level financial and business metrics.

Another important section of a project charter identifies key stakeholders, team members, anticipated business benefits, and the timeframe for completing a project. Key stakeholders include customers, suppliers, and various organizational functions, which provide information to define a project, provide its resources, or help a team to implement its solutions. A project team's members should be selected based on their relationship to a project's goals and objectives. In addition to key stakeholders and team members, projects may also require several other useful roles and responsibilities. Examples include process owners for whom the work is being done and project champions. Project champions help project teams define projects from a business perspective, and obtain critical resources and organizational support from key stakeholders. These are the critical elements of a project charter that ensure organizational support.

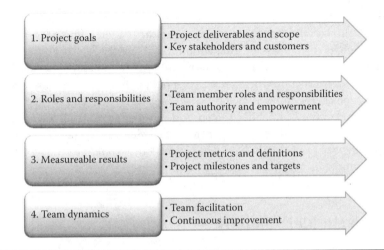

Figure 3.3   Creating team authority and clarity.

Team Authority and Clarity

A project team is formed after a project charter has been created by managers and champions. Figure 3.3 shows four basic elements of team authority and clarity. Once a team has been formed, one of its first important activities is to review the project charter and related information to clarify its authority, responsibilities, goals and objectives, scope, key stakeholders, customers, and related aspects of a project. This approach enables a team to modify its project charter to make it more focused relative to its goals and objectives, key stakeholders, and other information. A second important activity is to assign roles to its members and decide on their responsibilities. Additional team activities include breaking down a project's deliverables into work activities using a work breakdown structure (WBS). Once these initial team activities have been completed they are time phased for implementation using tools such as Gantt charts (large projects) or activity backlogs (smaller projects or subcomponents of larger projects). Once properly defined, a project's work activities can also be aggregated into milestone events to enable a team to track its completed work against its project schedule.

Team dynamics also impact a team's work activities as well as team facilitation and continuous improvement. Team dynamics move through a maturation process consisting of four stages. These phases include the forming, storming, norming, and performing stages of team formation. In the forming stage, team members meet for the first time. In these initial group interactions, people begin to learn about one another and they do not engage in in-depth project discussions. As a result, interpersonal relationships are superficial but also friendly. After their initial meetings, team members begin to discuss specific topics related to their project. It is at this point in the team maturation process, that significant differences of opinion may begin to develop regarding how to define and approach a project's execution. This is called a team's storming stage. Facilitation is important to bring a team through its storming stage. Facilitation recognizes the fact that different team members will have different perspectives regarding how to best define and execute a project's work activities. Therefore, rules should be created to promote respectful interactions between team members. This approach will tend to help to either prevent team conflicts or, if they should occur, to more effectively manage them. Finally, as a project team learns proper rules of conduct and its project deliverables are efficiently and consistently executed, mutual trust should be created between a team's members, its customers, and key stakeholders.

Key Stakeholder Analysis

Key stakeholders include internal and external organizational groups that support a project or are impacted by one or more of its solutions. A stakeholder analysis helps to identify important key stakeholder needs and requirements, such as anticipated project benefits, expected project costs and resources, execution and implementation risks, and known issues and similar factors that impact stakeholders. An understanding of stakeholder needs and requirements is important because they provide resources such as team members, support specialists, materials, equipment, or similar resources to a project team, or they help implement its solutions.

In a stakeholder analysis, stakeholder needs and requirements, issues, and risks are identified for subsequent analysis. The work activities necessary to meet stakeholder requirements or eliminate known project issues and risks are also identified and prioritized by a project team. In this requirements translation process it is important that the information gathered through a stakeholder analysis is passed on to the software design team so that a system's features and functions are frequently tested and approved by users and stakeholders to avoid performance and related problems. This is why the APM with scrum management approach is so useful to a team.

Table 3.2 shows a simple example of a stakeholder analysis applied to the design and deployment of an Internet-based e-commerce portal (which was also discussed in Chapter 2 and shown in Figure 2.6). The stakeholders used in this example include intended users of the Web site, internal management who is responsible for the use of the Web site, IT people who are building the site, marketing and sales, and communication people who represent external and internal customers. The requirements, known issues, and project risks of these stakeholders are shown with their associated work activities in Table 3.2. It should be noted that a project risk has a probability of occurrence. As a result, it may or may not occur. In contrast, a known project issue will occur. Known project issues and risks must be managed, mitigated, or eliminated to the greatest extent possible by a team to minimize their impact on a project's schedule, cost, and other objectives. The fourth column of

Table 3.2 Stakeholder Analysis: Creating an E-Commerce Portal

Stakeholder Group	Key Requirements/Issues/Risks	Team Activities to Eliminate or Mitigate Issues/Risks	Success Probability
1. Users	• Site must be easily accessible through a few clicks of the computer mouse. • Customizable by users. • Have excellent search capability. • Should be Web based.	Ensure information is passed on to the development group and that the system code is tested as it is created. Bring users in for frequent focus group sessions.	High
2. Management	• Must be in compliance with all organizational policies. • Must be cost effective. • Must be available on schedule. • Must have a standardized format and be integrated with other IT systems.	Maintain project budgets and schedules through scrum sprints and frequent project reviews.	High
3. Information technology (IT)	• Site code must be well documented. • Its capacity should be correctly estimated to provide acceptable response times. • It should be Internet based. • It should link to other organizational sites.	Follow organizational policies regarding software development. Insist code is created modularly and is functional at every sprint iteration and its documentation becomes part of the software code for easy access. Test its response time and link functionality.	High

continued

Table 3.2 (continued)   Stakeholder Analysis: Creating an E-Commerce Portal

Stakeholder Group	Key Requirements/Issues/Risks	Team Activities to Eliminate or Mitigate Issues/Risks	Success Probability
4. Marketing and sales	• Should be multilingual. • Include all suppliers and products. • Site available to all users at any time. • All organizational branding and logos must be correctly displayed. • All prices must be updated on time. Information must be accurate.	Include sales and marketing on review teams. Continually verify information accuracy and supplier representation. Bring in translators to work with marketing to ensure correct translation of information. Create subteams within the impacted countries.	High
5. Communication	• Users must be notified of the site's benefits. • Users must be trained to use the site. • Users must be notified of changes to the site.	Once a pilot is ready, update training and communication materials. Develop a training and communication schedule.	High

Table 3.2 provides a current estimate of the project's success probability. This success probability is the team's consensus of how successful their work activities will be relative to meeting stakeholders' expectations. The example shown in Table 3.2 uses an ordered ranking of low, medium, and high. More rigorous ranking systems can also be used to support a risk analysis. In the current example all rankings are thought to be high.

An analysis of Table 3.2 shows the requirements for each of the key stakeholder groups. As an example, the four key user requirements are that the Web site must be easily accessible through a few clicks of a computer mouse, be easily customizable, have excellent search capability, and be Internet based. Meeting the first three requirements will enable users to conveniently search for their needed products and services. Also, designing an Internet e-commerce Web site as opposed to creating an internal payment system should reduce software design and development costs, and increase the system's flexibility. This approach will enable users to purchase products and services, which are always up to date by suppliers. This system design approach to system design will tend to be more timely and efficient since the number of manual work activities will be significantly reduced. Key needs and requirements of the management stakeholder group are that the Web site be in compliance with all organizational policies, that it is cost effective, it be implemented on schedule, and it use a standardized format with respect to user features and functions to facilitate its integration with other IT systems. The IT stakeholder group requires that the new e-commerce portal have well-documented software code, sufficient capacity to provide acceptable response times, be Internet based, link to other organizational sites, and follow all organizational policies regarding software creation and deployment. To accomplish these IT objectives, planned work activities include creating software code in a modular manner, ensuring that key features and functions are delivered on time at the end of every scrum sprint, ensuring documentation is easily accessible to users, and that all software code is fully tested and reviewed as it is created to ensure the e-commerce Web site response time meets all expected user performance requirements. Marketing and sales stakeholders have different but complimentary requirements. These requirements are focused on increasing revenue by having the site be multilingual and available to as many users as possible at convenient times, using clear and consistent branding and logos that are correctly displayed, and ensuring the prices for products and services are accurate. Finally, the communication stakeholder group is concerned that clear and consistent messages are sent to the larger organization relative to the Web site's benefits, that users be trained to use the Web site, and that users be notified of changes to the site as they occur. This requirements listing is brief in that an actual e-commerce Web site will have a more extensive requirements listing.

Table 3.2 also provides strategies to meet stakeholder requirements or eliminate and mitigate project issues and risks. One overall mitigation strategy, which is common across all requirements, is to ensure that key stakeholders are on scrum sprint review teams. This will ensure they see the features and functions as they are completed at the end of each sprint. This will enable customers and key stakeholders to provide feedback. Other strategies to capture and implement key stakeholder requirements are also described in Table 3.2. For example, the marketing and sales group has identified several ways to meet user requirements. These include continually verifying information accuracy and supplier representation of the databases being used by a software system, and ensuring the Web site is available in the required customer languages by retaining translators and perhaps including people from the impacted countries to ensure local dialects and cultural factors are considered when building the Web site. The information gained using a stakeholder analysis will subsequently be translated into detailed product and service specifications. This translation process will be discussed in Chapter 4.

Analyzing Promoting and Restraining Factors

It has already been mentioned that stakeholders should be engaged throughout a project. An important first step in a project's engagement is to understand stakeholder requirements. An important second step is to review the many factors that either promote or restrain a team's work activities relative to achieving requirements. Some of these factors are common from one project to another, whereas others are project specific. Two examples are organizational culture and organizational infrastructure, which could become either promoting or inhibiting factors depending on how they are managed by a team. Figure 3.4 describes several common promoting and inhibiting factors. As an example, an important promoting factor is alignment of a project's goals and objectives with an organization's strategy. This is important to ensure that a project will be supported and be provided with resources for its work activities. A formal team project charter also helps document organizational alignment. In this context, it was mentioned earlier in this chapter that a well-defined project charter describes a project's business benefits, costs, and resource requirements as well as other important information. Once a project charter has been created, its team members are selected. After team chartering and formation, its work plan and schedule must be established. In most improvement projects APM with scrum will be useful to manage a project's work activities. However, APM may also be used within a larger and more formalized project management system such as RUP. Recall that RUP provides a highly structured project management framework to ensure complex customer and key stakeholder requirements are managed across several work teams. An integrated APM approach can also be used to ensure that the subcomponents of the larger system are efficiently created. Integral to promoting a project's objectives is ensuring that communication occurs with its key stakeholders on a frequent basis.

Team empowerment is also an extremely important promoting factor. Other promoting factors include ensuring that all team members are properly trained relative to their specific knowledge domain tools and methods, and integrating

Promoting Factors	*Inhibiting Factors*
1. Alignment of project's goals and objectives with strategic objectives.	1. Conflicting priorities due to nonalignment of a project with business goals and objectives.
2. Well-defined project charter showing business benefits versus resource requirements.	2. Fear of the unknown relative to project resource requirements, benefits, or impact on employees or stakeholders.
3. Developing a diverse and balanced project team.	3. Bureaucratic policies which inhibit communication and stakeholder support for resources and implementation of improvements.
4. Establish clearly defined roles and responsibilities.	
5. Using Agile Project Management (APM) methodology with scrum (If necessary use APM within the context of a larger more formalized approach such as IBM® Rational Unified Process (RUP))	4. A poorly formed project team lacking diversity and proper facilitation or leadership.
	5. Poorly defined roles and responsibilities which create confusion between team members or key stakeholders.
6. Communicate all relevant aspects of a project to its key stakeholders as required on a frequent basis.	6. Limited training on new tools and methods such as Agile Project Management (APM) with scrum and technical specializations.
7. Empower the project team using APM and scrum methods.	
8. Ensure all team members are properly trained on their specific knowledge domain tools and methods as well as APM and scrum.	7. Lack of effective rewards and recognition systems which promote project support or which inhibit support by rewarding the wrong behavior.
9. Ensure reward & recognition systems are integrated with organizational policies to promote effective and efficient project execution.	8. Technical, political, cultural, legal, or regulatory barriers to a project.

Figure 3.4 Analyzing stakeholder resistance.

reward and recognition systems with organizational policies to promote effective and efficient project execution.

There are also factors that inhibit a project team in the execution of its work activities. In this context, eight common inhibiting factors are listed in Figure 3.4. The first three factors refer to the existence of conflicting priorities. These conflicts are caused by a nonalignment of a project with key stakeholder goals and objectives, the existence of bureaucratic policies that complicate and inhibit decision making, as well as a fear and mistrust of a project's solutions on employees and stakeholders. A poorly formed project team that lacks diversity and is not receptive to different viewpoints and perspectives also inhibits a project's work activities. Poorly defined roles and responsibilities will also create confusion between team members and their key stakeholders, which tends to slow a team's work activities. Another inhibiting factor is limited training on new tools and methods, which are necessary to support a project. By way of example, applicable tools and methods may include APM with scrum as well as various technical specializations. A lack of effective reward and recognition systems will also inhibit support for a project by rewarding the wrong behavior. Wrong behavior would include not supporting a project, although it has a high priority within its organization. It should also be noted that there may be significant technical, political, cultural, legal, or regulatory barriers to completing a project's work activities. One or more of these inhibiting factors will have a stifling effect on a project since they negatively impact communications between a project team, stakeholders, and the larger organization.

Analyzing Organizational Structures

Table 3.3 shows seven key components of issues associated with an organization's infrastructure. Because projects compete for scarce organizational resources, it is useful to analyze how organizational structures either promote or inhibit a project's work activities. Structures include available resources for projects, the types and relationships of organizational functions, the types of available IT systems and similar technical enablers, the level of employee training, organizational reward and recognition systems, communication systems, and organizational policies regarding personal development. These basic structural factors impact the ability of a project team to collect and analyze project information as well as implement solutions within its organization. As an example, if a team cannot obtain prioritization for the use of equipment or key support people then its project schedule will slip. Also, if organizational reward and recognition systems do not encourage employees to embrace a project's solutions, which change products and services as well as their associated process workflows, then an organization will not realize a project's business benefits.

Table 3.3 also describes examples of several common issues associated with each of the organizational structures. For instance, the availability of resources may become a project issue or risk for several reasons. There may be several competing initiatives being simultaneously deployed by an organization or budgetary reasons might be the cause for resource scarcity. There might also be conflicting goals and objectives between one or more organizational functions. For example, conflicts may be created when different locations compete for common resources

Table 3.3 Analyzing Organizational Structure

Organizational Structure	Potential Issue
1. Available resources for project	• Competing initiatives • Lack of materials
2. Organizational functions and relationships	• Conflicting goals • Different locations • Personality issues
3. Information technology systems and similar enablers	• Systems are poorly interfaced • Systems are obsolete • Systems are not available
4. Employee training	• Employees require training • Lack of training resources • Training requirements are not known
5. Organizational rewards and recognition	• No reward and recognition program • Misaligned rewards and recognition
6. Personal development	• Lack of clear goals and objectives at individual level • No employee performance review • Ineffective employee performance review
7. Communication systems	• No communication system • Professionals trained in communication

or if there are personality issues between key stakeholders. IT systems and similar technological enablers may also be poorly interfaced, obsolete, or not available. Training is another very important organizational structure since employees who lack training make mistakes. Training may become an issue or risk to a project if there is a general lack of training resources or if training requirements are not known in advance. A lack of formal reward and recognition systems is also a common inhibitor of change initiatives. Employees work on activities that are aligned with their goals and objectives. To gain their support, management must structure reward and recognition systems to support changes. This may be easy or difficult depending on the available reward and recognition infrastructure. In other words, some organizations are more apt to change than others based on their available infrastructure. A particularly poor situation is one in which reward and recognition systems are misaligned causing the wrong people to be rewarded. The result is that other employees cannot see a clear linkage between their work activities and reward and recognition. In these situations, the right things may not get done by disillusioned employees. There may also be situations where personal development is poorly managed by an organization because there is a lack of clear goals and objectives at an employee level or ineffective employee performance reviews. Finally, an organization's communication systems may be nonexistent or ineffective. These infrastructure problems have been shown to inhibit project execution and organizational change in many organizations.

Managing Project Risk and Issues

Projects have several types of risks that may adversely impact their cost, schedule, or performance of the products and services being created and commercialized. These project risks may be minor or major depending on the scope of a project as well as the number of stakeholders and organizational functions impacted if the risks occur or the issues are not well managed. In this context, project risks have an occurrence probability. As an example, we could say that the probability of losing a major customer is low, medium, or high. We could also assign a probability range to the occurrence of this risk event such as its range is between 10 percent and 20 percent. Another example would be that software code is fully developed and tested by a certain date with an expected probability range. In addition to project risks, there are usually one or more known project issues. Key stakeholders will usually help a team identify project issues. In contrast to project risks, issues are not probabilities; they will occur and must be managed by a project team. An example of a project issue would be a critical hardware supplier that is going out of business. This issue has a 100 percent probability of occurrence. Now it needs to be managed by a team by identifying another source of supply. Both project risks and known issues can impact a project. As a result, project teams need to identify and manage them.

The next step of a risk analysis is to categorize risks and issues into the general categories of cultural, technological, scheduling, customer and supplier, economic, legal, and regulatory. Rating scales may also be very useful in these analyses. A rating scale describes the relative importance of one category relative to another. The impact of a risk or issue on a project is another analytical factor that can be rated and included within a risk analysis. Using these concepts, a weighted risk score can be developed to help prioritize a project's risks and issues for each category so that they can be managed by a team. Management strategies include the elimination, prevention or creation of mitigation strategies. Mitigation strategies include developing contingency plans, which become operational if a project risk or issue actually occurs.

Table 3.4 provides several examples of the different types of risks and issues, broken into seven categories, that may impact a project. For example, cultural risks

Table 3.4   Managing Project Risks and Issues

Category	Project Risk	Project Issue
1. Cultural	• A market research survey has not been done for a new cultural market segment.	• Sales have not materialized for a new product sold in another country.
2. Technological	• Technology will not exist. • Technology must be modified.	• A competitor owns license to a key technology. • Certain algorithm must be modified for use.
3. Scheduling	• Project milestones will not be completed on schedule.	• Project is already late by ten days. • Critical materials will not be delivered on time.
4. Customer	• A customer might not sign a contract. • Customer might not agree to software changes.	• A major customer has chosen a competitor for a contract. • A customer has declared bankruptcy.
5. Supplier	• A new supplier might not successfully scale up a new process. • A supplier might become bankrupt. • A supplier went out of business.	• A supplier has quality problems and cannot deliver 100 percent of an order.
6. Economic	• Demand for a product may decline. • Currency valuation may fluctuate.	• Demand has decreased by 25 percent in the past six months. • Currency valuation has decreased by 10 percent in the past 30 days.
7. Regulatory and legal	• New regulations may be implemented that obsolete a product.	• A new law requires that several safety features be added to a product prior to its sale.

occur if market research has not been conducted with potential customers who are culturally different from current ones. A failure to properly conduct market research may result in product or service commercialization problems. Cultural issues often occur because assumptions are made that one market segment has similar preferences to another. Reducing the probability of cultural risks requires that a project team correctly identify its market segments and the customers within the segments, and work with them as well as other relevant stakeholders when identifying requirements. Creating a culturally diverse project team is useful in these situations. If market research indicates that sales will not be strong with a particular cultural group, then various actions can be taken to increase the probability of high sales. These include advertising, visiting customers, creating promotional literature, and planning promotional events. These actions are designed to reduce a project's commercialization risk. In contrast, after a product or service has been commercialized, its actual sales will become known to an organization. If sales have not materialized, despite market research efforts, an organization could take a range of actions to increase sales. Low sales have now become a project issue that must be managed. Similarly, a technological risk would exist if advanced technology must be created or modified because there is an uncertainty of its success. In contrast, a failure to successfully commercialize a new technology is an issue that must be managed by an organization. A second example of a project issue would be known testing failures for a new algorithm. As a third example, scheduling risks would be related to uncompleted project milestones. In contrast, a project milestone that is already behind schedule by ten days can become a project issue. As a fourth example, submitting a quotation for a new contract, requesting that a customer agree to several critical software changes, and similar situations in which the final outcome is not known with certainty would be customer risks. In contrast, customer issues would include not being awarded a contract by a major customer who has chosen a competitor and a customer who has declared bankruptcy. In both situations, the event has occurred and is a known issue that must be managed by a team.

Examples of common supplier risks may include a new supplier who may not be able to successfully scale up a new technology or a supplier who may become bankrupt. In contrast, known issues would include a supplier who has known quality problems, a supplier who cannot deliver 100 percent of an order, or a supplier who just went out of business. Contingency plans should be made for project risks in case they may occur and mitigation plans created if project issues are known with certainty. Economic risks may include a potential decline in demand for a product or service in the future or potential currency valuation changes that adversely impact revenues. In contrast, known economic issues would be that product demand has actually decreased or currency has increased in value. Finally, an example of regulatory risk would be that new environmental regulations may be implemented that obsolete a current product versus the known issue of passage of a new law that requires several safety features be added to a product prior to its sale.

Planning Project Communications

Project communications are very important to a project team's success. Effective communications provide a clear and consistent message that customers, key stakeholders, and an organization can easily understand. Table 3.5 describes communications planning for various stakeholders using the e-commerce portal example, which is also shown in Table 3.2, but from a different perspective. Several important elements of good communications include the consideration of the target audience, the goals and objectives of a message, the content of a message, and how and when a message is delivered to stakeholders. Team communications can be sent to their target audience using focus groups, e-mails, newsletters, and similar types of communication channels. It should be noted that APM with scrum exhibits several characteristics of effective communication planning. One of the most important characteristics is the team and stakeholder reviews, which are held at the end of every scrum sprint. Table 3.5 also describes several other elements of good communication from the perspective of other stakeholders of the e-commerce portal example.

Managing Lean IT Projects

Lean IT projects are often managed within diverse organizational environments. These environments have differing degrees of promoting and inhibiting factors that impact a project team's change activities. In addition, organizations also have differing infrastructural strengths and weakness. As mentioned earlier in this chapter, organizational change has a higher chance of succeeding when stakeholders, the larger organization, and an organization's infrastructure support it. In turn, organizational support depends on a project's alignment. Properly utilizing the change tools and methods that were discussed in this chapter and engaging professional facilitators, if necessary, will help a Lean IT team to efficiently execute its projects. Figure 3.5 attempts to capture these key concepts. First, every project management method must successfully integrate effective change tools and methods at several organizational levels. Second, the type of project management structure used to manage a project within a Lean system should always be flexible. In this approach, utilizing key elements of APM with scrum will facilitate flexibility. This is true even when project management activities are complicated and require the use of highly structured project management methods such as RUP. It should also be noted that the complexity of project management work activities is often dependent on specific designs. Finally, Lean IT projects should follow Capability Maturity Model Integration (CMMI)® as defined by the Software Engineering Institute (SEI), as well as best practices of the Information Technology Infrastructure Library (ITIL)® of the UK Office of Government Commerce and similar organizations. We will dis-

Table 3.5 Planning Project Communications: Creating an E-Commerce Portal

Target Audience (Stakeholders)	Goals of Communication	Message Content	Message Delivery	Schedule
1. Users	To ensure system design reflects user requirements.	System features and functionality to meet user requirements.	Focus groups, e-mails, and newsletters.	At the end of every scrum sprint (20 to 30 days).
2. Management	Communicate project budgets and schedules.	Budget and schedule status by major milestone.	Scrum sprints and frequent project reviews.	At the end of every scrum sprint (20 to 30 days).
3. Information technology (IT)	Follow organizational policies regarding software development.	Recent code creation including its degree of modularity and functionality. Documentation, response time, and link functionality.	At every scrum sprint iteration, e-mails, and meetings.	At the end of every scrum sprint (20 to 30 days).
4. Marketing and sales	To ensure system design reflects user requirements.	Include sales and marketing on review teams.	At every scrum sprint iteration, e-mails, and meetings.	At the end of every scrum sprint (20 to 30 days).
5. Lean IT team	Project status and comments from key stakeholders.	Work activities completed, activities remaining, issues and concerns.	At every scrum sprint iteration, e-mails, and meetings.	At the end of every scrum sprint (20 to 30 days).
6. Supporting functions	Project status and anticipated support for the project.	Work activities completed, activities remaining, issues and concerns.	At every scrum sprint iteration, e-mails, and meetings.	At the end of every scrum sprint (20 to 30 days).

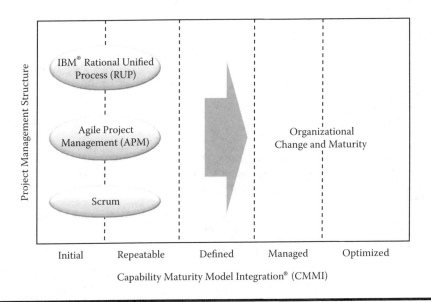

Figure 3.5   Managing Lean IT projects for change.

cuss the ITIL framework in Chapter 8 in the context of measuring and improving IT performance within Lean systems.

Summary

Every organizational initiative relies on the use of effective change management tools and methods for successful implementation of new products and services. This chapter discussed several common tools and methods that will enable Lean IT teams to manage their projects. Perhaps the most effective IT project management methodology is the use of APM with scrum. This is because the basis of APM is that there be frequent customer and stakeholder reviews of a Lean IT project's status, which serves as the basis for dynamically modifying a team's work activities based on a project's current schedule, cost, and performance status. In addition to customer and stakeholder meetings, which are held as part of scrum sprint reviews, there are several useful tools a Lean IT team can use to exchange project information with customers and stakeholders in an organized manner. These tools include project charters, clarifying team authority and clarity, analyzing stakeholder resistance, analyzing organizational structures, analyzing project risks and known issues, and developing effective communication plans. Finally, if a team finds it is having communication problems with its customers, key stakeholders, or other people within an organization, then a professional team facilitator can be added to the project team.

Suggested Reading

Augustine, Sanjiv. 2005. *Managing Agile Projects*. Upper Saddle River, NJ: Prentice Hall.

Behr, Kevin, Gene Kim, and George Spafford. 2007. *The Visible Ops™ Handbook-Implementing ITIL® in 4 Practical and Auditable Steps*. Eugene, OR: IT Process Institute.

DeMarco, Tom, and Timothy Lister. 1999. *Peopleware: Productive Projects and Teams*. New York: Dorset House Publishing.

Martin, James William. 2008. *Operational Excellence: Using Lean Six Sigma to Translate Customer Value through Global Supply Chains*. Boca Raton, FL: Auerbach.

Martin, James William. 2009. *Lean Six Sigma for the Office*. Boca Raton, FL: CRC Press.

Schwaber, Ken. 2004. *Agile Project Management with Scrum*. Redmond, WA: Microsoft Press.

Chapter 4

Translating Customer Requirements

If you can't explain it simply, you don't understand it well enough.

—Albert Einstein

Overview

The accurate translation of customer requirements into the design of products and services is a formal process in which frequent communications between external customers and key internal stakeholders is essential. In this translation process, there are several key measures of the efficiency and effectiveness of an organization's design process as it relates to external customer, internal stakeholder, and the larger organizational needs and requirements. One of the more important measures of a design process is its overall cycle time. Cycle time measures the length of time a project team requires to gather customer requirements, translate them into detailed specifications, and create new products and services or modify existing ones. The goal is to produce a product or service that meets market requirements relative to its features, functions, cost, and other requirements. Cycle time is so important that in some industries the first organization to commercialize a new product or service will obtain a significant percentage of the market shares for the entire life cycle of the product or service. Life cycle refers to the demand for a product or service as measured in units sold or sales revenue relative to its introduction, growth, and maturity and decline phases. Commercializing a new product or service on schedule is one important goal, but products and services must also be commercialized at a high quality level to meet their performance and cost targets and be within a project's budget. Another important measurement of a design project's success is the number of changes made both prior and after a new or modified design has been commercialized. A higher number of design changes to a new or modified product will lower its profitability, increase its commercialization cycle time, and lower customer and stakeholder satisfaction. It should be noted that these types of issues can be minimized or prevented by following good software design practices. In this chapter, we will discuss the translation of external customer and internal stakeholder needs and requirements using the concept of Kano needs and value analysis in the context of several prioritization tools. These will be discussed using the e-commerce portal example, which was introduced in earlier chapters. At the end of this chapter, we will link the requirement's translation process to Agile Project Management (APM) and scrum.

After a product or service has been commercialized, an organization may experience field failures. Key measurements related to these failures include percentage of warranty costs to revenue and the percentage of maintenance costs to revenue. Warranty costs are incurred when customers return, replace, or repair products prior to the product's normal end of life. Higher warranty costs are due to several factors, which can be arranged into a hierarchy. First, the failures may be related to design and production issues or be caused by customer error. If the failures are the result of poor design or production methods, then the causes could be due to one or several reasons and their interrelationships may be complex. Customer errors occur when customers do not know how to properly use a product or service. Examples include not understanding how to properly operate a system or causing damage to a system. Effective communication and training on the use of products and service may be as important as their design. Another good goal of good design practice is to prevent or minimize the occurrence of warranty costs. Warranty costs are lagging indicators of customer dissatisfaction and may eventually negatively impact a product's or service's sales. Maintenance costs also adversely impact profitability and customer satisfaction. They are directly related to the ease of replacing a system's components once a system has been sold. Some systems are less costly to maintain than others because they are designed in a way that makes their ongoing maintenance easy. How a product or service is designed impacts its repair frequency as well as the complexity and cost of the repair. Products and services having fewer and simpler subcomponents will usually have fewer maintenance requirements. There are also many best practices that can decrease maintenance costs. A common design approach is to use modules within a system so they can be easily removed and replaced by maintenance people. Two other important measures of the efficiency and effectiveness of a product or service design are their disposal or recycling costs.

At a high organizational level, there are several metrics that help a design team to measure the performance of its new product development process. These metrics include the percentage of market share of new products introduced within the past five years, actual versus target cost, the percentage of excess and obsolete inventory due to frequent design changes, the cost of designing a product as a percentage of its total sales revenue, and the function-to-cost ratio of a new design when compared to competitive products. A product team could also use additional metrics to measure its effectiveness and efficiency.

An organization should continually refresh its product portfolios with newer products and services to increase its profitability, cash flow, and market share. A metric that measures the percentage of new products introduced within the past five years avoids an organization's design process becoming stagnant. Measuring the cost ratios of features and functions of new products and services is also very important, because products and services should be commercialized in a way that ensures their sales price meets market requirements as well as internal profitability targets. The measurement of design cost as a percentage of total sales revenue can often be misused by an organization. This occurs when design costs are reduced to a point where the performance of a product or service is marginal. Therefore, it is important to measure costs to ensure that they are in line with those of comparative organizations. In some situations, additional resources may need to be allocated to an organization's design process. As an example, it has been shown that increasing the resources allocated to a product's design process up front tends to shorten a product's development time and reduces design errors. However, just throwing money at a design process does not guarantee success. Success can only be achieved by properly resourcing a design process in the right ways to minimize commercialization problems (such as a loss of market share, high warranty costs, and returned goods expenses) and lower customer satisfaction.

Key Design Goals

In this chapter we will discuss several tools, methods, and concepts useful in the translation of customer needs and requirements into software features and functions using the e-commerce Web portal example. This discussion will then be expanded in Chapter 6 to the design of software, and the concepts will be applied to several information technology (IT) applications within manufacturing and service processes. At the most basic level, the goal of good design is that a product or service meet customer requirements to ensure that it will have the relevant features, functions, and standard costs to meet customer requirements in a competitive manner within its target markets.

A second important design goal is that products and services be produced and delivered to customers both on time and defect free. However, this may not be an easy goal to achieve since customer disappointments are commonly encountered in the purchase and use of products and services. These disappointments are to some extent avoidable and can be mitigated to a large extent when good design practices are employed. In fact, there are best-in-class methods commonly used to design products. Examples include designing products for easy assembly and disassembly through simplification, standardization, and the use of modular design concepts. The goal of these decision methods is to ensure high product reliability, promote easy product delivery and installation, ensure ease of use by customers, and ensure ease of maintenance. At the end of a product's or service's life cycle, other important considerations include ease of disposal and recycling. These common design methods have analogues in the development of services including software design.

Translating Customer Requirements

Organizations provide products and services to different types of customers. Therefore it is useful to classify customers by their market segment, Kano needs, and required value expectations or elements. This concept is shown in Figure 4.1. Market segmentation classifies customers using several dimensions, including classifications of direct and indirect customers, sales volumes, and the types of purchased products. Direct customers purchase products and services directly from an organization and are called first-tier customers. Secondary customers purchase from those comprising the first tier. These are indirect customers. Additional indirect

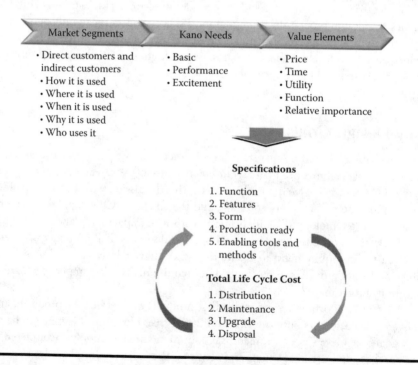

Figure 4.1 Translating customer requirements.

customers include key stakeholders such as regulatory agencies. Once a market segment has been defined, then additional information can be obtained from the customers who comprise it. For example, questions can be asked regarding how a product is used, where it is used, when it is used, why it is used, and who is using it. The answers to these questions will enable a design team to create new products and services that customers will find useful. Observing how customers use current products or services might show areas where the products and services can be improved or perhaps how they could be used more efficiently to increase customer satisfaction. This approach is different from sitting in an office and guessing how a customer might use a product or service.

Understanding where a product is used might also provide new insights into how to create or modify products. Customers might be using products in places not envisioned in the original design process. There may also be better ways to design a product's features and functions for use in these unanticipated environments. The time when a product is used and frequency of use might also provide helpful information on how to modify it to a design team. An example would be a service that is required at certain times of the day and by certain customers. It may also be useful to understand why customers are using a product or service. It might be found that their use is different from what was originally intended, or there might be additional features and functions customers would find to be useful. Finally, understanding who is using a product or service may reveal additional ways to improve these products and services or create new ones. It is also important to segment customers, because different market segments will have different needs and values. These needs and values can then be summarized as requirements. Requirements can then be translated into product specifications, which determine the design of products and services.

Kano Needs

What are Kano needs? A history review is required to understand the answer to this question. Dr. Noriaki Kano, a Japanese professor, was asked to help obtain customer feedback on a new Konica camera design. Previously, engineers had designed Konica's cameras based on internal requirements or using limited feedback from their customers. These requirements were developed as a substitute for the voice of the customer (VOC). However, it was shown through several on-site customer visits that the requirements did not accurately capture the VOC. In fact, customers were dissatisfied because many of the camera features and functions they needed had not been fully developed by Konica; for example, problems with picture quality (e.g., blurring and discoloration) and the time it took to develop the pictures. Kano, through a series of on-site customer visits and interviews, classified customer needs into five categories: attractive, one-dimensional, must-be, indifferent, and reverse. In turn, these five categories can be converted into basic, performance, and excitement needs. Basic needs are those requirements a product or service must have to function. Customers define products at a minimum performance level by their basic needs. For example, if you visit a physician's office for a routine annual checkup, you would expect basic services such as the doctor arriving on time, pleasant service, feedback on your medical condition, and related service attributes. You would become a dissatisfied patient if any of these basic needs are missing. This is a basic test to determine if a need is basic: Would a customer be dissatisfied if it were missing entirely? In contrast, performance needs differentiate one supplier from another. Relative to the previous example, services that would differentiate one physician from another would include the time spent answering patient questions, the use of advanced diagnostic equipment for testing, associations with highly rated hospitals, and graduating from a highly rated medical school with specializations. Measuring and improving the performance needs, while meeting basic needs, increases customer satisfaction and enhances organizational competiveness. Organizations typically compete within this space.

However, if an organization also obtains information that enables it to understand its customers' excitement needs, then new and exciting products and services can be developed for customers. Examples of excitement needs are all around us. This can be seen in the unique and useful products and services that were not anticipated by customers such as flat-screen televisions, iPods, computers, and FedEx overnight service. Excitement needs vary by customer market segment, but if after a product or service has been experienced for the first time a customer makes a statement such as, "Wow! I didn't know I needed that!" then the probability is high that one or more features and functions of this new product or service have fulfilled an excitement need. A design team determines customers' Kano needs through a series of interactive interviews. In these interviews, questions are asked from two perspectives. First, customers are asked how they would feel if the product or service attribute was present, and then how they would feel if it was absent. In this process, basic needs are identified when customers say they would be dissatisfied if an attribute was missing or would not be surprised if it were available. Performance needs would be identified by finding that more or less of an attribute was better than a baseline level. Excitement needs would be identified by a high level of customer enthusiasm for a product's or service's features and functions. If a design team understands how its customers' needs can be classified in a Kano sense, then its design work will be more efficient and customer satisfaction will be higher.

Value Expectations

In addition to Kano needs, customer value expectations should be understood and cross-referenced to Kano needs. In this cross-referencing analysis, a matrix by market segment is created using the dimensions of need type versus value expectation. From one perspective, value can be defined as price and convenience. A typical example would be for a customer to shop at a convenience store and pay higher prices to save time. Convenience can be further broken down into elements of cycle time and perceived benefits. Perceived benefits can be broken down into elements of function, usefulness, and relative importance to a customer. In summary, customers place higher value on a product or service if its price is low, the time to acquire it is short, it functions according to need, its perceived usefulness is high, and its relative importance is high. A design team can obtain a much better idea of customer requirements by using the concepts of Kano needs and these five value elements by market segment.

Collecting the Customer Information

After market segmentation, the next step for a design team is to collect actual information from customers and other relevant stakeholders to identify their Kano needs and value elements. In this investigation, a three-by-five matrix would be developed for each market segment. Then the customers within each market segment would be contacted through a variety of passive and active methods. A passive method takes advantage of information that is currently available to a team. This information consists of logged customer complaints, tracked failure costs such as warranty issues, returned goods, lost contracts, and similar types of information. Other examples of passively collected information include internal management reports, external industry reports, and benchmarking information obtained from other sources. Actively gathered information is obtained through customer interviews, focus groups, and surveys. Surveys may include face-to-face meetings, phone interviews, Internet surveys, and mailings to customers. A modification of face-to-face or phone interviews is visiting a customer's work site to observe how products and services are used under a variety of conditions. For example, it is useful to understand the how, where, when, why, and who uses a product or service. This type of information is usually not captured by internal management reports. Also, customers may not be aware of the full range over which a supplier's products and services are used in practice.

Although an important aspect of IT projects is that formal design reviews are held to identify customer requirements and translate these into specifications, this may not be sufficient to properly balance all customer and stakeholder requirements. For example, a customer may request specifications that dramatically increase the complexity of a design. In other words, requirements could become overly complicated relative to those actually needed to provide the necessary features and functions. In these situations, it can be really useful for a design team to engage its customer in an interactive dialogue relative to requirements that are directly aligned with the required features, functions, and aesthetics of a new product or service. Focus groups, face-to-face meetings, and on-site visits should also be integral to a design review process. In summary, obtaining accurate information about customer needs and requirements will usually be useful to a design team and facilitate the translation of customer needs and requirements.

Specifications

In Figure 4.1, specifications follow from the identification and translation of customer requirements using the concepts of market segmentation, Kano needs, and value elements. Specifications can also be broadly classified into functions, features, form as well as specifications a customer may not be able to see but are necessary to produce a product or service. Specifications are also needed to support production operations relative to the use of tools, equipment, and operational work tasks. An organization's profitability will also be higher if its products and services are cost effective relative to their distribution, maintenance, upgradability, and disposal. These are also controlled by specifications. As a final comment, specifications also help describe requirements for packaging, documentation, and other related product and service attributes. For example, a product's packaging must be strong enough to prevent damage in transit, clearly describe the product, and be attractive to customers.

Reasons for Poor Specification of Requirements

It may be useful to review several reasons for poor specification of customer and stakeholder requirements prior to a discussion of developing specifications for products and services. Ten common reasons for poor specification of requirements are listed in Table 4.1. The first reason is not accurately obtaining the voice of the customer (VOC). This situation occurs when the customers who will use a product or service have not been integrally included in the requirements definition phase of a project. Unfortunately, this is a very common problem. Customers need to be included in defining their needs and requirements for several reasons. First, customers help provide information that shows which features and functions have the greatest value. This enables a design team to focus on what is important to its customers, rather than become distracted with design concepts that do not directly meet customer requirements as represented by the VOC. This is important because not getting the VOC right could result in a useless product or service. Second, the VOC could greatly expand the design options available to a design team. Customers may provide ideas and concepts that are actually better than those that were originally under consideration by a project team. Involving customers in a design project creates ownership and will result in greater acceptance of its final features and functions. This implies they have an open invitation to attend design review meetings starting from the concept phase of a project through to the final testing and deployment of a product or service. To facilitate this review process, a meeting schedule of these review meetings should be published far enough in advance to avoid scheduling conflicts. Including customers in these meetings will also avoid situations in which sales and marketing are forced to substitute their voices for their customer's. In summary, not accurately identifying customer requirements by

Table 4.1   Ten Reasons for Poor Specification of Requirements

1. Not obtaining the voice of the customer (VOC) as represented by their requirements both qualitative and quantitative.

2. Not properly balancing the competing priorities and interests of key project stakeholders.

3. Poor translation of requirements into specifications resulting in incomplete, inconsistent, or untestable specifications.

4. Not using automated systems to design and test software code.

5. Not elevating the abstraction level of software design to facilitate the use of reusable assets to ensure system architecture has been fully discussed and reviewed prior to its selection.

6. Not testing system functionality under anticipated user conditions.

7. Not using proper statistical analysis to account for testing variation and limited sample sizes.

8. Not obtaining frequent user feedback as system functionality is developed by the Lean IT team (functionality is demonstrated in an iterative manner).

9. Too little or too much flexibility relative to incorporating user requirements into an ongoing system design.

10. Poor project management methods resulting in poor team coordination and collaboration, inefficiency and ineffective work activities, and poor risk assessment and management.

market segment using the concepts of Kano needs and value elements will distort a design team's objectives and priorities. The inevitable result of ineffective VOC communication will be poor product sales as well as modifications to newly created products and services.

A second failure point in product development is not properly balancing the competing priorities and interests of key project stakeholders. Priority balancing should be carried out in an objective manner to ensure broad stakeholder support. To facilitate this goal, customer requirements should be included in all analyses. However, even if a design team accurately obtains customer requirements, a third issue could be poor translation of requirements into specifications. This situation may result in incomplete, inconsistent, or untestable specifications, which delay a product's launch or create an unsalable product. However, to avoid these situations a design team can use best-practice tools and methods to efficiently translate the VOC into necessary features and functions and then into the required specifications. A fourth consideration is that it is also important that best-in-class design methods are used to take advantage of automated testing of software code. Not being able to create and test software code using automated testing systems could contribute to the creation of design flaws that cannot be detected until full functional testing. The inevitable result will be an increasing number of quality issues causing system failures. Fifth, it is also important to elevate the abstraction level of software to facilitate its use as a reusable asset and to ensure that a system's architecture will be completely reviewed prior to its final selection.

A sixth reason for poor specification of requirements is not testing a system's functionality under a full range of anticipated test conditions and environments. One example of designing a test to evaluate customer use under actual operations conditions would be to design a Web portal and test it over a range of expected demand to evaluate its capacity and response time. A quantitative comparison would then be made to verify that the actual response times meet the original customer requirements. In this test and evaluation process, the use of proper statistical analysis is also necessary to account for testing variation as well as the use of limited sample sizes. As an example, operations research methods such as queuing analysis can also be important when analyzing a system's capacity to operate within the range of expected demand.

An eighth reason for the poor specification of requirements is not obtaining user feedback on a frequent basis. Recall that an advantage of using APM with scrum is that a system's features and functions are created during each scrum sprint. This enables their evaluation prior to creating additional software code. This helps to quickly isolate and identify hardware and software problems. The application of APM with scrum project management methodology reduces product development cycle time since mistakes and rework are found quickly.

The ninth reason for poor specification of requirements is allowing either too much or too little flexibility regarding the incorporation of user requirements into a system. Not incorporating critical user requirements or incorporating too many nonessential requirements will negatively impact the design of an entire system. For example, failing to incorporate critical requirements may result in an unsalable product, but adding unnecessary features and functions will increase costs, degrade product performance, and increase a project's cycle time. In these situations, if a design team understands its customer's requirements it will be able to efficiently prioritize them. The tenth reason for poor specification of requirements is poor project management. The use of poor project management methods will result in poor team coordination and collaboration as well as inefficient or ineffective work activities.

Translating Critical-to-Quality (CTQ) Requirements

The translation of customer requirements is a straightforward but time-consuming process. In this section, we discuss creating lower-level specifications using the list of the customer requirements shown in Figure 4.2. We also introduce several useful tools and methods that will help facilitate the prioritization of customer

Stakeholder Group	CTQ Requirements	Specification "Y"	Design Criteria
1. Users	1.1. Site must be easily accessible through a few clicks of the computer mouse.		Function
	1.2. Customizable by users.		Feature
	1.3. Have excellent search capability.		Function
	1.4. Should be web based.		Form
2. Management	2.1. Must be in compliance with all organizational policies.		Production ready
	2.2. Must be cost effective.		Production ready
	2.3. Must be available on schedule.		Production ready
	2.4. Must have a standardized format and be integrated with other information technology (IT) systems.		Function
3. Information Technology (IT)	3.1. Site code must be well documented.		Function
	3.2. Its capacity should be correctly estimated to provide acceptable response times.		Function
	3.3. It should be web based.		Form
	3.4. It should link to other organizational sites.		Feature
4. Marketing and Sales	4.1. Should be multilingual		Feature
	4.2. Include all suppliers and products		Production ready
	4.3. Site available to all users anytime		Feature
	4.4. All organizational branding and logos must be correctly displayed.		Form
	4.5. All prices must be updated on-time. Information must be accurate.		Production ready
5. Communication	5.1. Users must be notified of the site's benefits.		Production ready
	5.2. Users must be trained in use of the site.		Production ready
	5.3. Users must be notified of changes to the site.		Feature

Figure 4.2 Translating critical-to-quality (CTQ) requirements.

requirements. Our goal is to translate high-level critical-to-quality (CTQ) requirements into specifications. Figure 4.2 classifies CTQ requirements based on several
types of design criteria. These criteria describe a product's functions and features,
its form or general appearance, and whether it is production ready or suitable from
an internal viewpoint. Functions are specifications that describe and control how
a product operates. In this context, functions consist of either individual or several
interacting hardware and software components. The concept of function also helps
define the various performance requirements of a product or service. A product
should meet its basic functional requirements. For example, an automobile should
have a running engine, a waterproof compartment, and basic safety functions. But

to the extent that it has additional functions that differentiate it from competitors, a customer's value perception of it will be higher. Features are additional differentiating mechanisms that add to a product's value from a customer's perspective. Using the automobile as an example, its color, type of interior, and various options are considered features. Form is reflected in a product's styling, including its size and overall appearance. Production-ready implies that a product can be produced according to customer and internal requirements. Internal requirements are related to efficiency targets, including how long it takes to produce a project, its standard cost, and expected yield.

Figure 4.2 shows several common CTQ requirements that an organization may consider important in the design and use of a Web site to manage its e-commerce activities. It divides key stakeholder requirements into several major classifications. These classifications include users who may be external or internal customers, the management of organizations, the IT group designing the Web site, marketing and sales, and communication professionals. It should be noted that this is only a partial stakeholder listing. Additional stakeholders may include suppliers, regulatory agencies, and internal or third-party production facilities. CTQ characteristics are cross-referenced to each stakeholder group. Some of these CTQ requirements will be expanded later in this chapter to illustrate the CTQ-to-specification translation process.

Some of the typical requirements often mentioned by users of e-commerce Web portals include that the site should be easily accessible through a few clicks of a computer mouse; be easily customizable by users relative to data input, analysis, and reporting; have an excellent search capability based on key search terms; and it should be an Internet (as opposed to an intranet) system. Some typical management requirements are that the system be in compliance with all organizational policies, be production ready or easy to use and maintain by internal or third-party users, be cost effective and developed within its budget, be delivered or available to users as originally scheduled, and have a simple and standardized system architecture that can be integrated with existing IT systems as necessary. The IT group has a technical focus. Its requirements are that the software code used to construct the Web site be well documented, the Web site should have sufficient capacity to provide acceptable response times, and it should be Internet-based and link to other organizational Web sites, both internal and external. This list of technical requirements would be greatly expanded for projects that represent actual Web-based applications.

Marketing and sales stakeholders have additional requirements that help to ensure easy customer access to the Web site regardless of language or the time of day and week. Once a customer signs onto the Web site, its content should be easy to understand to facilitate the product ordering process. All organizational branding and logos used on the Web site should also be correctly displayed and positioned. Finally, product and service prices and ordering information should be up to date and accurate. The assistance of communication professionals is also very important throughout the software development process. For example, potential users need to be told of the Web site's benefits and trained in its use. In summary, it is important that a design team properly obtains the VOC from all relevant stakeholders and accurately translates this information into product requirements.

Using the Analytical Hierarchy Process (AHP)

Once a team has carefully listed and defined its stakeholder and customer requirements, the requirements must be prioritized and organized for assignment and execution by local work teams. In this prioritization, work activities should be organized in a way to deliver discreet system functions or groups of related functions. This is especially important if the project management methodology is APM with scrum. There are several tools and methods that can be used in this prioritization work. The analytical hierarchy process (AHP), which is shown in Figure 4.3, is one of the more useful prioritization methods. The AHP method provides pairwise comparisons between all requirements to rank them relative to their importance. The requirements shown in Figure 4.2 are rearranged in a matrix format in Figure 4.3. This modified format enables a comparison between every possible two-way combination of requirements. We will use this tool to rank customer requirements and then use a Pugh matrix to select design alternatives that provide the greatest value to customers and stakeholders. We will discuss the Pugh matrix later in this chapter. The information gained from these analyses will be useful when prioritizing software features and functions during scrum sprints. We will show the AHP method for the partial listing of user requirements shown in Figure 4.2 because the example, although very simple, has many pairwise comparisons.

Analytical Hierarchy Process (AHP) Ranking Scale

Prior to discussing the AHP method, we will provide some context to show how the pairwise comparisons will be made using the ranking scale shown in Table 4.2. The scale is used to compare every requirement against every other requirement in a pairwise manner. When a requirement is compared to itself, the ranking is 1. If a requirement is highly preferred to another, its ranking is 9. The other requirement is ranked inverse to the first, or $1/9 = 0.11$. How does this ranking system work in practice? Figure 4.4 shows a partial view of the pairwise comparison matrix shown in Figure 4.3 for user CTQ requirements. Notice that the four requirements mentioned by potential users of the system are compared to each other using the ranking scale shown in Table 4.2. The rankings in this example were made by row. As an example, CTQ 1.1 (site accessibility) was ranked as a 3 when compared to CTQ 1.2 (customizable by users). The inverse ranking resulted in CTQ 1.2 being ranked as 1/3 or 0.3 relative

CTQ	1.1. Site must be easily accessible through a few clicks of the computer mouse.	1.2. Customizable by users.	1.3. Have excellent search capability.	1.4. Should be Internet based	2.1. Must be in compliance with all organizational policies.	2.2. Must be cost effective.	2.3. Must be available on schedule.	2.4. Must have a standardized format and be integrated with other information technology (IT) systems.	3.1. Site code must be well documented.	3.2. Its capacity should be correctly estimated to provide acceptable response times.	3.3. It should be Web based.	3.4. It should link to other organizational sites.	4.1. Should be multilingual	4.2. Include all suppliers and products	4.3. Site available to all users anytime	4.4. All organizational branding and logos must be correctly displayed.	4.5. All prices must be updated on-time. Information must be accurate.	5.1. Users must be notified of the site's benefits.	5.2. Users must be trained in use of the site.	5.3. Users must be notified of changes to the site.	Prioritized Ranking	Normalized Rank
1.1. Site must be easily accessible through a few clicks of the computer mouse.	1																					
1.2. Customizable by users.		1																				
1.3. Have excellent search capability.			1																			
1.4. Should be Internet based				1																		
2.1. Must be in compliance with all organizational policies.					1																	
2.2. Must be cost effective.						1																
2.3. Must be available on schedule.							1															
2.4. Must have a standardized format and be integrated with other information technology (IT) systems.								1														
3.1. Site code must be well documented.									1													
3.2. Its capacity should be correctly estimated to provide acceptable response times.										1												
3.3. It should be Web based.											1											
3.4. It should link to other organizational sites.												1										
4.1. Should be multilingual													1									
4.2. Include all suppliers and products														1								
4.3. Site available to all users anytime															1							
4.4. All organizational branding and logos must be correctly displayed.																1						
4.5. All prices must be updated on-time. Information must be accurate.																	1					
5.1. Users must be notified of the site's benefits.																		1				
5.2. Users must be trained in use of the site.																			1			
5.3. Users must be notified of changes to the site.																				1		
Total																						

Figure 4.3   Using the analytical hierarchy process (AHP).

Table 4.2 Analytical Hierarchy Process (AHP) Ranking Scale

Judgment	Ranking	Inverse Ranking
Highly preferred	9	0.11
	8	0.13
Strong preference	7	0.14
	6	0.17
Moderate preference	5	0.20
	4	0.25
Minor preference	3	0.33
	2	0.50
Equal preference	1	1.00

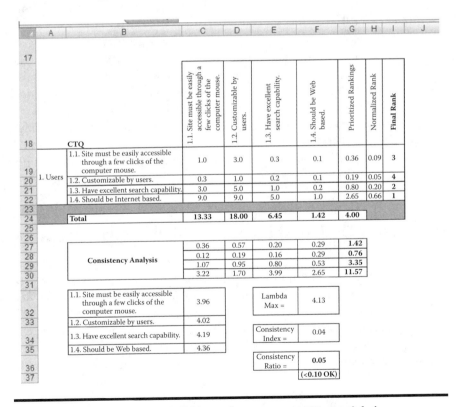

	A	B	C	D	E	F	G	H	I	J
17										
18		CTQ	1.1. Site must be easily accessible through a few clicks of the computer mouse.	1.2. Customizable by users.	1.3. Have excellent search capability.	1.4. Should be Web based.	Prioritized Rankings	Normalized Rank	Final Rank	
19	1. Users	1.1. Site must be easily accessible through a few clicks of the computer mouse.	1.0	3.0	0.3	0.1	0.36	0.09	3	
20		1.2. Customizable by users.	0.3	1.0	0.2	0.1	0.19	0.05	4	
21		1.3. Have excellent search capability.	3.0	5.0	1.0	0.2	0.80	0.20	2	
22		1.4. Should be Internet based.	9.0	9.0	5.0	1.0	2.65	0.66	1	
23										
24		Total	13.33	18.00	6.45	1.42	4.00			
25										
26										
27			0.36	0.57	0.20	0.29	1.42			
28		Consistency Analysis	0.12	0.19	0.16	0.29	0.76			
29			1.07	0.95	0.80	0.53	3.35			
30			3.22	1.70	3.99	2.65	11.57			
31										
32		1.1. Site must be easily accessible through a few clicks of the computer mouse.	3.96		Lambda Max =	4.13				
33		1.2. Customizable by users.	4.02							
34		1.3. Have excellent search capability.	4.19		Consistency Index =	0.04				
35		1.4. Should be Web based.	4.36							
36					Consistency Ratio =	0.05				
37						(<0.10 OK)				

Figure 4.4 Using the analytical hierarchy process (AHP): Partial view.

to CTQ 1.1. Figure 4.5 shows the Excel formulas for the AHP method. These formulas provide weighted rankings for each of the requirements being analyzed for the user stakeholder group. The final weighted ranking of each CTQ based on the AHP prioritization is in the following sequence from most important to least important requirement: CTQ1.4 > CTQ 1.3 > CTQ 1.1 > CTQ 1.2.

These rankings must also be checked for their evaluation consistency to ensure that the decision maker's judgments relative to the pairwise rankings are not contradictory. Consistent means that for all pairwise comparisons if a choice A compared to a choice B has a rank of 2 and choice B compared to a choice C has a rank of 4, then choice A should have a rank compared to choice C of 8 to ensure consistency between the three choices. A consistency ratio (CR) of less than 0.1 implies that the rankings are consistent relative to one another and the prioritization is accurate. A CR is calculated by first calculating the average priority of a requirement and then calculating a consistency index (CI). The CR is calculated as the CI divided by a random index (RI). The RI is the CI of a pairwise matrix that has been generated randomly, and it is based on the number of requirements being compared. The RI for a few pairwise comparisons is: RI = 0.58 for n = 3; RI = 0.90 for n = 4; RI = 1.12 for n = 5; and RI = 1.24 for n = 6. In this example, since there were four requirements, the RI = 0.9 and the consistency ratio is 0.05 < 0.10 (cell F36), which indicates that pairwise evaluations were ranked in a consistent manner.

The prioritization information obtained using the AHP method can be used to directly manage scrum sprints, because it helps to prioritize customer and key stakeholder requirements. But the AHP information can also be used with another tool called a Pugh matrix to compare several competing design alternatives in a consistent manner based on how they impact several requirements. Additional information describing the AHP and its calculations can be found in operations research textbooks such as the one written by Anderson, Sweeney, Williams, and Martin titled *An Introduction to Management Science: Quantitative Approach to Decision Making*.

Prioritizing Design Alternatives Using a Pugh Matrix

In most situations, a design team must evaluate several competing design alternatives, each with differing software features and functions. In this evaluation process, it will often be the case that some alternatives will satisfy certain customer and stakeholder requirements more efficiently than other alternatives. However, regardless of the design alternative selected as the best, in the sense that it satisfies most of the requirements, it may also be possible to incorporate the best features of each of the several alternative designs into a final design. As an example, in Figure 4.6 the user CTQ requirements from the e-commerce Web portal example are compared across several alternative designs versus a baseline system using a Pugh matrix.

CTQ		1.1 Site must be easily accessible through a few clicks of the computer mouse.	1.2. Customizable by users.	1.3. Have excellent search capability.	1.4. Should be Web based.	Prioritized Rankings	Normalized Rank	Final Rank
1. Users	1.1. Site must be easily accessible through a few clicks of the computer mouse.	1	3	0.25	0.11	= AVERAGE((C7/$C$12)+(D7/$D$12)+(E7/$E$12)+(F7/$F−G7/$G$12)		3
	1.2. Customizable by users.	0.333	1	0.2	0.11	= AVERAGE((C8/$C$12)+(D8/$D$12)+(E8/$E$12)+(F8/$F−G8/$G$12)		4
	1.3. Have excellent search capability.	3	5	1	0.2	= AVERAGE((C9/$C$12)+(D9/$D$12)+(E9/$E$12)+(F9/$F−G9/$G$12)		2
	1.4. Should be Internet based.	9	9	5	1	= AVERAGE((C10/$C$12)+(D10/$D$12)+(E10/$E$12)+(F−G10/$G$12)		1
	Total	= SUM(C7:C11)	= SUM(D7:D11)	= SUM(E7:E11)	= SUM(F7:F11)	= SUM(G7:G10)		

Consistency Analysis				
=C7*$G$7	=D7*$G$8	=E7*$G$9	=F7*$G$10	=SUM(C15:F15)
=C8*$G$7	=D8*$G$8	=E8*$G$9	=F8*$G$10	=SUM(C16:F16)
=C9*$G$7	=D9*$G$8	=E9*$G$9	=F9*$G$10	=SUM(C17:F17)
=C10*$G$7	=D10*$G$8	=E10*$G$9	=F10*$G$10	=SUM(C18:F18)

1.1 Site must be easily accessible through a few clicks of the computer mouse.	= G15/G7	Lambda Max =	= AVERAGE(C20:C23)
1.2. Customizable by users.	= G16/G8	Consistency Index =	= (F20−4)/(4−1)
1.3. Have excellent search capability.	= G17/G9	Consistency Ratio =	= F21/0.9
1.4. Should be Web based.	= G18/G10		(<0.10 OK)

Figure 4.5   Analytical hierarchy process (AHP): Formulas.

	CTQ	Importance Ranking (From AHP)	Alternative 1	Alternative 2	(Baseline)	Alternative 3	Alternative 4
1. Users	1.1. Site must be easily accessible through a few clicks of the computer mouse.	1	−1	1	B	1	1
	1.2. Customizable by users.	2	1	1	B	1	−1
	1.3. Have excellent search capability.	3	−1	−1	B	1	−1
	1.4. Should be Internet based.	4	1	0	B	−1	−1
	Weighted Total		2	0	B	2	−8

Note: Alternatives 1 and 3 are superior to the current baseline design. However, a design team can analyze the alternatives for ideas to create a superior final design.

Figure 4.6   Prioritizing design alternatives using a Pugh matrix.

In this evaluation, it should be noted that the ranking information from the previous AHP analysis is used to prioritize the CTQ requirements. In the Pugh analysis shown in Figure 4.6, each of the alternative designs is compared with the baseline system by assigning −1 if it is worse or a 1 if it is better than the baseline. Also, if an alternative is significantly worse or better than the baseline, it is assigned either a −2 or 2 respectively. Also, notice that the relative rankings from the AHP analysis shown in Figure 4.4 are preserved in Figure 4.6. For example, in the AHP analysis, the CTQ 1.4 (Web based) was ranked first with a 1. This highest rank order is preserved in the Pugh matrix by now assigning a weight of 4 in Figure 4.6. Also, CTQ 1.2 (customizable) had the fourth lowest AHP rank and now its weight is set in Figure 4.6 as a 1.

Reviewing the weighted total of the Pugh analysis, we see that alternatives 1 and 3 are superior to the baseline design. Also, alternative 2 is neutral and alternative 4 is worse than the baseline system. However, a more detailed analysis of Figure 4.6 shows that the baseline design is superior to alternative 1 relative to CTQs 1.1 and 1.3 but not CTQs 1.2 and 1.4. Also, alternative 3 is superior to the baseline design relative to CTQs 1.1, 1.2, and 1.3. It may make sense to combine the best features of alternatives 1 and 3 to create a superior design. Perhaps alternative 3 can be modified to incorporate alternative 1's solution to CTQ 1.4, that is "Should be Internet based," to create an overall superior design.

Stakeholder Group	CTQ Requirements	Specification "Y"	Type	System 1	System 2	System 3	System 4	System 5	Competitor Performance
1. Users	1.1. Site must be easily accessible through a few clicks of the computer mouse.	1.1.1 Less than 5 clicks.	Function	1	5				8
	1.2. Customizable by users.	1.2.1 Fields 1–10 have standard options menu.	Feature			5	10		7
	1.3. Have excellent search capability.	1.3.1. Will return 100% of available items in catalog using standardized search terms.	Function	5	10				6
	1.4. Should be Internet based.	1.4.1 Accessible both internally and remotely by computer systems on an approved list.	Form					5	5
	1 = Weak		Target (s)						
	5 = Medium								
	10 = Strong		Performance Gap (s)						
			Actions to Improve Perfomance						

Figure 4.7 Mapping specification to systems.

Mapping Specifications to Systems

Recall that customer needs and value elements are translated into CTQ characteristics. In Figure 4.7, the CTQ requirements associated with the user stakeholder group users have been defined quantitatively. As an example, the CTQ stating "site must be easily accessible through a few clicks of a computer mouse" has been quantified as a specification of "less than 5 clicks." How a team might develop the functionality to enable fast searches will be discussed in Chapter 6. But, at a high level, it would require reviewing standardized algorithms and integrating these, as applicable, into a project's software code. Notice that the matrix shown in Figure 4.7 cross-references specifications to the software systems that enable them. This type of mapping of specifications to systems is also called quality function deployment (QFD). The matrix representing Figure 4.7 is often called the house of quality.

In addition to mapping customer requirements to specifications and to the systems that enable them, the relationships between the enabling systems are also shown in the QFD matrix. Relationships between systems are shown at the top of the QFD matrix as shaded cells. For example, system 1 is impacted by systems 2 and 5. However, the exact form of these relationships must be determined through an analysis of the design or its testing. These relationships may be linear or nonlinear as well as additive or negating. Weights are also used to describe the degree of correlation between systems and specifications. The weighting scale is 1 (weak relationship) through 10 (strong relationship). As an example, we see that system 1 has a weak relationship or impact relative to the specification 1.1.1, whereas system 2 has a medium impact. In addition, there is also a column titled "Competitor Performance," which rates each specification against the performance of one or more competitors. Competitive information may be obtained though testing and evaluation of purchased competitive products. Competitive information may at times be very useful to a design team. This would be especially true if a current version of a new design could not meet one or more specification targets. In the lower section of a QFD matrix, actual performance of each system is compared against its specifications to identify gaps that need to be closed prior to releasing a product to production. The QFD matrix is also useful in translating design specifications across an organization's supply chain, including operations and suppliers. This concept is shown in Figure 4.8. In this more extensive translation process across a supply chain, the outputs of one QFD matrix become the inputs to lower-level QFD matrices. Once customer requirements have been effectively prioritized and translated into specifications, a project plan is created to execute work activities using APM scrum sprints. This concept is captured in Figure 4.9 and it will be discussed in Chapter 5 using Figure 5.9.

Summary

The accurate translation of customer requirements into the design of products and services is a formal process that requires frequent communication between external customers and key internal stakeholders. Several tools, methods, and concepts were presented to help translate customer needs and requirements into design features and functions. This discussion used an e-commerce Web portal example. The translation process begins with classifying customers by their market segment, Kano needs, and required value expectations. This information is converted into CTQ requirements. Once a team has carefully listed and defined its stakeholder and customer requirements, the requirements must be prioritized and organized for assignment and execution by local work teams using APM and scrum. Failing to properly identify customer and stakeholder requirements will result in the creation of specifications that do not reflect what customers and key stakeholders need and value. In this prioritization of requirements, work activities should be organized so they deliver discreet system functions or groups of related functions at the end of every scrum sprint. The prioritization information obtained using the AHP method can also be used to directly manage scrum sprint activities since customer and key stakeholder requirements are prioritized. But, the AHP information can also be used with another tool called a Pugh matrix. It was shown that a Pugh matrix can be used to compare several competing design alternatives in a consistent manner

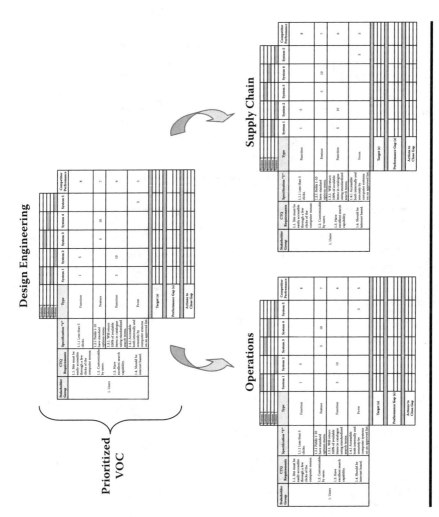

Figure 4.8 Translating requirements through a supply chain.

Sprint	Discrete System Function
1	1.1. Site must be easily accessible through a few clicks of the computer mouse (less than 5).
2	1.2. Customizable by users (fields 1–10 have options menu).
3	1.3. Have excellent search capability (will return 100% of items).
4	4.1. Should be multilingual (languages A, B, and C).
	4

Figure 4.9　Mapping system functions to a sprint schedule.

based on how they impact requirements. Finally, it was also shown that a QFD matrix was useful to map customer and stakeholder requirements to their specifications as well as the systems that enable them. Once customer requirements have been effectively prioritized and translated into specifications, a project plan can be created to execute a project's work activities using APM and scrum.

Suggested Reading

Anderson, David R., Dennis J. Sweeney, Thomas A. Williams, and R. Kipp Martin. 2008. *An Introduction to Management Science: Quantitative Approach to Decision Making.* Mason, OH: Thompson-Southwestern.

Augustine, Sanjiv. 2005. *Managing Agile Projects.* Upper Saddle River, NJ: Prentice Hall.

DeMarco, Tom, and Timothy Lister. 1999. *Peopleware: Productive Projects and Teams.* New York: Dorset House Publishing.

George, Michael L., James Works, and Kimberly Watson-Hemphill. 2005. *Fast Innovation.* New York: McGraw-Hill.

Martin, James William. 2008. *Operational Excellence: Using Lean Six Sigma to Translate Customer Value through Global Supply Chains.* Boca Raton, FL: Auerbach.

Martin, James William. 2009. *Lean Six Sigma for the Office.* Boca Raton, FL: CRC Press.

Prasad, Biren. 1997. *Concurrent Engineering Fundamentals*, vols. I and II. Upper Saddle River, NJ: Prentice Hall.

Schwaber, Ken. 2004. *Agile Project Management with Scrum.* Redmond, WA: Microsoft Press.

Suh, Nam Pyo. 2001. *Axiomatic Design: Advances and Applications*. New York: Oxford University Press.

Yang, Kai, and Basem El-Haik. 2003. *Design for Six Sigma: A Roadmap for Product Development*. New York: McGraw-Hill.

Chapter 5

Understanding Lean Concepts

Everything should be made as simple as possible, but not one bit simpler.

—Albert Einstein

Overview

The purpose of this chapter is to discuss major Lean tools, methods, and concepts. Our goal is to show the similarities between Lean and current project management methods used to manage information technology (IT) projects with a focus on Agile Project Management (APM) with scrum. This discussion will show how Lean methods can be applied to the management of Lean IT projects. In this approach, the goal will be to show how Lean practitioners can blend IT project management tools and methods within already deployed Lean systems. A second goal is to discuss adaptable and flexible approaches to the management of Lean IT projects to create, modify, and deploy hardware and software systems in manufacturing and service processes to increase organizational productivity.

Figure 5.1 shows several key goals of a Lean system. This first key goal is to understand customer requirements by gathering the voice of the customer (VOC) relative to their needs and values expectations. Recall that discussions of the VOC appeared in earlier chapters. In these discussions, it was shown that understanding the VOC is essential to any improvement methodology including APM with scrum as well as Lean. Also, in Chapter 4 we discussed that customer requirements consist

1. Understand customer requirements.

   • Voice of the Customer (VOC)
   • Customer needs and value elements

2. Create simple, standardized, and mistake-proofed products and services.

   • Analyze product designs for their value content.
   • Value stream map service and manufacturing processes.
   • Develop performance measurements.
   • Continually eliminate waste from products and services.
   • Continually improve the performance of products and services.

3. Develop integrated networks of key stakeholders including customers and suppliers.

4. Implement visual control systems both in the design of new products and services as well as in their steady state.

5. Continually update technology to eliminate waste.

Figure 5.1 Key goals of a Lean system.

of Kano needs and value elements. We also discussed that value elements can be broken down into subcomponents of price and convenience, and that convenience can be broken down further into the subcomponents of time, utility, or usefulness and relative importance.

A second goal of a Lean system is to translate customer needs and value expectations when designing new products or services or modifying current ones. To help in this work, there are several common Lean tools and methods which can be employed by a design team to facilitate translation activities. First, product designs should be analyzed for their value content. Value content is evaluated relative to the VOC and voice of the business (VOB). Recall that the VOB includes internal organizational stakeholder needs and values. However, we want to ensure that the VOC has the higher priority and that the VOB does not contradict the VOC. Once the VOC and VOB have been analyzed to understand their required value content, this information is used to directly build value into a new product or service. If a product or service currently exists, then its design should be analyzed to determine the percentage of value-adding (VA) content. For example, in an existing service process, value can be identified and analyzed using the VOC to create a value stream map (VSM) of the process workflows. In contrast, in an evaluation of VA content of a product, a value analysis is used to determine the relationships between customer requirements and the features and functions of the product. Features and functions not valued by customers or required by internal stakeholders should be eliminated from a product's design if technically possible.

Performance measurements are used to measure system key attributes once product or service designs have been created or modified. Measurements include the percentage value content, specifications describing required product or service performance characteristics, unit cost, and overall cycle time. Design metrics help to measure and quantify how well customer requirements are being met in practice by a Lean IT team. It should also be noted that additional metrics help to measure how well a Lean IT team manages its project activities. In summary metrics are used to measure the effectiveness and efficiency of designing products and services as well as the management of a project's work activities. Once products and services have been created and their performance measured, the goal of an organization should be one of continuous improvement to squeeze out any remaining non-value-adding (NVA) work tasks for service processes, or NVA features and functions for products. This continuous improvement strategy will help to ensure that customer requirements are met using the simplest product and work process designs to reduce a Lean IT project's cost and cycle time.

A third major goal of a Lean system is to develop integrated networks of key stakeholders, which include customers, suppliers, and other groups. Integration facilitates the translation of customer and business requirements throughout an organization's supply chain. There are many ways to achieve supply-chain integration. First, all supply-chain participants should embrace Lean principles and create systems to eliminate NVA work activities from these systems. In this context, several enabling tools and methods will be discussed in this chapter, but at a basic level, Lean supply chains should use common metrics to identify process waste, make continuous improvements across organizational boundaries, provide visibility of demand for products and services, optimally allocate or position supply-chain assets, and increase their utilization efficiencies (measure of leanness). This must be done while simultaneously meeting all customer and stakeholder requirements. Ideally, the IT systems of the supply-chain participants will also be integrated to provide visibility to supply-chain demand and capacity at all levels and in real-time. In addition, the collocation of supply-chain participants is important to minimize travel distance and to facilitate communication. Finally, contractual relationships should reflect participant cooperation. These are several integrative characteristics of a Lean supply chain.

The deployment of visual control systems is a fourth major goal of Lean systems. Visual systems can be used to monitor and manage the day-to-day work activities within a process workflow. In a manufacturing system, in which materials and information move from one work operation to another, visual means that metrics related to the past, current, and projected status of materials and information can be seen at a glance. A common situation is that performance measurements are displayed for everyone to see on a daily or even minute-to-minute basis. Visual displays have different formats. First, some are manual, whereas others are highly automated. Manual systems include using poster boards located within production areas to show production status or marking off floor space to identify where materials should be placed to be near their points of usage. Other common visual controls include using lights and warning buzzers to signal abnormal production conditions. The goal of a visual control system is to quickly alert people to changes of process status. In highly automated systems, visualization is displayed using IT systems. An advantage of using this approach is that the IT system displays up-to-date information regarding the status of a product system. This information may also be gathered from geographically dispersed and disparate IT sources. In other words, all supply-chain participants will be able to easily see the demand on their portion of the system, available capacity, and the status of relevant work activities. Common examples include call centers that display operational metrics for facilities across the world, and airline and other transportation companies that identify asset status using radio frequency tagging or other IT platforms. Also, recall that Lean IT teams are managed using visual control systems. In this context, in Chapter 2, we discussed using an activity backlog and scrum sprints to provide visibility to a project's work activities. It was also recommended that project information describing the status of work activities be displayed using whiteboards with supporting documentation within a dedicated conference room. The review of a project's status at the end of a scrum sprint by customers and key stakeholders also facilitates the visual control of a project's work activities.

The fifth goal of a Lean system is to continually reduce waste. Continuous improvement depends on many supporting elements. These supporting elements include the systems discussed earlier in this section as well as others to be discussed later in this chapter. But at a basic level, improvement implies that effective process measurements exist and that an organizational infrastructure also exists to support and reward people for improving their products, services, and work processes. It should be noted that the activities associated with the management of IT projects within Lean systems also comprise a work process. To support waste reduction, people must be trained in the use of process improvement tools and methods such as Lean, Six Sigma, and APM with scrum, as well as key IT tools, methods, and concepts.

Seven Forms of Waste

Lean systems are deployed to increase the percentage of VA work activities within a process by reducing the seven common types or forms of process waste shown in Figure 5.2. These seven forms of process waste have analogues to the creation of products and services. The first type of process waste is the overproduction of work. If customer requirements should change, then producing work in advance of actual customer demand may result in wasted materials and labor. The impact of this type of waste can be seen as longer process cycle times and higher costs. In a Lean IT team, an example of overproduction would include producing software code in anticipation of customer needs or known requirements. A complicating impact of overproduction would be to overutilize available resources for the creation of

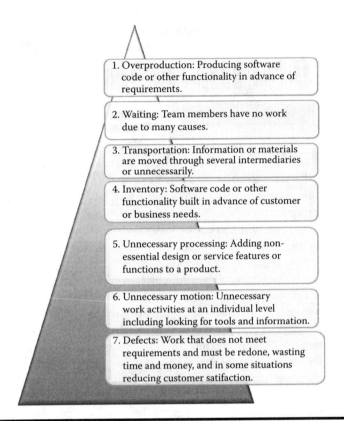

1. Overproduction: Producing software code or other functionality in advance of requirements.

2. Waiting: Team members have no work due to many causes.

3. Transportation: Information or materials are moved through several intermediaries or unnecessarily.

4. Inventory: Software code or other functionality built in advance of customer or business needs.

5. Unnecessary processing: Adding non-essential design or service features or functions to a product.

6. Unnecessary motion: Unnecessary work activities at an individual level including looking for tools and information.

7. Defects: Work that does not meet requirements and must be redone, wasting time and money, and in some situations reducing customer satifaction.

Figure 5.2   Seven major forms of waste.

products or services in which demand does not occur. Overproduction has a significant impact on production operations because systems have limited capacity. However, it should be noted that a relevant factor contributing to overproduction is the ability to quickly set up and move from one type of work activity or job to another. In other words, organizations are often forced by economic factors, related to limited capacity or high setup costs, to overproduce. This situation is more severe in some industries. Lean practitioners attempt to minimize or eliminate overproduction by matching available capacity to actual demand. The goal is to do work only when it is required and without overproducing. We will discuss this operational strategy later in this chapter relative to APM with scrum.

Waiting is a second form of process waste. When people wait for materials or information to do work, or if equipment is idle, process time is lost, and cycle time and production costs increase. There are many causes of waiting for materials, information, tools, equipment, or other resources. One major negative impact caused by waiting includes delays in moving production to downstream work operations. Relative to a project team, waiting waste occurs when team members are idle because they do not have the resources they need to start or finish their work.

Transportation waste occurs when information or materials are moved through several unnecessary intermediaries. Unnecessarily moving materials through a service system directly increases its cycle time and cost. Also, in highly automated systems, the impact may be exacerbated if unnecessary work operations are performed. Examples include doing a work task more than once due to rework or scrap, obtaining data extracts and analysis that are not needed, creating nonessential reports, or other situations where busy professionals are required to unnecessarily transfer materials or information between one or more work operations. In contrast, information should be moved directly to where it is needed and not routed through several intermediate locations. An example would be eliminating several unnecessary management reviews of a project's work objects. In a project management sense, transportation waste occurs when team members must travel to see one another, or people and information are unnecessarily moved from one location to another. In summary, whenever unnecessary work, inspection, or storage locations are added to a process, transportation waste is created.

Inventory waste occurs when a work object not immediately needed by a customer has been produced. In this sense, it is also related to overproduction when materials or information are excess and cannot be used until the future. An example would be software code or other system functionality built in advance of customer or business needs. The risk in creating inventory is that customer requirements may change or the work may become damaged or lost. Inventory waste varies by industry with one of the most extreme situations being perishable items, such as food, that must be carefully stored otherwise they will rapidly deteriorate. However, information within a service system also has a limited shelf life. For example, if management reports are created but not used, then their value rapidly decreases from its initial level. The best way to prevent inventory buildup is to carefully match demand to supply. However, this is not an easy task. It also becomes more difficult in systems that rely on forecasting models to estimate customer demand. As an example, it is common for a forecasting model to have an inherent percentage error between 5 percent to 25 percent or more of average unit demand. In a project management application, demand is directly related to various customer and stakeholder requirements and project schedule. Supply is represented by available resources, such as team members, support people, and equipment. A good strategy to match demand and supply is by assigning and balancing team resources using scrum sprints.

Unnecessary processing occurs as a result of several scenarios. First, unnecessary features and functions may be added to a product. This situation results in NVA work activities. The existence of unnecessary processing indicates that customer requirements have become disconnected from customer and key stakeholder needs and value expectations. Unnecessary processing increases the cycle time and cost of design and production processes when it occurs. Also, process complexity is increased. This may compound the problem by increasing the number of mistakes made during the production of products or services. In a project management sense, any work activities not related to a project's activity backlog will result in unnecessary processing. Also, any requirements added to an activity backlog that have not been specifically requested by customers or key stakeholders as being necessary to satisfy the VOC or VOB will result in unnecessary processing.

Unnecessary motion occurs when a specific work activity is not done efficiently. This situation will cause higher process cycle times and cost. Processing defects may also be created, which further decreases operational efficiency. There are several possible causes for this type of waste and several operational impacts. The best way to avoid unnecessary motion is to study work activities and their associated work tasks to determine the best way to do them day after day. This implies that each work task can be broken down into smaller and optimally sequenced work elements. As part of this analysis, all the necessary work materials, information, tools, and training are provided to employees. This enables them to do their work in a way that minimizes physical effort and the variation of time caused by not using an optimum work method. In other words, unnecessary work will exist at an individual work task level if an inordinate amount of time is spent looking for tools and information. It also is created when employees do not follow standard work procedures.

The seventh process waste is process defects. Defects are caused if work products do not meet customer requirements. When defects occur work must be redone (i.e., reworked) or thrown away (i.e., scrapped). The result is higher cycle time and production cost, as well as lower customer satisfaction. Defects occur for many reasons. These include poor communication of customer requirements as well as their translation into specifications. Additional reasons include measurement errors, poor workmanship, and problems with incoming materials. In fact, there is a long list of causes of process defects.

Lean Tenets

The development of a Lean system is based on three major tenets: the existence of relatively stable external customer demand; the application of simplification, standardization, and mistake-proofing activities to stabilize operational systems; and continuous process improvement (Figure 5.3). These tenets are also called the pillars of a Lean enterprise. Stable external demand implies that the flow of work, through a production system, is smooth and its variation is predictable. Smooth implies that material or information flowing through a system is sequenced as a fairly regular pattern. Predictable implies that an organization can estimate external demand and match its available capacity to demand regardless of its growth or decline, its seasonality, and its natural random variation. For example, in a stable production system such as automobile manufacturing, the magnitude of stable variation may be less than 10 percent of the average unit demand between each equivalent time period. Ideally, if the operational components of a system are properly matched to expected external demand patterns, then the work will be

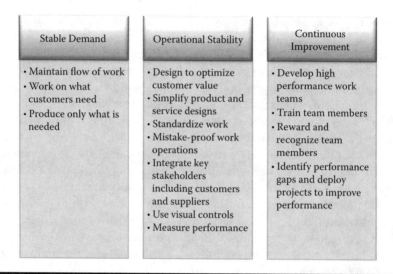

Stable Demand	Operational Stability	Continuous Improvement
• Maintain flow of work • Work on what customers need • Produce only what is needed	• Design to optimize customer value • Simplify product and service designs • Standardize work • Mistake-proof work operations • Integrate key stakeholders including customers and suppliers • Use visual controls • Measure performance	• Develop high performance work teams • Train team members • Reward and recognize team members • Identify performance gaps and deploy projects to improve performance

Figure 5.3   Lean tenets.

produced when, where, and in the quantity needed. A direct analogue to this concept is a scrum sprint. A sprint is designed to produce discrete levels of a system's features and functions, based directly on customer requirements. This strategy helps to prevent the overproduction of work. For example, recall that at the end of a scrum sprint, customers and key stakeholders review recently created product features and functions. This feedback mechanism matches supply (team resources) to demand (VOC and VOB requirements).

Operational stability is developed through the many programs and improvement activities designed to ensure day-to-day work activities are efficiently performed. An important basis of operational stability is the effective design of products and services. This implies an alignment of customer and stakeholder requirements and their accurate translation into the specifications and design of products and services. This will tend to ensure higher value content using simple, standardized, and mistake-proofed designs. The efficient design of products and their associated production processes is a central reason for higher operational stability since simple and standardized designs will be easier to produce. Also, the application of mistake-proofing strategies will tend to increase operational stability since defects will be eliminated. For example, software algorithms should also be designed simply, using standardized coding, and have mistake-proofing strategies applied. We will discuss this approach to software design in Chapter 6.

The third Lean tenet is that processes should be continually improved over time to increase the percentage of their value content. Continuous improvement activities depend on several factors. These include the development of high performance work teams; training team members to use appropriate tools and methods; and the creation of reward and recognition systems, which help align team members and their work activities with organizational goals and objectives. In summary, continuous improvement facilitates the identification of performance gaps and the deployment of project teams to improve product and service performance.

Lean versus Agile Project Management (APM)

There are several similarities between Lean and APM with scrum. This is also true for project management methodologies such as Extreme Programming. Table 5.1 lists fifteen common Lean tools, methods, and concepts, and cross-references these to APM. In this discussion of Lean and APM, we will show the similarities of Lean and APM from two perspectives. The first perspective is from that of Lean IT project management. The second is from that of designing or modifying IT products and services. Our discussion will then continue into Chapter 6 with a discussion of proven approaches to efficient software design. This will touch, in part, on the key Lean concepts of removing intermediaries, standardization, modularization, and reusability of software components. In Chapter 7, we will show how the concepts presented in Chapters 1 through 6 are applied in manufacturing and service applications.

Reorganize Work Environment

Reorganization of a team's work environment is important to facilitate communication between team members and minimize external distractions. Both of these situations reduce team productivity. The proper design of a work environment, based on known ergonomic principles, will not only ensure that a team is collocated in one place to enhance both group and key stakeholder interactions but also provide enough work space and quiet areas to satisfy the needs of individuals as well as the larger work group. Another important objective of work area reorganization is to ensure that team members have the materials, equipment, and information they need to effectively and efficiently execute their work activities. This reduces the wasted time required to search for these items.

Although experts should be consulted for recommendations for the design of employees' work spaces, there are several proven characteristics of a good workplace design. These are shown in Figure 5.4. There should be a minimum square footage per person to enable access to work materials and prevent the work space from becoming too cluttered with work materials. Also, it has been shown that overall noise levels within a work space decrease as the square footage of a work space increases. However, the square footage assigned per person should also not be too great since team members must interact and travel distance should be minimized. Also, excessive work space may be expensive. In addition to a minimum square

Table 5.1   Lean versus Agile Project Management (APM)

Classical Lean Tools and Methods	Agile Project Management (APM) Equivalent
1. Reorganize the work environment	Bring APM team together in one place and reorganize work space to enhance individual and group interactions. Ensure team members have the materials, equipment, and information they need to effectively and efficiently execute their work activities.
2. Create high-performance work teams	Ensure teams are empowered to do the work within their project's scope with minimum supervision except during sprint reviews. Ensure proper facilitation of conflicts.
3. Understand customer value	Review customer needs and requirements directly with customers and quantify all requirements. Translate requirements into specifications and system features and functions in an iterative manner using scrum sprints with frequent customer reviews.
4. Develop metrics and measurement systems	As part of the requirement translation activities, develop measures or metrics and testing systems to verify design features and functions, and compare performance to the original customer requirements.
5. Link work operations	All team work activities must be highly visible and linked using activity backlog whiteboards and scrum sprints to track and report project status. Frequent and accurate communication is the goal.
6. Level demand	Demand is managed using an activity backlog to ensure an APM team is level loaded with work during every sprint.
7. Simplify the work	The goal of APM is to develop the simplest product features and functions that meet customer requirements under expected user conditions.
8. Standardize the work	The goal of APM is to use standardized components in product design and standardized methods in project management.
9. Apply mistake-proofing methods	Mistake-proofing implies that even if a customer mistakenly uses a product, no adverse consequence occurs since a warning is issued or the system compensates for the error. Relative to project management applications, codeveloping key product functionality or having frequent sprint reviews will help to prevent errors from being incorporated into a product's final design.

Table 5.1 (continued)   Lean versus Agile Project Management (APM)

Classical Lean Tools and Methods	Agile Project Management (APM) Equivalent
10. Balance material and information flow (using a takt time)	Ensure team members have equal workloads and help team members who fall behind schedule.
11. Manage bottlenecks	Certain work activities control a project's cycle time. These are bottleneck activities.
12. Use transfer batches	Immediately transferring information to the next operation dramatically reduces project cycle time.
13. Reduce setup time	Reducing the setup time for work will also reduce a project's cycle time.
14. Maintain high system availability through preventive maintenance	Ensuring systems are designed simply, using standardized components, and are tested under actual usage conditions will help make certain they are reliable with a certain probability.
15. Implement a pull scheduling system	Sprint iterations use pull scheduling as a means to reduce the time to obtain team and key stakeholder feedback.

footage for each team member, there should be dedicated work areas where team members can interact. There should also be natural light in the work space. For example, people should not be placed in cubicles against walls without access to daylight since it has been shown that this situation lowers their productivity. Support services such as copiers, conference rooms, and administrative people should also be located in work areas to provide easy access to resources and to prevent excessive walking by team members. In other words, all materials and equipment should be readily available to a team. In addition to proper workstation design, there should be areas to display project status reports and related project information. In some situations conference rooms should be assigned to a team on a long-term basis.

In the book *Peopleware*, DeMarco and Lister describe some basic design principles originally proposed by Christopher Alexander. Alexander proposed that work spaces should be designed to provide for their evolutionary growth under the local control of the teams occupying them. In other words, the structure of a work space should not be imposed from outside a group. However, I would recommend that a modification be made to this original concept to provide for a standardized

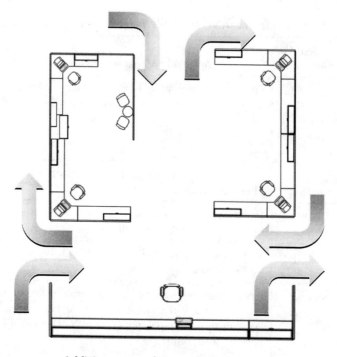

1. Minimum square footage per person
2. Quiet areas for development
3. Areas for group interaction
4. Windows for light
5. Close to support services to minimize walking
6. All materials and equipment available
7. Wall areas to display project status reports

Figure 5.4   Reorganize work environment.

approach to both workplace ergonomics and employee safety. In other words, evolutionary growth must be constrained to a degree. Unfortunately, it is common that many organizations bring together high-performance teams only to dissipate their energies through poor working conditions. It should also be noted that in addition to optimized elements of a team's working space, employee training and similar factors are important for increasing team productivity.

Create a High-Performance Work Team

The term *high performance* implies that a team is empowered to do the work within its project scope with minimum supervision or interference. In other words, recommendations by key stakeholders are only made during design or sprint reviews.

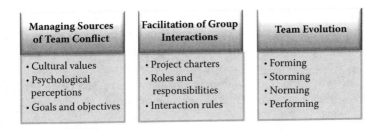

Managing Sources of Team Conflict	Facilitation of Group Interactions	Team Evolution
• Cultural values • Psychological perceptions • Goals and objectives	• Project charters • Roles and responsibilities • Interaction rules	• Forming • Storming • Norming • Performing

Figure 5.5   Create a high-performance work team.

This is an important concept because the creation of a high-performance work team is essential to creating and deploying Lean IT systems. Although there have been many books written on how to create high performance work teams, several common themes have emerged from these diverse sources of information. Figure 5.5 shows three major components forming the basis for the development of high-performance work teams. These components include the management of the sources of team conflict, the facilitation of group interactions, and their maturation or evolution. This classification recognizes the fact that an important characteristic of high-performance work teams, because they are diverse, is the proper facilitation of conflicts. Typical sources of conflict are caused by differences between team members' cultural values, psychological perceptions, and personal goals and objectives. However, diversity and differences of opinion, when properly facilitated, have been shown to increase a team's ability to solve problems. Also, diverse teams will tend to more fully evaluate different approaches to problem definition and solution.

The facilitation of teams is enhanced through the use of professional facilitators, the use of project charters, and the assignment of team roles and responsibilities. Project charters and the assignment of roles and responsibilities were discussed in Chapter 3. Facilitators are trained to use proven tools and methods to move a team through its four evolutionary stages. These stages are shown in Figure 5.5. As part of the facilitation process, facilitators work with a team to develop rules that help guide its interactions. Typical rules include only one person speaks at a time, and the rotation of team member roles and responsibilities. Team members also need to meet their commitments on schedule and they should have a mutual respect for each another.

The evolutionary process consists of four stages. These are the forming, storming, norming, and performing stages. In the forming stage, team members meet for the first time and begin to discuss one another's behaviors and expectations. If a team is highly diverse, then there may be interpersonal conflicts toward the end of this stage. The beginning of interpersonal conflicts initiates the storming stage. In this stage, team members openly disagree with one another. If these disagreements are not properly facilitated, then a team's cohesiveness may deteriorate. But with proper facilitation, team members begin to learn to positively interact with one another. In these interpersonal interactions, all team members are encouraged to express their viewpoints as part of the facilitation. A predominance of positive interactions indicates that a team has entered its norming stage. During the norming stage, mutual trust begins to develop among team members. Toward the end of the norming stage, a team enters its high-performance stage and it becomes a high-performance work team. In the high-performance stage, team members respect one another, value their differences, and consistently meet their commitments.

Understand Customer Value

Once a work space has been created and team facilitation is in place to move a team through its evolutionary stages, the concept of customer value must be explored in the context of the team's project charter, the product or process the team is focused on, and the project's goals and objectives. Recall from earlier discussions that identifying and analyzing customer value includes meeting with customers to determine their Kano needs and value expectations, and translating these into requirements and finally into specifications. This information should be gathered directly from customers and quantified to facilitate measurements, evaluation, and testing. Specifications are then used to create or modify IT systems to provide the necessary features and functions of products and services. This work is accomplished in an iterative manner using scrum sprints, and frequent customer and stakeholder reviews.

Figure 5.6 describes the VOC translation process from a Lean perspective, and it emphasizes the creation and modifications of IT systems. The VOC translation begins with an analysis of customer market segments, because different customers have different needs and requirements. In some VOC analyses, products and services may be highly differentiated by market segment, whereas in other analyses, they may be required to simultaneously satisfy several different market segments. In Chapter 4, we discussed that markets can be segregated using several factors. These include the type of customer, the type of industry, and how and where a product is used. It was also shown that a major benefit of market segmentation is that it forces a team to identify customers' requirements in a way that best captures their needs and value expectations at a local level. This is the best approach to ensure that products or services are efficiently created and that they will be purchased by customers when they are eventually produced and commercialized. It is also important to measure the VOC by market segment. Typical methods used to do this include face-to-face conversations, telephone surveys, e-mail surveys, and similar forms of communication. However, Lean IT teams will most likely find that face-to-face meetings are the best way to obtain the VOC and VOB requirements.

Once the VOC and VOB have been identified through various data collection methods, the information is brought together and analyzed to develop quantifiable customer requirements, and then translate these requirements into specifications. Specifications are used to guide the design of features and functions to ensure customer requirements are met in practice. There are also specific software tools

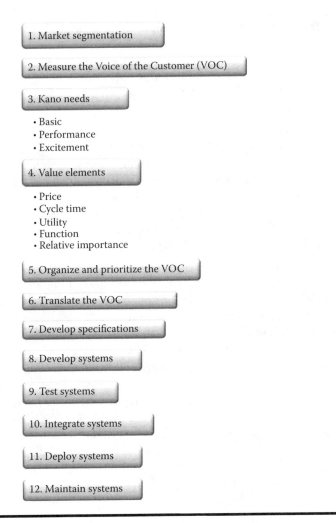

Figure 5.6   Understand customer value.

and methods that enable a team to move efficiently through its VOC translation process. In Chapter 4 we discussed several methods to do this and in Chapter 6 we will discuss several others.

Develop Metrics and Measurement Systems

In this section we will begin the discussion of metrics from a Lean perspective. In Chapter 8 we will continue this discussion with a focus on the development of metrics for the design of software products and services. The goal of this section will be to develop easily measurable metrics to verify that design attributes and performance meet original customer requirements, and that metrics are useful to manage Lean IT projects. In a classical sense, common Lean metrics include the percentage of VA time of a process, its production rate, its throughput rate, scrap and rework percentages, process downtime or the time not available for work, maximum available capacity, the setup time required to switch from one job to another, the average inventory level, and the floor space required for the process. These are classic operational metrics useful in any production system, although they may require some modifications. In addition to these metrics, Lean IT teams must also create metrics that can be used to manage their software development projects, as well as those that measure product and service performance and other design attributes. It should be noted that there is some overlap in these approaches. For example, the higher the percentage of VA activities in which a project team engages itself, then the lower a project's cycle time and cost in most situations. To some degree, VA percentages are driven by simple and standardized design strategies that make project management easier. Also, simpler designs should have fewer quality issues such as scrap and rework. As a result, understanding customer requirements when developing software systems to get them right the first time is also the best approach for successful project Lean IT project management. The other classical Lean metrics have been discussed in earlier chapters of this book.

A common classification strategy is to divide project metrics into business, financial, operational, and project metrics. This concept is shown in Figure 5.7 and it was introduced in Chapter 3. Recall that business metrics are linear and additive. Examples include continuous units of measurement such as time, hours, and monetary units. In addition, business metrics can be aggregated upward through an organization or disaggregated at lower organizational levels. They can also be represented as a percentage to show the relative contribution of one part of a system to another. As an example, we could measure lost time at several levels within an organization and aggregate these time components through a business unit to calculate

Figure 5.7 Develop metrics and measurement systems. Metrics must be consistent with customer needs and requirements, which are translated into a project's problem statement and objectives.

an overall estimate of lost time for an organization. Alternatively, we could create a metric representing hours lost as a percentage of total hours worked. These types of metrics when used together enable an organization to understand where process improvements should be made. In contrast, financial metrics are expressed in terms such as monetary units related to expenses, revenues, and cash flow. Since financial metrics are also continuous, they can be either aggregated or broken into smaller units and expressed as percentages. Financial metrics should also correlate to business operational metrics. For example, lost time should be correlated to higher, direct labor expenses.

In contrast, operational metrics could take several forms. But, regardless of their form, their relationships to higher-level business and financial metrics should be clear. As an example, time lost could be caused by several different types of process issues such as the breakdown of a machine, poor quality, a lack of materials, inexperienced employees, or scheduling problems. In turn, these issues would have lower-level root causes such as a scrap problem caused by paint blemishes or other quality problems. A Lean IT team will measure its performance using all four metric classifications. In summary, Lean IT teams use metrics to manage their software development projects and measure product and service performance and other design attributes.

Link Work Operations

In a lean system, work activities are linked with one another to enable local control of the flow of materials and information. An analogous characteristic of APM with scrum is that an APM team's work activities are highly visible and linked using activity backlogs and scrum sprints. In Chapter 2, we discussed that whiteboards are very useful in these project management applications because a team's work information is highly visible. However, even if a team is dispersed geographically, similar work activity prioritization, tracking, and reporting systems should be used to manage its activities. In other words, local work teams should display their work activities and this information should be available to other work groups around the world. The goal of the project team should be frequent and accurate communication to facilitate information sharing between all team members. The physical linkage of work activities and team members may also take on different physical forms, which vary by application. As an example, Figure 5.8 implies that it is important for a team to have a work space conducive to a high degree of team interaction but still provide quiet areas for work. In other words, work environments should reflect the types of work to be done within them.

The linkage of work activities within a production system ensures that the flow of work can be controlled using visual or other simple communication methods. This is also true for the management of projects in that a team's project status will be visible to both its team members and key stakeholders. This is a major characteristic of a Lean system in that process status is clearly visible to all participants

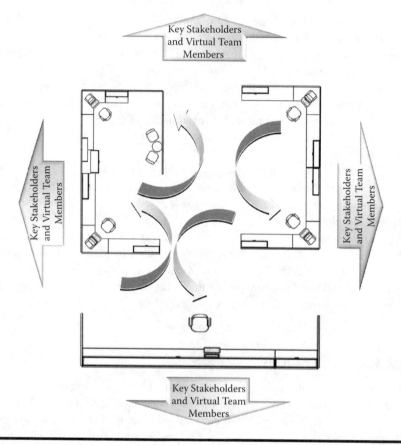

Figure 5.8 Link work operations.

without having to investigate or read lengthy management reports. Management reports may become quickly outdated or contain information that is not very useful. There are many ways in which team members can stay in touch with one another. Collocation using effective supporting tools and methods is a major enabler. In this regard, although remote teams cannot be collocated with one another, they can use video or audio conferencing on a frequent basis.

Level Demand of a Scrum Sprint

A major goal of Lean systems is to level the external customer demand on a system so it can produce products at a constant rate. This constant production rate is called its takt time. A takt is calculated as the time available for production divided by the required production. For example, if there are 8 hours (480 minutes) available and 100 units of production need to be produced, then the takt time is 4.8 minutes per unit. In other words, every 4.8 minutes one production unit must exit the process.

All the resources of a process are then balanced to achieve this target takt time or production rate. A stable takt time requires a stable production schedule and system, which in turn requires that the demand on a system is also stable within capacity limits.

In an analogous manner, a Lean IT project team should also attempt to level the workload of its team members. For example, the workload taken from an activity backlog and broken into scrum sprints should also be leveled between sprints. Figure 5.9 shows an example of this leveling concept. Notice that the activity backlog has been divided into four sprints, whose objective is to deliver a discrete level of system functionality. The functionality will be created through various work activities, each requiring a certain number of person days. An alternative project management strategy might be to combine sprints 2 and 3 to balance the required resources or person days with sprints 1 and 4. However, this may not be possible if the functionality to be delivered by sprint 3 depends on the functionality provided by sprint 2. Sprint 4 provides a different challenge to a Lean IT team in that there is apparently a higher degree of variation relative to required resources or person days. This situation should be managed to ensure the work is level across team members. It should be noted that the graph shown in Figure 5.9 is a control chart which has been modified as a simple time series chart. This chart shows the sequential work activities as well as the person days required to complete them. LCL is the lower control limit. UCL is the upper control limit. X-bar is the average of person days across all work activities.

Simplify Work

The concept of work simplification applies to project management activities as well as to the design of products and services. In fact, there is synergy with respect to the design of products and services and their work activities. For example, the greater the complexity of a product or service, the greater the number of project work activities necessary to bring it through its design activities. Also, its production process will be more complicated. As a result, an organization's goal should be to use good design practices to simplify its product and services because high complexity reduces operational efficiency. A major goal of designing products and services should be to create the simplest product features and functions that meet customer requirements under expected usage conditions. Using a similar perspective, simple project management systems such as APM with scrum should be used to manage design projects to the greatest extent possible since their project management methods are simple and visual.

The focus of the first step shown in Figure 5.10 is on accurately translating customer requirements. The second is the simplification of product and service designs. It should be noted that work simplification depends on accurately translating the VOC and VOB when initially creating a product or service design. This approach ensures that a design team focuses on features and functions important

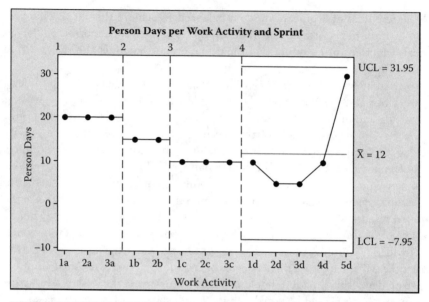

Sprint	Discrete System Function	Work Activities	Person Days	Person Days per Sprint
1	A	1a	20	
		2a	20	
		3a	20	60
2	B	1b	15	
		2b	15	30
3	C	1c	10	
		2c	10	
		3c	10	30
4	D	1d	10	
		2d	5	
		3d	5	
		4d	10	
		5d	30	60
	4	13	180	

Figure 5.9   Level demand during sprint.

to customers and key stakeholders. The simplification of features and functions is achieved through a combination of best-in-class design practices. These best-in-class design practices share several common philosophies, and their actual applications differ by industry. Software development is a specific example in that its design tools and methods differ from those used to manufacture durable products. In summary, product and service designs can be simplified using a variety of methods including component elimination and combination as well as other

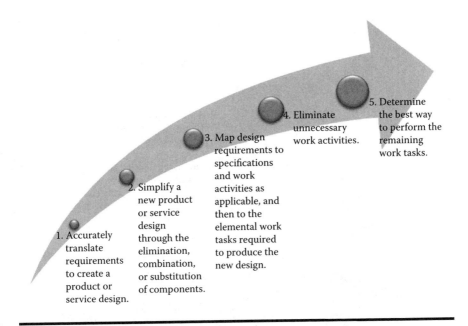

Figure 5.10 Simplify work.

methods such as substitution. Once a product or service design has been simplified, the work activities necessary to produce it are analyzed to identify additional simplification opportunities but from a process perspective. This concept is represented in Figure 5.10 as steps 3, 4, and 5.

Standardize Work

Once a product or service and its production work activities have been simplified relative to the VOC and VOB, work activities, materials, and all other design and production factors should be standardized. The goal of standardization is to ensure that all work activities are done the same way to reduce work variation. This approach reduces the overall cycle time to produce products and services as well as the frequency and extent of processing errors. A major goal of APM with scrum is to use standardized project management procedures to ensure a standardized approach to the design of software.

Figure 5.11 shows a 5S approach to simplifying and standardizing process work activities and their associated lower-level work tasks. Our assumption is that these lower-level work tasks are optimized and are the best way to do the work. The 5S's are sorting, setting in order, shining, standardizing, and sustaining. Sorting requires removing materials or information not needed to do the current work tasks from a work area. The logic behind this practice is that extraneous materials distract employees from important work. Distractions result in mistakes

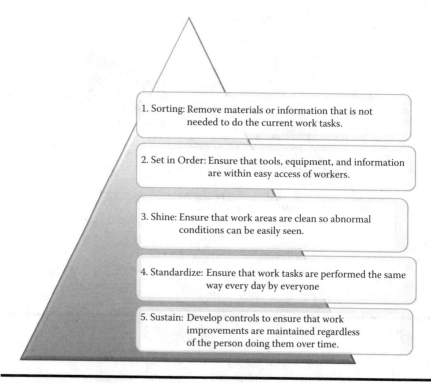

1. Sorting: Remove materials or information that is not needed to do the current work tasks.

2. Set in Order: Ensure that tools, equipment, and information are within easy access of workers.

3. Shine: Ensure that work areas are clean so abnormal conditions can be easily seen.

4. Standardize: Ensure that work tasks are performed the same way every day by everyone

5. Sustain: Develop controls to ensure that work improvements are maintained regardless of the person doing them over time.

Figure 5.11   Standardize work.

being made and lost time spent searching for materials and information. A common example in a service process would be a poorly organized sharepoint. In these situations, it is difficult for employees to quickly find the information they need. As a result, their searches take an inordinate amount of time. Other sharepoint issues may include accessing incorrect or outdated information. In summary, sorting requires the removal of extraneous materials and information from a work area. The second 5S—setting in order—organizes the remaining materials and information for easy access and usage. The practice of setting in order ensures that tools, equipment, and information are visible, and employees have easy access to it. This practice results in fewer mistakes and reduces cycle time. The third 5S practice is called shining the work area. A work area should be kept clean once extraneous materials have been removed from it and the remaining items have been properly organized. Clean work areas enable employees to see abnormal processing conditions very easily and to continuously improve their work areas. As an example, in manufacturing processes, clean work areas enable teams to identify faulty machines that leak oil or exhibit other maintenance problems. Also, in a service process, sharepoints may contain extraneous pieces of information such as old data files, poorly organized folders, inaccurate and redundant information, or missing folders and files. The fourth 5S practice is standardization of the work tasks to minimize process variation. It is at this point in the process improvement work that a detailed analysis can be made of remaining work tasks. The goal is to standardize around the best way to do the work. This implies that the work tasks are done the same way every time. It is also important to continually improve all work tasks once they have been simplified, set in order, cleaned, and standardized. A proven strategy to continually improve a process is through the use of local work teams to collect and analyze process information to identify ways to apply 5S and other Lean methods.

Apply Mistake-Proofing Methods

Mistake-proofing is a series of interrelated strategies and applications that are used to prevent or minimize the impact of failures on either an end user of a product or service, or internal work operations. Mistake-proofing strategies are broadly divided into three major areas. These are prevention of errors through the design of process controls, the detection of errors before defects are created, and the immediate detection of defects after they are created or during processing. These strategies are shown in Figure 5.12. Since a failure occurrence has been made either impossible or easily detectable, mistake-proofing implies that if a customer mistakenly uses a product or service, then no adverse consequence will occur. In addition to mistake-proofing strategies used in the design of products and services as well as production operations, mistake-proofing strategies are applicable to effective project management. Project management examples include codevelopment of key product features and functions rather using more than one team member to prevent programming errors, and frequent sprint reviews to prevent error conditions from being incorporated into subsequent iterations of a product's or service's final design.

There are several other proven methods to help prevent error conditions and defects from occurring. First, a system's subcomponents or work operations can be eliminated or combined with one another. Eliminating one of more components ensures there are fewer opportunities for an error. A second method is to reduce the

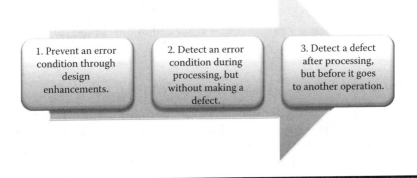

| 1. Prevent an error condition through design enhancements. | 2. Detect an error condition during processing, but without making a defect. | 3. Detect a defect after processing, but before it goes to another operation. |

Figure 5.12   Apply mistake-proofing strategies.

number of product or service features and functions to only those required by end users. Fewer features and functions reduce the probability that an error condition or defect will occur. A third mistake-proofing method requires using best-in-class design practices to ensure subcomponents can be assembled or put together in an approved manner. In manufacturing applications, mechanical product designs used asynchronous mating parts to ensure that subcomponents can only be assembled one way. This design approach prevents assembly errors. Depending on the industry and function within an industry, there are many other mistake-proofing methods.

The second mistake-proofing strategy is the detection of errors during processing. In these applications, process conditions are monitored and if a particular combination of process conditions having a high probability of failure occurs, then the error condition is flagged and an alarm is triggered or the process is shut down. For example, when drilling a hole, the power required can be monitored to detect dullness of a drill bit. This monitoring enables a machine to be shut down prior to breaking a drill bit. In a service process, incoming call volume, staffing levels, and the time customers must wait for an agent can be monitored to ensure the service level of the process is maintained. If customer waiting time increases to a predetermined limit, then additional capacity can be brought online to reduce the waiting time. Detecting error conditions requires that a system model exist to enable the identification of failure conditions prior to the creation of a defect.

The third mistake-proofing strategy requires that a process has controls sufficient to identify a defect if it occurs. As an example, in manufacturing, inline sensors can be placed on machines to measure the production of work objects to identify defects if they should occur. In an office environment, a project's sign-off review is designed to find defects and prevent them from moving through a process. In software development, a beta test of a new product or service is another example where error conditions or defects can be identified before they impact significant numbers of customers. The quality of work of a project can also be monitored at predetermined control points, called review gates or activity milestones. During a gate or milestone review, a project team can check the status of all work activities to identify failures. This enables a project team to develop strategies for failure elimination. APM with scrum sprints go one step further in the project management process because there is a project review at the end of each scrum sprint in which feature and function errors can be quickly identified and eliminated.

Balance the Flow of Work between Team Members

Balancing the flow of work and information within a process or across a project team depends on effective communication. Communication is facilitated through a variety of tools and methods, many of which have been discussed in previous chapters of this book. For example, it is important that team members have up-to-date project information relative to planned work activities assigned to other team members. In these applications, communication is enhanced through the use of scrum sprints,

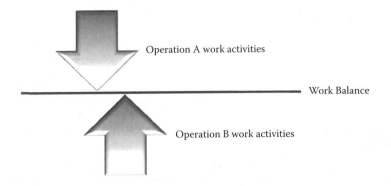

Figure 5.13 Balance the flow of work between team members.

daily team review meetings, and sprint review meetings between all key stakeholders and a project team. In this section, we will focus on the mechanics of balancing the flow of work and information between a project's team members to ensure sprint targets are achieved on schedule without overloading team members.

There are several relevant aspects to balancing work. Balancing begins by breaking a project's activity backlog down into sprints, which are created to deliver discrete levels of system features and functions. A sprint consists of several work activities and their lower-level work tasks which are arranged as a work breakdown structure (WBS). The mechanics of WBS were discussed in Chapter 1. Figure 5.13 qualitatively describes the concept of work balancing between team members with a view that they should have equal amounts of project work. To properly balance its workload, a Lean IT team should calculate the total time per day to do the work after an initial assignment of work tasks has been made to team members using the activity backlog and scrum sprint WBS. This concept was shown in Figure 5.9. Team members who are overloaded should have their work tasks assigned to other team members.

There are several advanced Lean methods that may help a Lean IT team to more effectively manage its project activities. These include using customer requirements to pull work through a team, managing bottlenecks, using transfer batches to move materials and information, reducing work setup times, increasing system availability, and creating stable operational work procedures so work does not need to be done more than once. It should also be noted that APM with scrum integrates several of these tools and methods into its project management activities. As an example, the work activities listed on an activity backlog and assigned to scrum sprints are pulled by team members based on their perceived capacity for additional work. In other words, capacity is determined at an individual level by available time, experience, and education or skill level of each team member. A pull system enables team members to balance their work in a manner described by Figures 5.9 and 5.13. The balance of Lean tools and methods needs further discussion prior to showing their relationships to APM with scrum.

Manage Bottlenecks

The concept of managing a "bottleneck" resource gained popularity in the 1980s through publication of a landmark book written by Goldratt and Cox titled *The Goal*. This book brought into play several operational methods to increase a system's throughout. Throughput is the time required to convert purchased materials and labor into sold products or services. It is an important measure of a system's effectiveness as opposed to efficiency, because it emphasizes an integrated approach to the production of products and services. As an example, prior to publication of *The Goal*, a production operation optimized the efficiency of a process operation by operation. This resulted in very high local efficiency but also much inventory waste. As an example, inventory waste occurs if external customer demand does not exist or if high levels of in-process inventory buildup in a downstream operation because it cannot use the materials created by an upstream operation having a higher production rate. In Goldratt and Cox's approach, a system's throughput was calculated based on the slowest operation within a system on its critical path. The flow of materials and information was balanced relative to the production rate of this bottleneck resource. The resultant process improvement efforts were also applied to the system's bottleneck, because increasing its efficiency would increase the throughput of the entire production system.

This concept is quantitatively shown in Figure 5.14. The bottleneck resource is shown as the second operation having a production rate of 50 units per day. Notice that the first operation that supplies the bottleneck has a production rate of

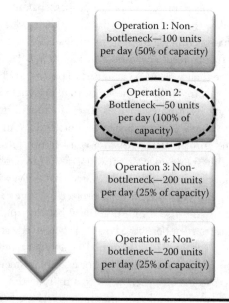

Figure 5.14   Manage bottlenecks.

100 units per day. Also, the third and fourth operations have production rates of 200 units per day. The throughput of this process is restricted to 50 units per day due to the presence of the system's bottleneck. Also, if the first operation produces at a rate greater than 50 units per day, then inventory will build up in front of the bottleneck operation. This simple example implies that a production strategy is necessary to increase the bottleneck's production rate, to match a system's takt time, prior to utilizing other operations at their maximum production rate. Another important consideration is that the production rate of a bottleneck resource should match the external demand placed on a system, which should also be reflected in the system's takt time.

Several strategies can be employed to increase a bottleneck's production rate or capacity. First, a second operation (same as the bottleneck) can be deployed in parallel to the bottleneck operation to bring the effective production rate of the bottleneck process up to 100 units per day to match the first operation and increase the throughput of the system to 100 units per day. Second, any drag on the bottleneck's capacity such as scrap, rework, or maintenance issues could be investigated and perhaps reduced or eliminated to improve the bottleneck's production rate. The bottleneck concept is also applicable to the management of Lean IT teams. As an example, a bottleneck resource could be a team member who cannot keep up with assigned work activities or a specific set of work tasks. In this situation, additional team members could be used to take on some of the work. Alternatively, team members could be trained or provided with tools to increase their productivity. Also, in situations in which work tasks are known to require significantly more time than others, perhaps work hours can be temporarily extended so the sprint backlog remains balanced over all work tasks and team members. In summary, nonbottleneck resources should be balanced with respect to the throughput rate of a bottleneck resource. Higher production rates of a process or a Lean IT team can only be achieved by increasing the capacity of its bottleneck.

Use Transfer Batches

The concept of transfer batches is related to the important Lean principle of single-unit production or flow. There are many advantages of using single-unit production. These include preventing the buildup of inventory between work operations, significantly lowering cycle times since materials are not batched, and achieving higher quality since defects are found immediately when they interrupt the flow of work. However, the ability to attain single-unit production depends on several supporting systems, some of which have already been discussed in this chapter. These include process simplification and standardization as well as incorporating design features and functions that are production friendly, creating flexible workers and equipment, level loading demand on a system, maintaining a level of high availability or capacity, and implementing process improvements to

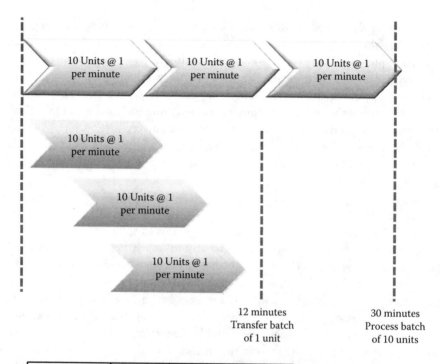

Time (Minutes)	Operation 1	Operation 2	Operation 3
1	Unit 1		
2	Unit 2	Unit 1	
3	Unit 3	Unit 2	Unit 1
4	Unit 4	Unit 3	Unit 2
5	Unit 5	Unit 4	Unit 3
6	Unit 6	Unit 5	Unit 4
7	Unit 7	Unit 6	Unit 5
8	Unit 8	Unit 7	Unit 6
9	Unit 9	Unit 8	Unit 7
10	Unit 10	Unit 9	Unit 8
11		Unit 10	Unit 9
12			Unit 10

Figure 5.15   Use transfer batches.

achieve high quality. Without these supporting systems, the flow of work will be interrupted and inventory may be necessary to buffer work operations.

Figure 5.15 illustrates the basic concept of transfer batching using three production operations. Each operation requires one minute for completion of its work task. By way of example, 10 units are shown to move through this simple system. If the work is batched, it will take 30 minutes for the job to be completed. However, if the work is transferred to subsequent operations as soon as it is finished, then the total time to complete the job will be only 12 minutes. In a transfer batch production system, quality issues will also be easier to see because a downstream work operation will immediately receive work completed by an upstream work operation. If a defect has occurred then it will be immediately detected at the downstream work operation. As noted earlier, a significant reduction in a system's cycle time can be obtained using this concept. In the example, shown in Figure 5.15, the cycle time was reduced by approximately 60 percent over the original production batch system. The transfer production batch concept also has application to the management of a Lean IT team at two levels. First, team members should transfer their completed work to other team members as soon as it is completed rather than batch it for future release. Second, the assignment of work activities should be organized to facilitate their transfer as soon as they have been completed to reduce a sprint's cycle time.

Reduce Setup Time

The setup time of a job consists of several time elements, which in combination represent the setup activities that are necessary to get a job ready to begin processing. Setup work activities can also be simple or very complex depending on the products or services being produced. For example, in a service system, a simple setup may consist of setting up work orders using readily available information and templates. However, a more complicated series of setup activities would be required to bring together team members to begin a project. Relative to creating a software system, a simple setup may involve turning on a computer to access common files and software programs, whereas a more complicated setup would be to modify software and its associated hardware systems to begin testing an algorithm. It should also be noted that setup time is one of several time components found in the production of work. These other time components include processing, inspection, waiting, transfer, and the storage of work objects. Jobs or work operations may also have these components arranged in different sequences. These sequences may also consist of several repeated components. As an example, a work operation could consist of a sequence such as waiting, inspection, setup, inspection, processing, inspection, waiting, transfer, waiting, and storage.

Processing of work consists of the various VA work activities that produce products and services. Waiting represents a component of NVA time. Waiting time should be minimized or eliminated from a system. Transfer (or movement) time represents the movement of materials and information through a system. This time component should also be minimized or eliminated from a system to reduce its overall cycle time. Inspection is also an NVA time component. To minimize inspections, quality should be designed into a product or service and the design mistake-proofed. Setup time is more complicated in that it consists of VA as well as NVA work elements. However, the longer the time required to set up a job, the longer an employee or system must wait to begin producing work. For example, prior to creating an invoice, several pieces of information must be available. These include information describing the customer being invoiced, the work performed, and the cost of doing

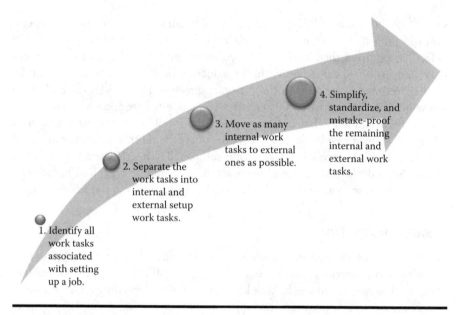

1. Identify all work tasks associated with setting up a job.

2. Separate the work tasks into internal and external setup work tasks.

3. Move as many internal work tasks to external ones as possible.

4. Simplify, standardize, and mistake-proof the remaining internal and external work tasks.

Figure 5.16   Reduce setup time.

the work. Additional information may include materials, tax rates, and various organizational approvals. Ideally, this information will be readily available prior to doing the work. As an example, in work operations in which invoicing is automatically done by IT systems, the IT system should not need to wait for information except for planned data feeds. In a similar manner, a Lean IT team should not have to wait before it can start its work activities. Rather it should have all the materials, information, and equipment needed to immediately begin work on schedule.

Lean practitioners have developed several strategies to identify, analyze, and reduce the number of work tasks required to set up a job. The strategy is to externalize internal setup work tasks and improve the efficiency of the remaining internal and external work tasks. Internal setup work tasks must be completed before a process can begin. In contrast, external work tasks can be done offline and at any time, and do not directly impact the time it takes to set up a job. Figure 5.16 shows several sequential approaches to reduce setup time. These include the identification of the work tasks associated with setups and the elimination of unnecessary ones, the separation of internal and external work tasks, and the movement of work tasks from internal to external setup as well as the simplification, standardization, and mistake-proofing of all remaining internal and external setup work tasks.

How is this done in practice? And how does it apply to the work activities of a Lean IT team? First, let's consider a manual invoicing example. The start of a job begins with the receipt of information that authorizes an invoice be sent to a customer if service was performed or a product was delivered. In some systems, the invoice is automatically created and sent to the customer. The setup work tasks are automated in these systems and the time the system requires to send an invoice is negligible. However, if the process is manual, then an employee must work through several operations prior to sending an invoice. First, customer information must be found, and then matched to the completed work or the product sold. Then an invoice is created using a computer or work form, placed in an envelope and mailed to the customer. In summary, a major tool in improving setup efficiency is to externalize internal setup work tasks. In the manual setup example just discussed, setup efficiencies could be increased by enabling employees to mark a data field in advance with the type of service or product delivered and the customer's information would either be readily available or preprinted making invoicing easy and fast. Work simplification, standardization, and mistake-proofing should also be investigated to improve setup efficiencies in these situations.

Maintain System Availability

Ensuring that a system is available to do work is the result of applying preventive and corrective maintenance activities to a process. This requires specialized tools, methods, and concepts that ensure equipment, systems, and people are able to do their work at a required production rate to meet demand on a system with a predetermined reliability level. Maintenance tools and methods vary depending on the type of process. For example, in manufacturing processes, the maintenance focus is on ensuring that equipment is available for use with a predetermined probability level. In an analogous manner, using ergonomic principles, people should be available to do their required work when needed. Service industries rely heavily on IT systems to do work. In these situations, IT systems must also have sufficient capacity and reliability to ensure they meet availability targets. In Figure 5.17, availability is defined as a logical mixture of reliability targets and the maintenance activities necessary to achieve them in practice. Reliability implies the equipment is serviced at periodic intervals, based on its design and hours of use.

The three major goals of a maintenance strategy are shown in Figure 5.17. These are preventing unexpected disruptions, maintaining a stable production rate, and achieving high process yields. To attain these goals, equipment should be periodically serviced based on its design classification and hours of use. To achieve these goals in practice, organizations often employ maintenance experts to develop strategies and plans to ensure equipment is properly maintained. For example, in a well-deployed maintenance system, software is used to create and monitor maintenance schedules, resource availability, and related information to ensure that availability targets are met. Availability depends on reliability and maintainability levels. Maintainability can also be broken into subcomponents of preventive and corrective maintenance. The key concept behind preventive maintenance is that equipment has a failure rate that increases over time and is predictable (follows a known failure distribution), which enables maintenance professionals to create maintenance schedules or plans for periodic service and tc replace components to prevent unexpected failures. The

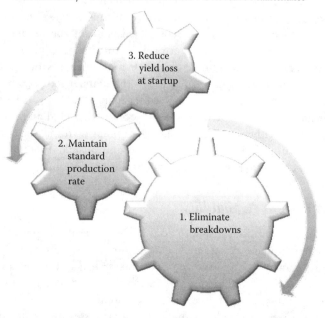

Availability = Reliability + Maintainability
Maintainability = Preventive Maintenance + Corrective Maintenance

Figure 5.17 Maintain system availability.

concept is that an unexpected failure will adversely impact a system's production rate. Another key consideration of an effective preventive maintenance program is that the cost of failure prevention is usually less than the cost of allowing a failure to occur and correcting it after it has failed. However, the application of this principle varies by production system. For example, if the failure impact is minimal then it may make economic sense to allow a certain number of failures before applying maintenance. A classic example is replacing lights in a work environment. As long as lighting standards are being met, a good strategy would be to replace all lights at the same time since their replacement cost is low when compared to the labor cost of replacing one bulb at a time.

A common strategy used in manufacturing systems is to develop a maintenance schedule for each piece of equipment by considering the required percentage of unscheduled (corrective) versus scheduled (preventive) maintenance activities necessary to ensure the equipment will be available at its target reliability. As part of this maintenance analysis, a maintenance team must identify the failure probabilities for equipment by its major classification. For example, equipment could be classified by its basic design characteristics (i.e., pumps, motors, trucks, etc.). In IT systems common classifications of related equipment would include servers, desktop computers, and similar equipment classifications. It should be noted that employee roles and responsibilities is another integral component of an effective maintenance program.

In this context, employees should be properly trained to perform their work and have assigned work roles and responsibilities. Budgets should also be developed for each equipment classification to ensure resources are available to meet scheduled maintenance activities over time.

Implement a Pull Scheduling System

A pull scheduling system ensures that resources are activated only when demand is placed on a system. In other words, resource activation is not dependent on forecast demand. It should be noted that there is a difference between resource activation versus utilization. Activation implies that a resource is doing work needed by an external customer and that there will be times when a resource may be idle. In contrast, the utilization of a resource may exceed its activation level, which implies its work is not needed downstream and inventory is building up downstream within a production system. Organizations that measure their performance using utilization metrics may overproduce work. In contrast, systems that activate their resources will match their capacity to external demand. As a result, the previous tools and methods discussed in this chapter are very important to meet external demand requirements

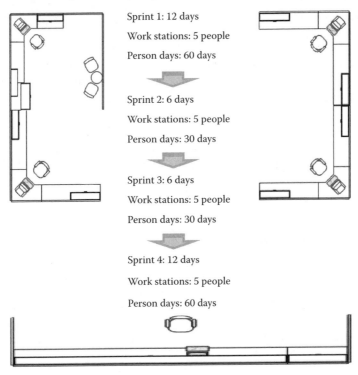

Sprint 1: 12 days

Work stations: 5 people

Person days: 60 days

Sprint 2: 6 days

Work stations: 5 people

Person days: 30 days

Sprint 3: 6 days

Work stations: 5 people

Person days: 30 days

Sprint 4: 12 days

Work stations: 5 people

Person days: 60 days

Figure 5.18   Implement a pull scheduling system.

since they help to stabilize a production system. Stabilization conserves a system's capacity to enable it to meet external demand in a flexible manner.

Figure 5.18 uses the APM with scrum example shown in Figure 5.9 with a pull scheduling system within an office environment. In this service example, external customer requirements determine the sequential work activities of an activity backlog. This approach reduces the probability that one or more of the process wastes described in Figure 5.2 will occur. The key concept shown in this pull scheduling example is that the work activities should be balanced across a team's project schedule, across its team members, and from sprint to sprint. Notice that the length of each sprint is adjusted, in this example, to ensure that five team members can complete the work activities of each sprint to deliver the required system features and functions. As an example, sprints 1 and 4 are twelve days and sprints 2 and 3 are six days, but they each require five people. Using a pull scheduling approach avoids overloading team members and keeps a steady pace of work across an APM team. In summary, pull scheduling systems have been used to control the flow of information and materials in production systems for years. But they are also applicable to the management of projects using APM with scrum sprints.

Summary

The application of Lean concepts, tools, and methods to IT projects is a straightforward and useful approach to project management. In fact, IT practitioners independently developed and currently use similar approaches in managing software projects. An example is APM with scrum. The direct application to project management practices is easy to see because Lean is a process-centric set of tools and methods. In the next chapter, we will discuss the creation of software features and functions in a preparation for a discussion of Lean applications in manufacturing and service systems. Lean concepts and principles will also be shown to be integral to the effective and efficient creation and deployment of software.

Suggested Reading

Augustine, Sanjiv. 2005. *Managing Agile Projects*. Upper Saddle River, NJ: Prentice Hall.
Fabrizio, Thomas, and Don Tapping. 2006. *5S for the Office: Organizing the Workplace to Eliminate Waste*. New York: Productivity Press.
Goldratt, Eliyahu M., and Jeff Cox. 1992. *The Goal: A Process of Ongoing Improvement*, 2nd rev. ed. Great Barrington, MA: North River Press.
Harmon, Paul. 2003. *Business Process Change: A Manager's Guide to Improving, Redesigning, and Automating Processes*. San Francisco, CA: Morgan Kaufman.
Hines, Peter, Richard Lamming, Dan Jones, Paul Cousins, and Nick Rich. 2000. *Value Stream Management*. New York: Prentice Hall.
Iwao, Kobayashi. 1995. *20 Keys to Workplace Improvement*. New York: Productivity Press.

Martin, James William. 2007. *Lean Six Sigma for Supply Chain Management.* New York: McGraw-Hill.

Martin, James William. 2008. *Operational Excellence: Using Lean Six Sigma to Translate Customer Value through Global Supply Chains.* Boca Raton, FL: Auerbach.

Martin, James William. 2009. *Lean Six Sigma for the Office.* Boca Raton, FL: CRC Press.

Morgan, James M., and Jeffrey K. Liker. *The Toyota Product Development System.* New York: Productivity Press.

Schwaber, Ken. 2004. *Agile Project Management with Scrum.* Redmond, WA: Microsoft Press.

Suri, Rajan. 1998. *Quick Response Manufacturing: A Companywide Approach to Reducing Lead Times.* New York: Productivity Press.

Womack, James P., and Daniel T. Jones. 1996. *Lean Thinking: Banish Waste and Create Wealth in Your Organization.* New York: Simon & Schuster.

Chapter 6

Software Development and Project Support

> Any intelligent fool can make things bigger, more complex, and more violent. It takes a touch of genius—and a lot of courage—to move in the opposite direction.
>
> **—Albert Einstein**

Overview

It was mentioned in earlier chapters that a major goal of this book is to provide tools and methods to enable Lean practitioners to support the application of information technology (IT) projects within Lean systems. Although there is a great deal of similarity between Lean and software project management methodologies, there are also significant differences. As an example, software development practitioners have created their own specialized tools and methods to simplify, standardize, and mistake-proof their specialized work. The purpose of this chapter is to discuss several important concepts that have proven to be useful in creating software and providing support to its development, release, installation, activation and deactivation, maintenance, and removal. These concepts are important because Lean systems rely on the efficient deployment of software systems to reduce process cycle time and cost as well as improve quality. The application of IT is very important in the design and improvement of service systems as well as in highly automated manufacturing systems.

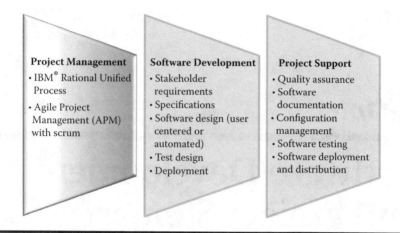

Project Management	Software Development	Project Support
• IBM® Rational Unified Process	• Stakeholder requirements	• Quality assurance
• Agile Project Management (APM) with scrum	• Specifications	• Software documentation
	• Software design (user centered or automated)	• Configuration management
	• Test design	• Software testing
	• Deployment	• Software deployment and distribution

Figure 6.1   Software design and deployment activities.

In previous chapters, we discussed two important software project management methods. These were the IBM® Rational Unified Process (RUP)and Agile Project Management (APM) with scrum. The RUP methodology was created to control the project activities associated with the management of very large hardware and software development projects. In contrast, APM with scrum was created to efficiently execute smaller software projects using scrum sprints. Recall that scrum sprints are characterized by frequent customer and key stakeholder project reviews to maintain a project's focus on satisfying design requirements. It was also previously mentioned that APM and scrum project management methods can be used within an RUP project management approach at a local level.

Also discussed in earlier chapters, and in Chapter 4 in particular, was the translation of customer requirements into product and service specifications and then into features and functions. Figure 6.1 captures these interrelated concepts. In this chapter we will discuss the basic concepts for the design of best-in-class software systems. This discussion will focus on software testing, its deployment, ongoing project support, configuration management, documentation, testing, quality assurance, packaging design, product and service distribution, and training. It should be noted that several issues associated with software design and its project management were described previously in Tables 1.4 and 4.1. Our goal in this chapter will be to discuss several tools and methods useful in preventing these types of design issues.

Development of System Specifications

The creation of detailed specifications that describe how to produce products and services is obtained from several sources of information. It should be noted that the required information varies by the type of product or service. As an example, some products are highly specified upfront by a customer, and as a result they require periodic and formal design reviews by all key stakeholders and a project team. Many software projects between large organizations, and especially governmental institutions, will usually follow this structured approach to specification translation. On the other hand, some software development projects are designed to create new products or services for consumers. These latter types of projects require the use of market surveys, focus groups, and similar marketing activities to identify customer needs and value expectations.

Capturing Stakeholder Requirements

Figure 6.2 is one example of how customer and key stakeholder requirements are captured when creating new products or services. It should be noted that there are several variations of this format and that is an example of the types of information that would be exchanged between a project team, key stakeholders, and customers. For example, additional information such as diagrams, prototypes, competitive examples, and similar information are exchanged to identify and further describe product or service requirements. Supporting information would also be attached to the example shown in Figure 6.2.

Key information captured by Figure 6.2 includes key functions and features as well as requirements related to software production, distribution, maintenance, upgrades, and disposal. This information promotes a holistic perspective of the requirements translation because it encompasses the entire life cycle of a product or service. In addition, the requirements shown in Figure 6.2 are cross-referenced to Kano needs as well as supplemental information regarding how, where, when, why, and who is associated with the product attribute. Finally, this information should be captured for each market segment as well as key stakeholders, such as end users, design engineering, project management, and project support and process management. The goal of capturing this information is to ensure that products and services are designed to meet customer and key stakeholder requirements and that they can be economically produced throughout their expected life cycles.

Table 6.1 describes some key components of a requirement's specification document. A design team should gather customer, key stakeholder, and supporting information to create a detailed specification document containing the information shown in Table 6.1. The administrative section of the table presents an overview that describes the important features and functions of a product or service. An index and revision control pages should also be inserted in this section of the requirements' specification document. An overview should provide background about the expected features and functions of a system from an end user and key stakeholder perspective. In this section of the specification document, high-level descriptions should be made of how, where, when, why, and who will use a system. This information helps guide the project team and serves as a communication vehicle for other people who interact with a team. A high-level overview of the

Stakeholders: 1. End user 2. Engineering 3. Project management 4. Project support 5. Process management	Basic (Must Have)	Performance	Excitement	How it is used	Where it is used	When it used	Why it is used	Who uses it	Comments
Key Functions									
Function A									
Function B									
Function C									
Key Features									
Feature A									
Feature B									
Feature C									
Key Production Requirements									
Requirement A									
Requirement B									
Requirement C									
Distribution Requirements									
Requirement A									
Requirement B									
Requirement C									
Maintenance Requirements									
Requirement A									
Requirement B									
Requirement C									
Upgrade Requirements									
Requirement A									
Requirement B									
Requirement C									
Disposal Requirements									
Requirement A									
Requirement B									
Requirement C									
Comments									

Figure 6.2 Capturing stakeholder requirements.

Table 6.1 Developing Specifications

Specification Category	Key Components
1. Administrative information	a. System overview b. Index and revisions
2. External interface	a. Interfaces between users and systems b. Hardware and software interfaces c. Communication rules
3. Data input/output description	a. Data structures, locations, and accessibility rules
4. Software/hardware features	a. Module performance b. Integrated system performance c. Security d. Reliability e. Maintenance
5. Supplementary information	a. Product specific

combined impact of specifications on features and functions is very useful since specifications are very detailed and can be complicated when they are discussed in isolation or at a technical level.

The next major section of a specification document describes the external interfaces between interfacing systems. External interfaces exist between users and they are associated with hardware, software, and communication rules and protocols. These specifications are especially important in Lean systems that integrate hardware and software from different sources. The third section of Table 6.1 describes data input and output. Input and output between algorithms within a system as well as between other hardware and software systems can be problematic if not properly specified in advance of software development. Key considerations include data structures, their locations, and the accessibility rules of the software. It should be noted that in these applications there are best-in-class design methods. The fourth section of Table 6.1 describes specifications that control features and functions related to software module performance and the integrated performance between software modules, as well as their associated hardware platforms and the specifications that control system security, reliability, and maintenance. The fifth section of a specification document will contain the supporting information a project team considers important in providing context for the first four sections of the requirement's specification document.

Use Cases

Software documentation can be very complicated and difficult to understand. This is especially an issue to nontechnical people, including customers and key stakeholders such as sales, marketing, finance, and senior management. In other words, it is often difficult to understand the complex interrelationships between specifications and their higher-level features and functions. One solution is to create communication documents, examples, and similar aids to help explain how a product and service is expected to perform. Product and service use cases have been found to be excellent communication vehicles for this purpose.

Several advantages of use cases are listed in Table 6.2. First, they help facilitate communication between end users, stakeholders, and the software design team by representing stakeholder requirements in easy-to-understand language using graphical examples. In this context, use cases describe a product relative to its underlying process and user applications. Also, application requirements are represented in business terms as discreet functions. In other words, users can see how process operations are related at a high level of abstraction. The clear and concise visual representation provided by use cases also facilitates the identification of alternative process flows and potential application issues prior to development of software code. If properly developed, use cases can also be generalized to similar applications. This approach reduces software development time for future business applications due to the high level of model abstraction. Finally, use cases can be translated into pilots or test examples to confirm that a software application will meet user requirements.

Figure 6.3 shows that the first step in developing a use case is to define the major actors of a process. Actors are defined by their basic roles within the process being created. For example, in an e-commerce application, typical actors would include buyers or customers, sellers or suppliers, and related supporting functions. Once the major actors of a process have been defined, their goals are listed in sequence. These goals consist of high-level user activities and the information requirements

Table 6.2 Benefits of Use Cases

1. Facilitate communication between end users, stakeholders, and a software design team

2. Describe process flow and application requirements in business terms as discreet functions

3. Identify alternative process flows and other potential application issues

4. Cases can be generalized to other related applications.

5. Can be translated into pilots or test examples to confirm an application meets user needs

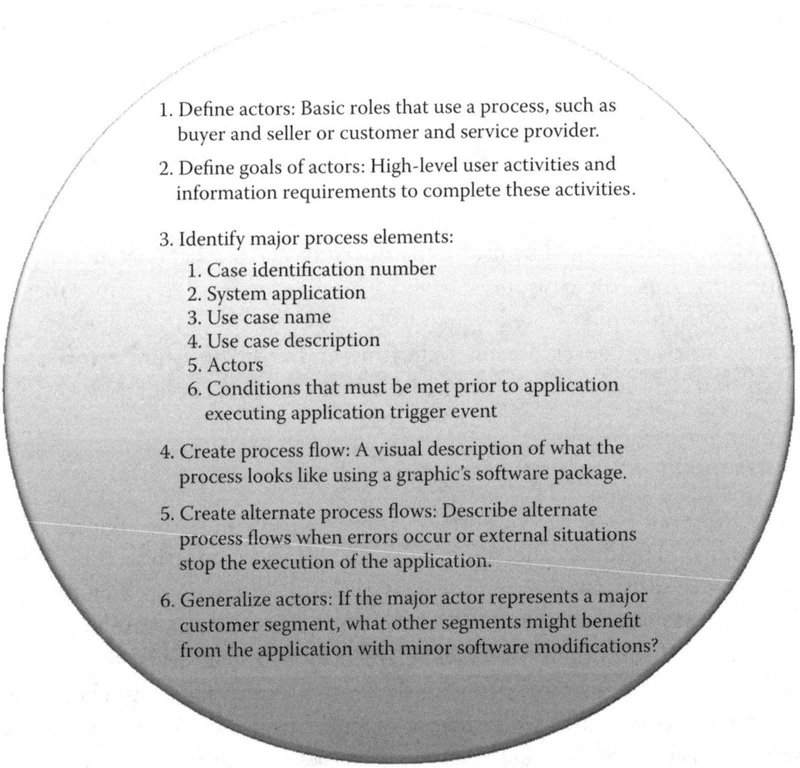

1. Define actors: Basic roles that use a process, such as buyer and seller or customer and service provider.

2. Define goals of actors: High-level user activities and information requirements to complete these activities.

3. Identify major process elements:
    1. Case identification number
    2. System application
    3. Use case name
    4. Use case description
    5. Actors
    6. Conditions that must be met prior to application executing application trigger event

4. Create process flow: A visual description of what the process looks like using a graphic's software package.

5. Create alternate process flows: Describe alternate process flows when errors occur or external situations stop the execution of the application.

6. Generalize actors: If the major actor represents a major customer segment, what other segments might benefit from the application with minor software modifications?

Figure 6.3   Developing use cases.

necessary to complete these activities. Customers may also have specific requirements that must be satisfied. Examples include the types of products they need to purchase and the sequence of activities used to access a system to purchase the needed products or services. In addition to purchasing products or services, supporting processes may also be described at a high level. These supporting processes may be related to financial transactions, complaint resolution, and similar supporting activities. Use cases also contain additional information such as the case identification number; the specific system application that is the focus of the project; and a clear and concise case name to help key stakeholders and customers to quickly understand the purpose of the use case, its summarized description to provide context for the project, the conditions (i.e., trigger events) that must be met prior to executing an application, and a visual description of the process. The visual description would preferably be constructed using a graphics software package. This combined information is incorporated into the use case to provide a high-level description of a new software application and to communicate its project requirements to customers and key stakeholders.

Another important benefit of a use case is that Lean IT teams can use its information to create alternate process flows. Creating alternate process flows is necessary when errors occur or other external conditions exist that could stop the execution of a software application. An evaluation of alternate process flows also enables a project team to identify unexpected process conditions that may adversely impact its algorithm's features and functions. Use cases are also useful in identifying generalized actors. As an example, if a major actor represents a specific customer segment it would be useful to understand how other customer segments might benefit from the new application with only minor software modifications. This is a generalization of the original use case. A benefit of this approach is that it reduces software development cycle time and cost. Software errors are also reduced since less software code must be written for new applications.

E-Commerce Example

Table 6.3 uses an e-commerce portal example to show how the concept of a use case is applied in practice. The example divides a project into two sections. The first section describes the product requirements as a use case with six elements. These include the case identification number, the system application, case name, actors, and the required conditions to trigger an application. The information is created to make it easy for nontechnical people such as users, stakeholders, and customers to understand what the software system is supposed to do. For example, the system described in Table 6.3 is being created as an Internet e-commerce portal to sell maintenance supplies in which product information is automatically updated. However, the various internal supporting systems are not shown in Table 6.3. Typical supporting systems would include user training, secure financial transaction systems, and quality controls. As a Lean IT team begins to develop the various algorithms necessary to create a working version of the use case, specifications are developed to describe and control successively increasing levels of product detail. The second section of Table 6.3 is not part of a typical use case. It is included to tie in the fact that a project team's work activities should to some extent reflect its assigned use case. In this context, the second section of Table 6.3 describes the project plan from an APM with scrum perspective. It should be noted that in practice, this example would be more extensive. Also, there would be more detailed documentation supporting the information shown in Table 6.3.

Key Concepts of Efficient Software Design

In this section we will discuss some key concepts of software design from a Lean practitioner perspective. In other words, this discussion will not be at a professional software programmer skill level. Rather, the information is intended for non-IT

Table 6.3   User Case: Creating an E-Commerce Portal

	Required Information— Major Case Element	*Project Phase*	*E-Commerce Portal Equivalent*
Product Description	1. Case identification number	Create use case	BR12345
	2. System application	Create use case	E-commerce application over the Internet using a Web browser
	3. Case name	Create use case	E-Commerce Portal for Maintenance Supplies
	4. Actor	Create use case	Users of the system and suppliers of products
	5. Required conditions	Create use case	Supplier creates a catalog of maintenance items having key search terms User signs onto system with approved user name and password
	6. Trigger event	Create use case	User inputs key words
Activity Backlog and Sprint Activities	1. Project sequence	Prepare for scrum sprint	Identify the key activities necessary to create the e-commerce portal into an activity backlog
	2. Priority	Prepare for scrum sprint	Prioritize the activities on the activity backlog and organize them into sprints
	3. Major activities	Prepare for scrum sprint	Within each sprint, assign activities to team members in a balanced manner
	4. Estimated person days	Prepare for scrum sprint	Estimate person days by team member and rebalance work activities if necessary

Table 6.4   Ten Key Goals for Efficient Software Design

1. New features and functions should be easily added to a product without major changes to the underlying software code (flexible).
2. Software can be upgraded, fixed, and restored easily and ideally automatically from remote locations (maintained).
3. Software is interchangeable with previous versions and enables backward compatibility regardless of the current revision level (compatible).
4. Software is designed for use in other systems as modular components (reusable).
5. Security features are incorporated into the software to detect and withstand external impact.
6. Software operation is not impaired by other factors such as input outside normal operating ranges.
7. Ideally, software can be designed and run automatically without manual intervention.
8. Software is well documented without requiring extensive external supporting documentation.
9. Software can be automatically tested under conditions reflecting actual as well as extreme use conditions.
10. Reliability is calculated using statistical methods that provide failure probabilities as well as the effects of interacting test conditions and system elements.

Note: Expansion of Table 4.1 and item 4 "Not using automated systems to design and test code."

people who are members of Lean IT teams deploying hardware and software within a Lean system. Therefore, some of the discussion will be easily recognizable since it incorporates several elements also common in the design of products and services as well as Lean applications. This information is not readily available to Lean practitioners, but is very important to ensure that software is developed efficiently, is flexible and adaptable to changing system requirements, well documented, and modifiable by future project teams. A Lean IT team should fully understand these basic design concepts to help reduce the cycle time and cost of hardware and software development.

Table 6.4 is a high-level expansion of item 4 of Table 4.1. It is a listing of ten key goals of efficient software design. We will include additional background to provide a more complete perspective of software design and how it supports the ten goals as we move through this chapter. The first goal shown in Table 6.4 is new features and functions should be easily added to a product without major changes to the underlying software code (flexible). This concept encourages design flexibility, which is a common theme both in Lean systems and classical product design. For example, over the past few decades, manufacturers of automobiles have developed strategies to create common product designs to provide numerous variations of a model to satisfy diverse consumer preferences. These preferences include color, trim, and various options that can be selected at an additional cost to a consumer, but they can also be easily incorporated into a production schedule. However, to achieve any degree of production schedule flexibility there are many interrelated and complicated systems that must be deployed in advance of production. This requires designing a product up front in a way that makes modifications to its original design easy and also designing its associated production equipment and process in a way that supports the building of flexibly designed products. In this context, creating an adaptable and flexible product infrastructure facilitates the addition or elimination of various product components based on changing customer preferences. Software designers use a variety of tools and methods to ensure that their algorithms are simple, standardized, and mistake-proofed. This approach is analogous to the basic Lean methods used in manufacturing.

A second key goal of software development is to ensure that software can be upgraded, fixed, and easily restored when necessary. Ideally these features can be automatically executed from remote locations that make system maintenance activities efficient, error free, and cost effective. But, to have these types of features and functions, software must be designed properly using best-in-class methods. This approach to software design has become very common. For example, Microsoft Windows® automatically checks for software updates and downloads them to computers. Another example is when a help desk fixes software problems remotely. A third example is satellite communications systems in which software updates or patches are uploaded and downloaded as necessary.

Third, software should also be interchangeable, in that newer versions should be backward compatible with earlier versions. This compatibility feature should not depend on the current version of a software system. However, this does not imply users having lower software versions will have all the features available in newer versions of the software. People with older software should be able to read files if they are saved at the correct lower version. This has been a common feature available in software for many years. At a more advanced level, the software should automatically save files so they are compatible.

A fourth important software design goal is that a product's features and functions be designed so they can be used with little modification within different products. In other words, they should be modular in that they can be used in different products. This design practice will promote software standardization. The benefits to an organization will be lower cost and development time as well as fewer mistakes. There are several other key goals listed in Table 6.4 that are associated with the efficient design of software. The fifth goal is that software should have security features that enable it to detect and withstand hostile attempts to access or modify its structure. There are many specific tools and methods used to secure software systems.

Sixth, it is also important that software operations not be impaired by conditions, such as data inputs that are outside their normal operating ranges, so that modules efficiently transform inputs from one module into the required outputs of a second one without leaving files open or causing other system-related problems.

The seventh goal of efficiently designed software is that it can run automatically without manual intervention, and self-check and repair itself if execution-related problems occur. To facilitate system maintenance, it is important that software be well documented, but also not require extensive external supporting documentation. Well-documented software is important because it helps in debugging future problems or when making modifications to its original software coding. Once software has been designed, it is important to verify that it meets its specifications by testing it automatically under simulated conditions that reflect all expected usage conditions. Finally, system reliability should be specified up front in the conceptual phase of a product's design and verified using statistical methods that calculate the probability of a system's failure. For example, experimental design methods may also be useful in estimating the effects of interacting test conditions and subsystems.

Whereas Table 6.4 described ten key goals of efficient software design, the balance of this chapter will present tools and methods that will help a Lean IT project team better manage the efficient design of its software. Table 6.5 describes ten specific tools and methods useful in designing software. It should be noted that, to a great extent, they reflect the goals of system simplification, standardization,

Table 6.5   Ten Key Concepts for Efficient Software Design

1. Maintain independent software components (orthogonal relationships) having a well-defined function.

2. Use a software object only once (i.e., no redundancy) and enhance its reuse by other functions and algorithms.

3. Create general software code that accesses detailed data tables for specific functions.

4. Modules should be able to access data tables without interference.

5. Remember Demeter's law for functions.

6. Use a software code editor that can be programmed and used on several applications.

7. Build in tests of software coding as the code is written and refractor (test and rewrite software code) frequently.

8. Use source code control to maintain an ability to restore software to earlier functioning states.

9. Programmers should be familiar with several applicable software languages to ensure the best one is used in a given application.

10. Use efficient methods to analyze software problems (i.e., bugs).

and mistake-proofing, but in applications regarding the design of software. The first key concept is to maintain independent software components with each having a well-defined function. Independence implies that changes to one software component will not impact another one. This is a useful design feature because many software algorithms are continually updated. Algorithm and component independence also enables future software programmers to make changes to a system's legacy code without creating unexpected problems or software bugs within existing algorithms.

A second key concept is to use a software module only once to avoid system redundancy and enhance its reuse by other functions and algorithms. In other words, it is located at only one place within the software coding. If a software module is in just one location it is easier to make changes once, at that location, rather than search what may be several million lines of software code for the same software module. In these nonoptimum situations, programmers who are tasked with making future software modifications may not be able to find and modify every redundant software module. Using a module only once will also enhance its reuse by other functions and algorithms. Lean practitioners will recognize the logic associated with these two best-in-class design practices as related to the classical Lean concepts of process standardization, simplification, and mistake-proofing.

A third key concept is to design software code using a general format to increase its flexibility relative to future modifications. To facilitate generality and flexibility features, one good design practice is to ensure that data tables are located at one location. This design practice makes data tables more accurate and it facilitates the updating of these tables in the future since they are updated once. A fourth and related concept is that algorithms should be able to access data tables without interference. This requires that software code be written in a way that ensures data files are accessed, opened, and closed by the same function as it exits its routine. In other words, tables should not be left open by algorithms or routines. These housekeeping rules are coincident with the general Lean principles associated with 5S (sorting, setting in order, shining, standardizing, and sustaining).

Demeter's law argues that the larger the size of a set in a specific calling class, then the larger the number of software coding errors likely to be found through testing. In other words, an algorithm should not attempt to directly access a module within another module. However, although a system's error rate decreases by avoiding the practice of nesting algorithms within one another, the runtime costs of this design approach for a specific application may significantly increase. As a result, this design practice needs to be used judiciously and analyzed for its trade-offs for each software application.

The sixth key concept described in Table 6.5 is to use a software coding editor that can be programmed to edit software. Hunt and Thomas, in their book *The Pragmatic Programmer: From Journeyman to Master*, argue that it is better to know one versatile editor very well than several only superficially. The seventh key concept is to build in algorithm tests as software code is being written and refractor (test and rewrite software code) frequently. It should be noted that refactoring software code is related to Lean's transfer batch concept that errors and defects should be detected as soon as possible to more quickly identify their original source. Refactoring is also facilitated by using APM with scrum since sprints create key system functions, which are then immediately evaluated by users and other stakeholders. The eighth key best practice of software design is to use version control and maintain an ability to restore software to earlier functioning states. This is important in situations in which newly created or modified software code creates issues with a system's features and functions, but it cannot be easily seen or detected using available testing routines. A ninth key concept is that programmers should be familiar with several applicable programming languages to ensure that the best one is used to design a software application. This will ensure the most efficient programming language is used to design software rather than using an inappropriate software language to develop an application. The tenth key best-in-class design concept is to use the best available debugging methods to efficiently debug software. Debugging software is a very complicated but essential task. Even experienced programmers have difficulty debugging software coding. As a result, debugging software can be considered to be both an art as well as a science. There are several references listed at the end of this chapter that contain useful information describing how to approach these types of investigative analyses. These include *The Pragmatic Programmer* and *Refactoring: Improving the Design of Existing Code.* In summary, it is important to ensure that a team has programmers with the knowledge and experience to efficiently design and debug software.

Software Quality Assurance

There are several organizations that develop and promote software standards. In the United States three key organizations are the United States Department of Defense, the National Institute of Standards (NIS), and the Object Management Group (OMG). These organizations are shown in Figure 6.4 with several of their stated goals. These goals include ensuring that a minimum number of vulnerabilities exist that can be exploited by external threats, that software generally executes and performs as intended to provide predictable outputs for specified ranges of inputs, and that standardized criteria for software evaluation are developed to enable industry participants to interact in a fact-based manner. There are also several basic characteristics an organization's software quality systems should exhibit in addition to these higher-level organizations, to create and manage software standards and best practices. These characteristics include the creation of effective quality management and audit systems as well as internal and external policies, standards, and quality control plans. Other important work activities include data collection and analysis, the testing for software requirements, system reliability analysis, and continuous process improvement using fact-based tools and methods.

1. Quality management and audit systems
2. Policies, standards, and quality control plans
3. Collection and analysis of data
4. Testing for requirements and reliability
5. Continuous improvement using fact-based tools and methods

Figure 6.4 Software quality assurance.

Quality management and assurance systems span numerous software design and testing activities. These activities include working with sales, marketing, and engineering to help identify the voice of the customer (VOC) as well as the voice of the business (VOB). The VOC and VOB are then translated into product specifications with the assistance of quality assurance to ensure that the original VOC and VOB requirements are met in practice prior to releasing newly designed software to customers, internal production operations, and other organizations. Quality management systems also help identify, analyze, and correct process problems if there are issues when either designing or commercializing software products.

In summary, these audits, policies, procedures, and control plans are the tools that support quality management systems.

Software Documentation

Software documentation provides a record of customer requirements as well as the systems that translate these requirements into software features and functions. Figure 6.5 shows that software documentation includes the supporting documents created for different target audiences. These audiences include users, production operations, sales and marketing, and other stakeholder groups. Documentation includes user manuals, technical aids, sales and marketing literature, and very detailed and sophisticated specification manuals. Although there are many versions of this type of documentation, they have several similar components. Their common goal is to communicate relevant information to various groups in a consistent manner. As an example, from an end-user perspective, system and product documentation describes features and functions using high-level diagrams and descriptive language. Sales and marketing documentation describes differentiating product features and functions using comparisons between current products and competitive products. Documentation for the design of a software product will include information describing the software coding and algorithms. Also, a best practice is documenting software code as it is being created is a best practice.

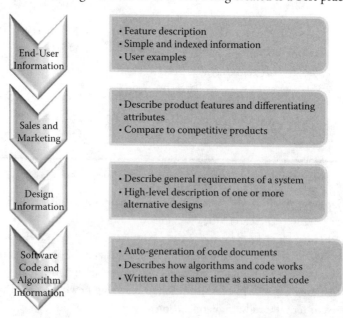

Figure 6.5   Software documentation.

Table 6.6 Configuration Management

Key Activity	Subactivities
1. Library control	Software code creation and revision control
2. Configuration management planning	Controlled specifications including features and attributes Revision control Roles and responsibilities Audits
3. Status reporting and verification	Features and functional requirements met by the system

Configuration Management

Configuration management consists of several integrated activities and work products that ensure a system's hardware and software subcomponents will function as planned. Table 6.6 shows three key configuration management activities and their subactivities. These key activities are library control, configuration management planning, and status reporting and verification. Library control refers to a set of activities related to the creation and revision control of software code. Configuration management planning develops plans to control a system's specifications. Specifications describe features and functions of software. These subactivities also include revision control of specifications as well as the roles and responsibilities of the people associated with revision management. Status reporting and verification reports the performance of a system against its required specifications.

Software Testing

Software design follows a sequential approach. It begins with the identification of user requirements, the creation of the necessary hardware and software systems, and the final release of software to users. In this approach, it is also important to ensure that a system's requirements are specified in a format that facilitates subsequent testing of algorithms, subcomponents, modules, or an entire system. Ideally, to facilitate the correct formatting, software testing can be automated to some extent since more extensive testing will be possible and work objects can be tested as they are created to verify they meet minimum expected-performance requirements.

The information from a review of a system's requirements and specifications is used to develop test plans, procedures, equipment, and related activities designed to test software features and functions. In test planning, one or more of the testing strategies described in Table 6.7 and Table 6.8 are used. It should be noted

Table 6.7 Software Testing

General Testing Method	Specific Methods	Testing Level	Final Testing
Black-box testing: Software is tested without an understanding of its internal functioning. White-box testing: Software is tested with knowledge of its algorithms, software coding, and data structures.	1. Equivalence partitioning 2. Boundary value analysis 3. All-pairs testing 4. Fuzz testing 5. Model-based testing 6. Traceability matrix 7. Mutation testing 8. Fault injection	a. Unit or module level for a specific function b. Module-to-module testing c. Full system test for internal and third-party systems	i. Alpha testing by a software development team and a few potential users of the software ii. Beta testing by a larger group of users to create a larger sample size and a more extensive set of testing conditions

that although there may be no predetermined combination of tests that can be used across all software development projects, a design team should agree up front on the sequence and testing strategies that will be necessary to qualify a system. Another consideration in software testing is an agreement on reporting formats, frequencies, and the actions to be taken based on the testing results. It is critical that both suppliers and users of software use exactly the same testing scenarios and conditions to evaluate and qualify software for its intended use. APM with scrum teams routinely report this information to customers and key stakeholders at the end of every scrum sprint.

Software testing should also be completed when an algorithm's software code has been written. This approach helps to quickly identify software coding errors and eliminate them before other components are dependent on their functions. In fact, it has been shown that there is a multiplier impact on a system because undiscovered software errors require increasingly greater amounts of time to identify and fix the closer they are to commercialization. These situations increase the cycle time and cost of a project. In other words, the costs to find and eliminate software errors is significantly less in the early phases of a project than at full system testing or commercial release. It should also be noted that a multiplier relationship has been shown to exist for numerous products and services produced by other industries such as manufacturing.

Table 6.7 lists several basic steps useful for developing a software testing strategy. First, a Lean IT team needs to agree on a generalized testing strategy for the

Table 6.8   Descriptions of Specific Testing Methods

Specific Method	Description
Equivalence partitioning	Using the minimum number of tests to evaluate an algorithm by dividing the range of an input so that both invalid and valid levels are chosen for testing
Boundary value analysis	Tests of algorithms where the inputs are near (either at or outside) their minimum and maximum levels
All-pairs testing	Inputs are tested pairwise in combination for their effect on an algorithm and to evaluate the defects created by the combination
Fuzz testing	Simulated data representing the full input specification range of an application is run through an algorithm to detect defects
Model-based testing	Developing functional tests based on abstractions of an application model
Traceability matrix	Using a two-way matrix to map one set of requirements into a second set
Mutation testing	Making small modifications to source code to mimic typical and known user errors
Fault injection testing	The intentional introduction of known coding errors (faults) to test software code. An important application is testing algorithms under atypical conditions.

algorithms, subcomponents, modules, and system functions. The choice is either white- or black-box testing and then moving toward one or more specific testing methods. In black-box testing, software is tested without an understanding of its internal algorithms and how they function. Rather, testing parameters or inputs and their associated ranges with their corresponding outputs are known. In contrast, white-box testing implies that software can be tested with a complete knowledge of its algorithms and data structures. Table 6.8 also describes several testing strategies that can be applied alone or in combination to evaluate the functioning of a software code. These include equivalence partitioning, boundary value analysis, all-pairs testing, fuzz testing, model-based testing, traceability matrices, mutation testing, and fault injection testing. Equivalence partitioning uses the minimum number of tests to evaluate an algorithm by dividing the range of an input so that both invalid and valid levels are chosen for testing. Boundary value analysis tests algorithms by evaluating inputs near (either at or outside) their minimum and maximum levels. All-pairs testing requires testing pairwise combinations of inputs for their effect on an algorithm and the defects created by their combination. Fuzz testing simulates data that represent the full specification range of an input and its impact on a software application when it executes an algorithm. Model-based testing develops functional tests based on abstractions of an application model. A traceability matrix uses a two-way matrix to map one column of information, such as user requirements, into a second column, such as reference tests for each requirement. Mutation testing makes small modifications to source code to mimic known user errors. Fault injection testing involves the intentional introduction of known coding errors (faults) to test software. Alpha testing focuses on evaluation of software by a few users, whereas beta testing expands the user evaluation population to gain higher confidence that software will function as expected under a larger set of actual usage conditions.

Software Deployment and Distribution

Once software has been created and tested, it is released to the general user community. This concept is captured in Figure 6.6. The user community may include only one organization, several related organizations, or direct consumers. In other words, depending on the software application, there may be different types of market segments. As an example, Microsoft Office® 2007 is sold to millions of individual people, whereas enterprise software is sold to organizations. After the release of software, it is installed at a user's site. Installation may be completed using specialized teams or directly by users. The specific approach depends on the sophistication of the software being installed as well as user experience. Software installation includes the activities associated with the configuration and setup for customer use as well as the activation of software using applicable system input commands. Once software is installed, it enters its maintenance phase. In this phase, software issues are resolved on an ongoing basis and newer versions of the software are either directly downloaded or manually installed at a user site. At the end of its life cycle, software will be removed from a system.

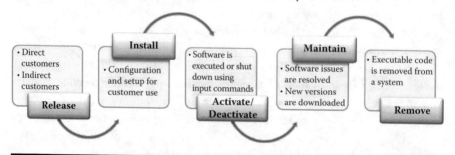

Figure 6.6 Software deployment and distribution.

Summary

The purpose of this chapter was to provide some insight into key design practices associated with the creation and deployment of software. The information is targeted at Lean practitioners who have little software design experience but who are involved with the creation or modification of IT systems within a Lean environment. It is obvious that there are many similarities between the efficient design of software and the classical Lean concepts, tools, and methods. For example, the basic concepts of accurate translation of customer and stakeholder requirements and the design of simple, standardized, and mistake-proofed systems in the context of APM with scrum has applicability across many technologies, industries, and organizations. In the next chapter we will use these concepts to understand how manufacturing and service systems can be created or modified to increase the efficiency of Lean systems.

Suggested Reading

Bustard, David, Peter Kawalek, and Mark Norris, eds. 2000. *Systems Modeling for Business Improvement*. Boston: Artech House.

Dunn, Robert H., and Richard S. Ullman. 1994. *TQM for Computer Software*, 2nd ed. New York: McGraw-Hill.

Fowler, Martin. 1999. *Refactoring: Improving the Design of Existing Code*. New York: Addison-Wesley.

Havey, Michael. 2005. *Essential Business Process Modeling*. Sebastopol, CA: O'Reilly Media.

Hunt, Andrew, and David Thomas. 2000. *The Pragmatic Programmer: From Journeyman to Master*. New York: Addison-Wesley.

LaPlante, Phillip A., and Colin J. Neill. 2006. *Antipatterns: Identification, Refactoring and Management*. Boca Raton, FL: Auerbach.

McConnell, Steve. 1996. *Rapid Development: Taming Wild Software Schedules*. Redmond WA: Microsoft Press.

McConnell, Steve. 1998. *Software Project Survival Guide*. Redmond WA: Microsoft Press.

Menasce, Daniel A., and Virgilio A. F. Almeida. 1998. *Capacity Planning for Web Performance: Metrics, Models, and Methods*. Upper Saddle River, NJ: Prentice Hall.

Thayer, Richard H., ed. 1997. *Software Engineering Project Management*. Los Alamitos, CA: IEEE Computer Society.

van der Aalst, Wil, and Kees van Hee. 2002. *Workflow Management: Models, Methods, and Systems*. Cambridge, MA: MIT Press.

Weill, Peter, and Jeanne W. Ross. 2000. *IT Governance: How Top Performers Manage IT Decision Rights for Superior Results*. Boston: Harvard Business School Press.

PROCESS
INTEGRATION

3

Chapter 7

Lean IT Applications in Manufacturing and Service Systems

Technology is so much fun but we can drown in our technology. The fog of information can drive out knowledge.

—Daniel J. Boorstin

Overview

The goals of this chapter are to show the importance of using Lean principles to manage information technology (IT) projects and to discuss ways in which IT can facilitate the deployment of Lean systems in manufacturing and service systems. Relative to the first goal, it has been demonstrated through several studies of IT project deployment that there are chronic breakdowns. Numerous authors and commentators have reported that a significant percentage of IT projects are not executed on time and within budget. Typical reasons for IT project failure include a failure to accurately capture customer and stakeholder requirements; conflicts between key stakeholders; a failure to use basic project management tools and methods (such as a work breakdown structure [WBS]) or scheduling models (such as Gantt charts); poor team member training, including a lack of education and experience; and poor project communication between team members leaders, customers, and key stakeholders. Many of the tools and methods discussed in earlier chapters will help to improve IT project management and increase the probability of successfully managing and executing IT projects.

In our discussion of Agile Project Management (APM) principles, it was shown that many of its major characteristics reflect classical Lean principles. For example, it was shown that translating the voice of the customer (VOC) and voice of the business (VOB) and using frequent design reviews helps to ensure that the features and functions created at the end of every scrum sprint meet requirements. IT software development tools and methods were also discussed in earlier chapters. Many of these tools and methods can be organized, from a Lean perspective, into simplification, standardization, mistake-proofing, and 5S (sorting, setting in order, shining, standardizing, and sustaining) methods, but also with a focus on best-in-class software design. The discussion in earlier chapters has been from two perspectives. First, IT project management is very important to Lean systems. Second, the use of best-in-class software design tools as well as project management methods helps to ensure successful IT projects.

In our current discussion, we will describe the relationships between Lean IT, as represented by APM with scrum, in the context of several manufacturing and service IT systems. Typical manufacturing systems include enterprise resource planning (ERP), manufacturing resource planning (MRPII), distribution requirements planning (DRP), master production schedule (MPS), forecasting, capacity requirements planning (CRP), manufacturing automation protocol (MAP), warehouse management systems (WMS), and advanced shipping notification (ASN). Typical service systems include workflow management (WM), enterprise application integration (EAI), business activity monitoring (BAM), business intelligence (BI), business process modeling and analysis (BMA), business process management (BPM), and business process management suite (BPMS).

Information Technology (IT) Applications in Lean Systems

In the past several decades, IT has continued to expand into key manufacturing and service production systems and, in particular, into their process workflows and supporting processes. This expansion has been seen in the form of several major applications that mirror those found in Lean systems. The associated productivity benefits are summarized in Table 7.1. Typical IT applications include process simplification, automation, integration, process monitoring, and the management and control of material and information workflows.

Process simplification is a basic goal of any Lean initiative. For example, at the process workflow level, the major improvement goal is to remove all non-value-adding (NVA) operations and their associated work tasks. Recall that NVA work tasks are identified, from an external customer perspective, as work tasks customers do not

Table 7.1 Information Technology (IT) Applications to Increase Productivity

Application	Productivity Increase
1. Simplification	Elimination of intermediaries
2. Automation	Elimination of manual work tasks to standardize and mistake-proof processes
3. Integration	Increases in system configurability, flexibility, and coordination
4. Process monitoring	Real-time data acquisition, analysis, and information sharing across supply chains
5. Management and control	Prioritization of work throughout a system based on real-time information (analyzed data)

need or value, and should not be included in a product or service offering. A related definition of NVA work tasks is those tasks customers will not pay for. It should also be noted that there is a third value classification called business-value-adding (BVA) work tasks. BVA work tasks are required to be performed due to technological or regulatory constraints, but they should be eliminated when it is practical to do so. IT tools and methods have proven to be very useful in simplifying processes by eliminating intermediaries from process workflows through automation of work tasks. For example, an organization's management controls could be streamlined by authorizing approval levels in advance of work. A second example would be streamlining a purchasing system by incorporating approval authorizations into electronic tables to reduce the cycle time and cost associated with approvals and sign-offs.

Automation can also be used to eliminate work tasks. In this regard, automation also helps to standardize and mistake-proof the remaining work tasks. Examples include the retrieval and evaluation of data across disparate IT systems and databases, matching data fields, communicating the status of work including system alerts, and creating and publishing management reports.

Much effort is also routinely wasted within an organization because its various systems are not integrated. The result is that time and effort must be expended at a local level to link them together to create work objects. In this context, IT systems refer to people, machines, materials, and information as well as the IT algorithms that transfer information across an organization. System integration, if properly designed and executed, increases a system's configurability and flexibility to create a more efficient coordination between all participants within an organization as well as its supply chain. This enables an ability to monitor processes in real-time through data acquisition and analysis and create information to share across a supply chain. Finally, the deployment of IT systems improves the management and control of

Table 7.2 Information Technology (IT) Applications in Lean Systems

Application	Productivity Increase	Lean Application[a]
Requirements analysis	Translation of customer requirements into specifications	Understand value through the VOC and the VOB
Simplification	Elimination of intermediaries	Simplify work
Automation	Elimination of manual work tasks to standardize and mistake-proof processes	Reorganize the work environment, standardize work, and apply mistake-proofing methods
Integration	Increases in system configurability, flexibility, and coordination	Link work operations, balance material and information flow (using a takt time), manage bottlenecks, use transfer batches, reduce setup times, maintain high system availability through preventive maintenance, implement pull scheduling system
Process monitoring	Real-time data acquisition, analysis, and information sharing across supply chains	Develop metrics and measurement systems
Management and control	Prioritization of work throughout a system based on real-time information (analyzed data)	Level demand and use pull scheduling as well as the visual control of work

[a] From Table 5.1.

workflow, including the prioritization of work to facilitate the availability of timely and accurate information.

Table 7.1 can also be expanded by linking it with several common Lean applications. This linkage is shown in Table 7.2 as a modification of Tables 5.1 and 7.1. As an example, a requirements analysis, if properly done, will accurately reflect the VOC and VOB. This VOC and VOB information will also be reflected by an accurate translation of requirements into quantitative or measurable specifications. In this way, IT and Lean approaches to project management and system design use customer and stakeholder needs and value expectations for their basis. This is particularly evident when APM and scrum methodologies are employed using activity backlogs and sprints. Recall that the objective of a scrum sprint is to produce clearly defined features and functions, which are immediately reviewed by customers and key stakeholders. In this project management approach, the VOC and VOB remains strongly aligned to the creation of software and its related systems. The simplification and automation of work tasks using IT applications is also analogous to the Lean goals related to the simplification, standardization, and mistake-proofing of work tasks. In fact, these basic concepts are useful in almost any application. Also, the critical Lean goal of supply chain integration, using pull scheduling systems, correlates well to the deployment of many IT applications designed for process improvement. The deployment of measurement systems and metrics to control processes is also an important characteristic of both IT and Lean systems. Finally, the deployment of automated systems should also facilitate the visual control of work and help to prioritize its flow through Lean systems.

Manufacturing Systems

In the next several sections, we will discuss the manufacturing IT systems, which are shown in Figure 7.1. These systems are presented generically because they are produced by different software organizations using different brand names. Manufacturing IT systems can be deployed either as turnkey systems or integrated into current IT infrastructure using interdisciplinary teams. Earlier chapters discussed Lean IT project management methods such as IBM®'s Rational Unified Process (RUP) and APM with scrum. Our goal in this chapter will be to show how these project management methodologies can be used, perhaps with some modifications, to support both the deployment as well as the day-to-day work activities within Lean systems. As an example, manufacturing resource planning (MRPII) systems are designed to push materials through a supply chain, but they can be modified to pull materials through portions of the same supply chain to increase its flexibility and responsiveness to lower inventory, reduce operational costs, and improve schedule attainment.

Figure 7.1 shows that the flow of materials and information through a manufacturing system begins with the estimation of external customer demand using either forecasting models or known demand, which is sometimes called "order book." Firm demand represents contractual obligations of customers to the organization. External demand by item and location is transmitted to a master production schedule (MPS) module for aggregation for all items by their location and offset by their due date. The aggregated production schedule is compared with capacity information using a capacity requirements planning (CRP) module. The aggregated demand is then also reviewed by an organization's senior management using a sales and operations planning (S&OP) team. The S&OP team also evaluates the available capacity by product group to determine which products can be produced within a given time period and location. Adjustments are usually made to

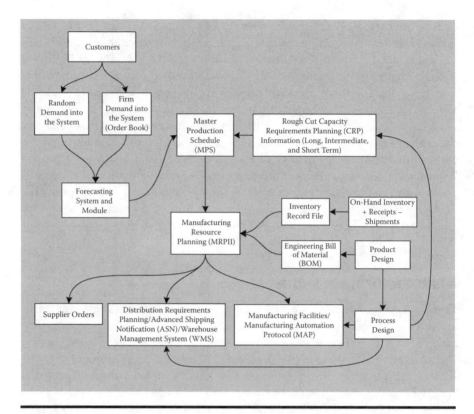

Figure 7.1 Relationships between manufacturing information systems.

the original MPS schedule to smooth future demand based on available production capacity. Once the MPS and CRP information has been finalized, the information is passed to the MRPII.

An MRPII system takes the aggregated external or independent demand for each item or product by its location and breaks it down into dependent-demand items using a bill of material (BOM). These dependent-demand items are the components of the higher-level independent-demand products. For example, if an MPS forecasts that 100 computers will be sold and if the assembly of a computer requires 100 screws, then the order would require 100 times the number of computers or 10,000 screws. After this calculation, an MRPII system would place an order for 10,000 screws with suppliers or create an internal production schedule to manufacture the screws based on a lead time offset. However, MRPII requirements are initially offset by any existing inventory identified by the inventory record file for each product. It should be noted that the production schedule of each dependent-demand item is determined by the sequence in which it is built, the lead time to produce or order it, and the available local capacity. Figure 7.1 shows that the BOM information is provided by design engineering based on how each product is constructed.

Table 7.3   Manufacturing: Enterprise Resource Planning (ERP)

Basic Functions	Some Known Issues	Lean Applications	IT Enhancements
• A more sophisticated version of an MRPII system that includes accounting-related information, as well as the resources needed to plan, manufacture, and ship customer orders.	• Incorrect relationships between independent and dependent-demand items. • Incorrect constants and parameters such as lead time, lot size, and similar inputs. • Database refresh intervals and sequencing. • Push demand using product forecasts.	• Reduce the complexity of the system by removing products that do not sell and redesigning others to reduce their subcomponent count. • Implement pull scheduling to the greatest extent possible. • Continually improve system accuracy and quality.	• Ensure system information is refreshed at correct intervals and in the proper sequence. • Ensure all system constants are accurate. • Modify current systems from push to pull scheduling. • Enhance visual control of processes by modifying fields and rules. Examples include hybrid MRP and kanban systems.

Enterprise Resource Planning (ERP)

Table 7.3 lists the basic functions of an ERP (enterprise resource planning) system including some known issues. Also shown in Table 7.3 are Lean applications and IT enhancements commonly used to either mitigate or eliminate the known issues within ERP systems. An ERP system is a more sophisticated version of an MRPII system in that it also manages information from accounting and financial systems and may integrate what used to be several standalone supporting modules. A modern ERP system includes basic manufacturing functions, such as the resources needed to plan, manufacture, and ship customer orders. Additional capability includes sales and marketing as well as accounting and financial management systems. In fact, a typical ERP system incorporates life-cycle management, which facilitates project management activities such as the planning and managing of the product development process. Additional capabilities support enhanced communication to facilitate collaboration between global teams using XML (eXtensible Markup Language)-based Web standards; quality management of the flow of materials and information; the management of assets through their entire life cycle; and the facilitation of environmental, health, and safety compliance to laws and regulations.

ERP systems also exhibit several common and chronic issues due to their complexity, and relative to software algorithms, data integrity, and diverse and integrated supply-chain functions. Some of these ERP issues are shown in Table 7.3. One issue is caused by errors in a product's BOM, which causes inaccuracies between independent- and dependent-demand subcomponents or items. In the previous example, the BOM required a ratio of 100 screws per computer. However, if this BOM ratio had been incorrectly set up in the BOM file, then there would either be not enough or too many screws to fully assemble the complete order for the 100 computers. If there had not been enough screws, this situation would have caused a missed production schedule, and screws would have had to be taken from other scheduled orders or they would have been expedited from a supplier. If too many screws had been ordered then inventory investment would have unnecessarily increased.

Another ERP issue includes the existence of inaccurate system parameters. Parameters provide information such as lead times, lot sizes, and similar information used by manufacturing IT systems to plan, manufacture, and ship materials and products. This information is used by algorithms to plan, manage, and execute ERP functions, such as calculating inventory quantities or placing supplier orders. Another major ERP issue is the sequencing or merging of files and the frequency of refreshing their databases. As an example, if receipt and shipment files are not periodically refreshed and current to each other, then inventory levels will not be accurate. This situation would result in over- or underordering inventory. Finally, the fact that an ERP system is a push rather than pull scheduling system that uses product forecasts, results in a disconnection between production schedules, actual external demand, and internally available capacity. The combination of these three system conditions, as well as other contributing factors, often results in higher inventory, missed schedules, and similar breakdowns within production processes.

However, Lean tools and methods can be used within an ERP environment to reduce the potential complexity of the system. Process simplification can be achieved by rationalizing the production of products that are not profitable, redesigning remaining products by eliminating subcomponents, and then standardizing the design of the remaining one. This approach can help to reduce the complexity of the work activities necessary to manufacture a product. Additional process improvements include mistake-proofing and deploying pull scheduling systems. Finally, Lean and related initiatives such as total quality management are also very useful to facilitate the continuous improvement of ERP systems.

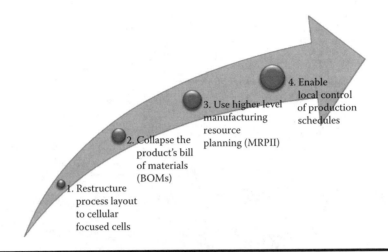

Figure 7.2   Quick Response Manufacturing (QRM).

IT enhancements also are very useful in improving ERP system performance by helping to ensure that system information is refreshed at frequent intervals and in their proper sequence and that all system constants are accurate. Advantages of IT enhancements include process automation, standardization, and mistake-proofing of work operations. In more advanced IT enhancements, ERP and similar systems can be modified, to varying degrees, to move from a push to pull scheduling system. Examples include Quick Response Manufacturing (QRM) shown in Figure 7.2 and the hybrid MRP and kanban system model shown in Figure 7.3. These models will be discussed later in this chapter. Also, the management and control of work can be enhanced through the visual control of materials and information moving through process workflows. This is done by modifying their data fields and decision rules, or creating dashboards, exception reporting, and similar systems.

Forecasting

Forecasting systems use time series algorithms and historical demand to predict future demand. Future demand represents unit quantities of a product by time period into a projected forecasting time horizon. Table 7.4 lists several common issues related to the use of forecasting systems. One issue is caused by using an incorrect form of a time series to build a forecast. As an example, the use of monthly shipment quantities rather than actual customer demand would cause forecasting errors. This is because if not all the original demand for a product was scheduled and built, then its shipment history would not accurately reflect a product's original demand. This situation could be caused if subcomponents or capacity are not available. It should be noted that there are many other reasons for a mismatch between a product's original quantities demanded versus its actual shipment history. In other

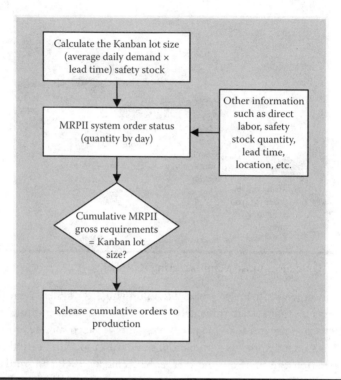

Figure 7.3 Hybrid MRPII/Kanban systems.

words, basing a product's forecast on its shipment history will tend to perpetuate backorders. Backorders represent the difference between original demands versus what was shipped to customers. Another forecasting issue is incorrectly specifying the length of a time series to build a forecasting model. For example, if a pattern of demand exhibits a high degree of seasonality, but an analyst only uses a single year of monthly demand to build a forecasting model, then year-over-year changes in monthly demand cannot be incorporated into a model and its resultant forecasts will not show the underlying seasonality pattern. As a result, its accuracy will be lower than if the correct model had been built using several years of monthly demand. A forecasting model may also be built using incorrect smoothing parameters or it may be incorrectly interpreted. Another major issue relates to not using a sales and operations planning (S&OP) team to review forecasts. An S&OP team should be used to create a consensus forecast based on current as well as projected considerations of supply and demand.

Useful Lean tools and methods to prevent some of these types of forecasting issues include creating multifunctional teams comprising customers and suppliers to improve the coordination and accuracy of communications across a supply chain, and moving toward local control of scheduling and resource management

Table 7.4   Manufacturing: Forecasting

Basic Functions	Some Known Issues	Lean Applications	IT Enhancements
• Uses historical demand and time series algorithms to predict future demand for each forecasting time interval over the forecasting time horizon.	• Incorrect time series is used for a forecast. An example is using shipment rather than demand histories. • Time series length is too short or too long. • Incorrect forecasting model is used to estimate future demand. An example is choosing a time series model rather than a regression-based model. • Incorrect smoothing parameters are used in a model. • An analyst incorrectly interprets a model's forecast. • Several forecasts are not properly aggregated by their product group. • The aggregated forecast is not reviewed by an S&OP team to agree on a consensus forecast based on current supply and demand considerations.	• Create multifunctional teams between customers and suppliers to improve coordination and communication across a supply chain. • Move toward local control of scheduling and resource management to increase operational flexibility as supply and demand factors change over time.	• Use point of sale information rather than forecasting models. • Integrate IT systems across the supply chain to provide all participant visibility to demand and supply as well as asset utilization by location.

to increase operational flexibility as demand and capacity change. Another important factor that can significantly reduce forecast errors is lead-time reduction. This is because reducing a product's lead time also shortens its forecasting time horizon. This is important because forecasts are built for shorter rather than longer time horizons and hence are built using more accurate information. In fact, it has been shown that forecasting error increases into the future as the square root of a product's lead time.

IT applications, which are helpful in reducing forecasting error, include using point of sale (POS) information that reflects actual customer purchases, rather than forecasts and integrating the demand and capacity, as well as asset utilization by location across a supply chain. As an example, major retailers have deployed POS systems in the past few decades to record customer purchases when they are scanned across a store's scanners. This POS information is then uploaded to central data warehouses where it is used to adjust a product's inventory level and to send orders to suppliers for replacement inventory. In addition to using POS information, suppliers or vendors may also be required to manage their own inventory. A common example is that a vendor receives POS information for each store location to adjust its production schedules. This helps to ensure that store shelves are properly stocked. This approach enables subsuppliers representing second- and third-tier suppliers to adjust their own production schedules. In summary, forecasting demand for products and services is heavily dependent on the accuracy of the available information.

Capacity Requirements Planning (CRP)

A capacity requirements planning (CRP) system uses MRPII information of open and new manufacturing orders, material routings, time standards, and other production information to estimate the required labor, materials, and machine time for production lines and facilities. Some common issues associated with these CRP activities are shown in Table 7.5. One major issue occurs when the routing or flow patterns of materials and subcomponents through a manufacturing process are very complicated. These process-related complications increase as the percentage of non-value-adding (NVA) work activities increase and excessive traveling between workstations occurs. In manufacturing, typical NVA work activities inclu2de excessive inspection of work, quality issues, excessive movements, storage of intermediate work called work in process (WIP), and similar manufacturing wastes, such as those described in Chapter 5 and Figure 5.2. Other manufacturing issues include inaccurate time standards or other production information that create errors when estimating local capacity and demand. These types of CRP issues result in inaccurate production schedules. The net effect on a process is lost capacity.

Lean tools and methods have been specifically designed and refined over the past several decades to stabilize and then increase a system's capacity. These include

Table 7.5   Manufacturing: Capacity Requirements Planning (CRP)

Basic Functions	Some Known Issues	Lean Applications	IT Enhancements
• Uses MRPII information related to open and current manufacturing orders as well as routings and time standards to estimate required labor and machine time across facilities.	• Complicated routings through manufacturing processes, which require excessive movement of materials. • Inaccurate time standards or other production information. • Inaccurate information related to demand or resource status.	• Simplify job routings by reorganizing job workflows. • Create multiskilled workers and use low cost and redundant equipment to increase operational flexibility. • When practical, control the routing and scheduling of jobs at a local work-team level.	• Decouple high-level IT systems to provide aggregate demand information, which is managed by local work teams at a product level based on current resource availability. • Provide visibility to actual customer demand and supply-chain resources.

the simplification and standardizing of job routings by reorganizing job workflows, training workers to become multiskilled, using low-cost and redundant equipment to increase operational flexibility, and, when practical, controlling the routing and scheduling of jobs at a local work-team level. These Lean applications help to match available capacity to current demand, which reduces process waste.

IT enhancements also help stabilize a system's capacity by providing local work teams visibility of their resources. Ideally, resources can be decoupled, to some extent, from higher-level IT systems, such as MRPII, which use push scheduling systems. In this approach, decoupling manufacturing schedules from high-level ERP systems enables local work teams to manage their product schedules at a product-family level using current information regarding available resources and capacity. Pull scheduling systems enhance these advantages since the activation of a system's resources is subordinated to external customers as well as available resources. This topic will be expanded in the section titled "Quick Response Manufacturing (QRM) Systems."

Master Production Schedule (MPS)

A master production schedule (MPS) receives and aggregates product demand and sales forecasts, and uses gross capacity estimates to develop a manufacturing schedule for every product and manufacturing location within its planning time horizon. Table 7.6 shows there are several common issues with MPS systems. These include product sales forecasts that do not reflect the demand, which actually occurred as measured using forecasting error metrics. In this context, there are several related metrics that measure forecasting errors. The most basic calculation subtracts forecasted quantities from actual quantities for each time period into the future. It should be noted that because customers change their original orders, a difference between forecasted and actual quantities are common. Also, the forecasting models themselves may have been poorly constructed by forecasting analysts. Other issues that occur within an MPS are related to inaccurate parameter information, such as available capacity or where products are actually manufactured.

A major Lean improvement is implementation of a pull scheduling system at a local level rather than MPS's push scheduling; however, it is difficult to deploy in practice. Additional enhancements may also include the stabilization of available capacity and lead times using Lean methods such as work simplification, standardization, mistake-proofing and continuous improvement activities, and the use of visual control systems to manage the flow of materials and information through a process.

IT enhancements include the use of actual customer demand such as point of sale information by item and location to aggregate demand rather than relying on product forecasts, and sharing demand and supply information across all supply-chain participants. If forecasting is required, then best-in-class modeling methods can be used and analysts properly trained in their usage. Finally, IT is also useful in locating and managing supply chain resources and assets. A typical example is the growing use of radio frequency identification (RFID) tags or responders, which are attached to assets, including materials and products, to track their flow through manufacturing systems and supply chains. These RFID tags contain an integrated circuit for receiving, storing, and processing information or then sending it via an antenna to other receiving systems.

Quick Response Manufacturing (QRM) Systems

Quick Response Manufacturing (QRM) methods consist of four major activities designed to decouple local production schedules from higher-level MRPII systems. These four major activities are restructuring a process layout and its workflows to create product-family-focused work cells; collapsing BOMs; continuing to use higher-level MRPII information, but only at a product-family level; and enabling the control of production schedules by local work teams (Figure 7.2). An advantage of using QRM methods is that in industries characterized by very high

Table 7.6 Manufacturing: Master Production Schedule (MPS)

Basic Functions	Some Known Issues	Lean Applications	IT Enhancements
• Uses the sales forecast and order book demand, gross capacity, and on-hand inventory to develop a final manufacturing schedule.	• Sales forecast does not reflect actual demand as measured by its forecasting error (actual minus forested quantity). • Customers change their original order quantities. • Available capacity changes. • On-hand inventory quantities are not accurately calculated, which increases net production requirements.	• Rely more on pull scheduling rather than forecasts. • Stabilize available capacity and lead times by using methods such as work simplification, standardization, mistake-proofing, and continuous improvement. • Use visual system to manage inventory and control the flow of materials and information.	• Use actual customer demand, such as point of sale quantities by item and location, to aggregate demand rather than rely on product forecasts. • Share demand and supply information throughout the supply chain using compatible IT platforms. • If forecasting is done, use best-in-class modeling and ensure analysts are trained properly in use of the models. • Use IT to locate and track supply-chain resources and assets.

manufacturing volumes and a diverse product mix, MPS and MRPII systems are necessary to control the scheduling of products within these systems. However, high-volume manufacturing systems differ from midrange systems, which were the initial focus of pull scheduling deployments. It should be noted that in both types of production systems, MPS and MRPII systems are utilized. But in midrange systems, manual interfaces and controls are easier to deploy and maintain over time.

An example is Toyota, which manufactures automobiles. Toyota successfully created and deployed the first pull scheduling systems. But, this was possible because Toyota also developed many of the Lean tools and methods discussed in Chapter 5 in an environment in which external customer demand for automobiles had low variation. For example, estimates of the monthly variation of unit demand are in the range of 10 percent of average monthly demand. This situation created a relatively stable production schedule. Stability was further enhanced using Lean methods, which simplified, standardized, and mistake-proofed production operations.

A benefit of using QRM is that some of the advantages of a pull scheduling system can be achieved in manufacturing environments where it is difficult to update MRPII and shop-floor scheduling systems, such as production activity control (PAC), to accurately reflect changes in local resources. These local resources include labor, equipment, and materials. QRM is useful in modifying production schedules to ensure an alignment of currently available resources to manufacture scheduled products. This is in contrast to some manufacturing systems where a product is built up to a certain point of its BOM hierarchy only to find it cannot be finished due to resource scarcity issues. These types of situations cause a buildup of WIP inventory. This increases manufacturing costs and exacerbates existing manufacturing schedules. Low-volume systems also benefit from deployment of QRM methods if their process workflows are inherently complicated and work must also be scheduled by higher-level MPS and MRPII systems.

Manufacturing Resource Planning (MRPII)

Figure 7.1 showed that an MRPII system converts independent demand into dependent demand. At its most basic level, an MRPII system uses a product's BOM, inventory record file, and MPS information to calculate and schedule the production of net requirements for materials and subcomponents used to build higher-level products. Net requirements are calculated by subtracting on-hand inventory from a product's initial requirements. Materials and subcomponent lead times and lot sizes are also used to schedule the production and receipt of these resources. Table 7.7 describes several known issues associated with an MRPII system as well as Lean solutions to these issues. Typical IT enhancements are also listed in Table 7.7. Issues associated with an MRPII system also correspond to its basic functions. For example, the presence of incorrect data files, and parameters or errors in algorithm logic impact operational and financial data conversions. Parameter inaccuracies include incorrect lead times and lot sizes. These types of errors occur when operational changes are not updated in an MRPII system or if the information was never correct. Related operational issues may occur when parameters are estimated rather than calculated using accurate process information. IT issues also occur if software algorithms improperly convert parameters, or calculate operational and financial statistics. As an example, constants may be rounded up or down with an effect of abruptly shutting down an operation prior

Table 7.7   Manufacturing: MRPII

Basic Functions	Some Known Issues	Lean Applications	IT Enhancements
• Includes operational and financial data conversion and enables business planning. • Uses BOM, inventory, and MPS information to calculate net requirements for materials and components for manufacturing and suppliers. These requirements are offset by material and component lead times. • Integrates functions related to sales and operations planning, master production planning, material requirements planning, and capacity planning.	• Data or algorithms may not be correct. • Calculations may be rounded up or down. • Databases may not be refreshed at correct intervals or in sequence. • BOM structure may be incorrect. • Conversion constants, such as lead time, lot size, and usage factors, may not be accurate. • Algorithms might not be correct. • Changes within a process such as inventory and capacity may not be reflected in net requirements. • Demand is incorrectly forecasted or aggregated. • Scheduling is pushed rather than pulled through the system. • Capacity is incorrectly calculated or not updated as manufacturing conditions change.	• Simplify production operations. • Standardize production operations. • Mistake-proof production operations and manual work operations associated with the MRP system. • Apply 5S to manual work operations associated with the MRP department. • Implement pull scheduling systems such as hybrid MRPII with kanban.	• Apply APM and scrum to system design. • Use good algorithm design methods. • Use continuous improvement teams to develop effective demand and supply strategies. • Design systems so that process status information is displayed in real-time as it occurs. • Modify data fields in current systems to implement pull scheduling. • Decouple lower-level systems from higher-level systems. An example would be collapsing a product group's BOM to provide local control of production to respond dynamically to changing process conditions.

to completing its work activities. For example, several years ago I was faced with a problem whereby a warehouse management system rounded up the weight of a trailer after it had been loaded to only a fraction of its weight or capacity. The IT system would not let the dockworkers add more weight to the trailer because it had closed the freight manifest. This situation resulted in higher freight costs because trailers went sent out only partially full and, as a result, additional trips had to be taken during a year. A second common IT error occurs if data files are not periodically refreshed in their proper sequence. In these situations, either too much or too few materials, subcomponents, or finished products will be manufactured or ordered from suppliers. The practical impact on an organization will be lower customer service if orders are not manufactured on schedule. Alternatively, there will be an increase of inventory. A second set of MRPII functions includes the integration of sales and capacity to schedule manufacturing operations. Independent-demand information from forecasting and MPS systems is also an important driver of MRPII calculations. However, a classical MRPII system uses demand to create a push scheduling system. In a push scheduling system, production and manufacturing schedules are planned and fixed in advance. However, if external demand or internal capacity change, then a demand–supply mismatch will occur between what is currently needed by customers and manufacturing schedules.

The Lean methods shown in Table 7.7 have been used to improve the operational performance of MRPII systems. In fact, these types of Lean tools and methods can be applied to most IT systems in the form of process simplification and standardization, as well as the application of other 5S methods and mistake-proofing methods. Lean tools and methods can help make the work tasks required to maintain an MRPII system more efficient and reduce work errors. The implementation of Lean methodology occurs in several major forms. First, just simplifying and standardizing work operations will tend to reduce the complexity of a process. This makes the use of an MRPII system easier. Also, these are specific projects that can be implemented to improve the communication between users of MRPII systems. This will also increase the accuracy of the demand and supply information used by such systems. A good strategy is to use an S&OP team to integrate demand and supply activities of an organization. Finally, software can be modified to create new or alter current MRPII functions. For example, we earlier discussed deployment of QRM systems as a way to schedule and manage local resources at a work cell level within an MRPII and MPS environment. We will expand on the QRM concept in the next section and introduce a second method that can be used to implement a pull scheduling system within an MRPII environment. This second method is hybrid/MRPII with kanban.

A kanban is a physical or electronic sign attached to inventory to show its status. In other words, kanbans signal the movement or production of materials and subcomponents. A kanban quantity of inventory is calculated based on an item's lead time, demand over lead time, and safety stock. Also, one or several containers may be needed to meet a kanban quantity for a given time period depending on the size of a container. For example, if a kanban quantity is 1,000 units but a container only holds 250 units, then a kanban quantity will consist of four containers. An important characteristic of a kanban is that it cannot move unless a downstream operation signals the material is needed. Once containers are signaled and leave an upstream work operation, the production of another kanban quantity, by the upstream work operation, is also authorized. Kanbans are pulled by an external customer demand through a manufacturing process using a takt time. This physical or electronic scheduling methodology balances demand with supply.

IT enhancements to improve the installation and maintenance of an MRPII system are also shown in Table 7.7 as two major areas of focus. The first area consists of the application of IT project management activities that can be best summarized as an application of APM with scrum to the design or modification of an MRPII system. Recall that APM with scrum can be successfully applied to manage almost any software development project. The second area of focus consists of best-in-class software design practices, such as those discussed in Chapter 6. As an example, using the simplest and most standardized algorithms will reduce the complexity of an MRPII system. Also, IT modifications to MRPII systems often include changes to its data fields to enhance functionality. For example, an MRPII system can be modified as a pull scheduling system using either QRM or an hybrid MRPII with kanban.

QRM was discussed earlier in this chapter and shown in Figure 7.3 and hybrid MRPII will be discussed in the next section. We now want to expand the QRM discussion in the context of MRPII systems. Recall that QRM was used to decouple lower-level work cells from higher-level MRPII and MPS systems. Decoupling is achieved by collapsing a product group's BOM as well as the other actions shown in Figure 7.2 to provide local control of manufacturing scheduling. This scheduling strategy enables a manufacturing system to respond dynamically to changing demand and capacity conditions. Although not a complete implementation of a pull scheduling system, a QRM scheduling strategy does create local flexibility in complex MRPII and MPS system environments. As an example, if a machine breaks down or deliveries of critical raw materials do not arrive on time, then a production schedule can be modified to produce different products without a major disruption to the larger supply chain. In summary, an advantage of using a QRM approach is that an MRPII system can still be used to control the manufacture of products, subcomponents, and other items at higher BOM levels; but because production conditions change at a local level, a production schedule can be modified by local teams based on available labor, materials, and equipment.

Hybrid MRPII with kanban systems are an excellent example of how IT can be successfully applied to an existing manufacturing system to maximize its benefits without significantly increasing hardware and software expenses. Figure 7.3 captures the basic elements of this type of system. In a hybrid MRPII and kanban system, kanbans are released to production to meet cumulative MRPII gross requirements. In effect, a hybrid MRPII system uses the MRPII push-demand information to automatically calculate a product's or subcomponent's kanban lot size, and then notify production scheduling of staffing and other capacity requirements. This approach is very useful in a manufacturing system in which there are hundreds or thousands of scheduled products, because it is impossible to manually create and manage kanban cards within these complex systems. When additional IT elements, such as bar coding, electronic data interchange (EDI), and similar methodologies, are added to a hybrid MRPII system, the flow of material and information can be further automated to increase its efficiency. Additional information describing hybrid MRPII and kanban systems can also be found in the book *Integrating Kanban with MRPII* written by Raymond S. Louis.

Other issues that adversely impact the functioning of MRPII systems occur when demand is incorrectly forecast or aggregated; capacity is incorrectly calculated or its status is not updated as conditions change; a BOM hierarchal structure is incorrect, or conversion constants such as lead time, lot size, and usage factors are not accurate; algorithms are incorrect; and changes to inventory and capacity are not properly recorded. It should also be noted that these issues also occur in ERP systems since they contain MRPII modules. A common approach used to mitigate these MRPII issues is to use S&OP meetings to integrate the manage demand and supply, as well as a supply chain's goals and objectives.

Manufacturing Automation Protocol (MAP)

Manufacturing Automation Protocol (MAP) systems use the International Standards Organization's (ISO) Open Systems Interconnection (OSI) standards to coordinate diverse software and hardware systems at a manufacturing shop-floor level. MAP standards enable communication between IT application systems from different organizations. Table 7.8 describes several common issues related to MAP. These include difficulty in integrating diverse systems in environments where there is a very high content of manual work tasks, data inaccuracies, and incompatible hardware and software platforms. Typical Lean tools and methods that accelerate MAP implementations are similar to those previously mentioned and include the simplification and standardization of work systems to increase operational stability prior to deploying automation, mistake-proofing strategies, and cross-functional teams to map out requirements and integrate software and hardware systems. In other words, simple and stable work operations contribute to the success of MAP implementations. An advantage of using IT enhancements includes the automation of work through the elimination of intermediaries as well as enhanced management and control of process workflows. Again in this regard, Lean methods will greatly accelerate manufacturing automation.

Table 7.8　Manufacturing: Manufacturing Automation Protocol (MAP)

Basic Functions	Some Known Issues	Lean Applications	IT Enhancements
• MAP standards enable communication between IT application systems from different organizations using the Open Systems Interconnection (OSI) standards of the International Standards Organization (ISO).	• Integration between all system elements may not be possible, especially in environments where there is a very high content of manual work. • System integration and functioning is only as good as the available data accuracy. • Incompatible hardware and software platforms.	• Simplify and standardize work systems to increase operational stability prior to deploying automation. • Mistake-proof production operations and manual work operations associated with the MRP system. • Use cross-functional teams to map out integration requirements and integrate system elements.	• Increased automation without manual intervention increases operational stability.

Distribution Requirements Planning (DRP)

Distribution requirements planning (DRP) is a system that matches capacity with demand throughout a distribution network. A very important function of a DRP system is inventory replenishment within distribution centers using an MRPII system and a time-phased order point for every item and location throughout a supply chain. Table 7.9 lists several common DRP issues. These issues include incorrectly estimating demand for items at a distribution center due to inaccurate forecasts, not accurately updating inventory estimates, using incorrect system parameters, incorrect software algorithms, and operational issues between suppliers and customers relative to supply and demand, respectively. These issues result in operational breakdowns such as inefficient order fulfillment, missed schedules, late deliveries, and quality problems. Other issues include excess and obsolete inventory, poor inventory location accuracy, and variations of demand and lead

Table 7.9   Manufacturing: Distribution Requirements Planning (DRP)

Basic Functions	Some Known Issues	Lean Applications	IT Enhancements
• Replenishes inventory at distribution centers using a time-phased order point. • Translates planned orders via MRPII to manufacturing and suppliers.	• Demand at distribution centers is incorrect. • Inventory locations and hierarchies are incorrectly specified during system design. • The changing levels of inventory and other assets are not accurately updated over time. • Typical process breakdowns include excess and obsolete inventory, poor order completion, poor inventory location accuracy, and lead-time variation. • System parameters and constants are inaccurate or not correctly calculated by algorithms. • Suppliers and customers may not meet their commitments relative to supply and demand respectively.	• Simplify systems to reduce products, components, and hierarchal levels. • Standardize production operations. • Mistake-proof production operations and manual work operations. • Bring suppliers and customers closer together. • Reduce inventory using pull scheduling and visual control methods. • Reduce lead time.	• Link IT systems to make demand and supply status transparent through the supply chain. • Reduce system complexity by giving visibility to the location and status of supply-chain assets. • Provide supply-chain demand, supply, and resource status as they change over time. • Reduce materials and information batching in favor of transfer batching to reduce lead time.

time. In many ways, DRP issues are similar to those described for MPS and MRPII systems.

Also, the Lean tools and methods previously discussed can be used to improve or eliminate some of these distribution center issues through process simplification, standardization, and mistake-proofing methods. But, at a higher level, to the extent that product and process designs can also be simplified and unprofitable products and services can be eliminated, system complexity will be reduced and a DRP system will become more stable. Additional Lean tools and methods include bringing suppliers and customers closer together to improve communication, deploying continuous improvement teams, and reducing inventory using pull scheduling and visual control methods. These process improvement activities will all help to reduce lead time.

In addition to applying operational improvements, including Lean, information IT applications can also enhance DRP systems. Key IT enablers include linking software and hardware platforms to ensure that the status of demand and capacity is transparent across a supply chain. Transparency implies that all supply chain participants know the locations and status of various supply-chain assets. IT applications can also help to reduce the batching of materials and information, and increase their continuous flow using electronic transfer batching to reduce lead times. IT applications such as QRM and hybrid MRPII and kanban can also be applied in practice with DRP systems.

Warehouse Management System (WMS)

A warehouse management system dynamically manages materials and subcomponents received from suppliers, and assigns them an inventory storage location. More advanced versions of these systems facilitate the efficient fulfillment of customer orders as well as inventory cycle counting by signaling workers to go to inventory storage locations to find items to complete customer orders. Table 7.10 lists several common operational issues associated with a WMS. These include the late arrival of incoming shipments; unusable or damaged inventory, which is either found at incoming inspection or later after it has been accepted into a warehouse; and missing items. Related issues are caused by inventory being placed into wrong storage locations or incorrect information entered into a WMS, which adversely impacts item descriptions as well as the accuracy relative to quantity and location. Also, software algorithms may not be correct resulting in data conversion errors.

Lean methods are particularly effective in a WMS because of the numerous manual work tasks and IT interfaces. For example, improvement teams can be very effective in a WMS. Typical improvement projects include improving the accuracy of filling customer orders, reducing the waste associated with extensive travel times around a distribution center, ensuring inventory is in the correct storage locations, and efficiently handling returned goods and customer complaints. There are numerous other areas within a distribution center where Lean tools and methods can be

Table 7.10   Manufacturing: Warehouse Management System (WMS)

Basic Functions	Some Known Issues	Lean Applications	IT Enhancements
• Dynamically manages received materials and components, and assigns an inventory storage location. More advanced versions of these systems facilitate efficient order fulfillment and cycle counting activities.	• Shipments arrive late. • Unusable inventory is received and accepted into the system. The inventory may be unusable due to poor quality, damage, incorrect type or quantity, or other reasons. • Inventory is damaged during storage. • Inventory is placed into wrong storage location. • Incorrect information is entered into the system. • The system parameters or constants are inaccurate. • Algorithms are not correct. Examples are assigning wrong part numbers and conversion errors.	• Simplify and standardize work tasks. • Mistake-proof manual work tasks. • Coordination of shipments with suppliers to ensure their on-time and accurate receipt. • Use simple systems to move and locate inventory to minimize errors relative to usability and location.	• Visual display of inventory status and location to facilitate management and control; and track items throughout their receipt, storage, and shipment to customers.

used well in practice. Also, distribution centers may have diverse functions that vary by industry. As an example, some distribution centers also contain invoicing and payment processes, packaging and kitting operations, order consolidation activities, and maintenance as well as other functions. Lean applications can be very useful in these situations.

IT can also help improve the efficiency of a WMS by helping to simplify, standardize, and mistake-proof distribution center operations by visually displaying the location and quantities of inventory; and by helping to facilitate the management and control of items through their receipt, storage, and final shipment to customers. Advanced versions of a WMS can also guide workers through a distribution center to find and select items to complete customer orders. Also, a WMS can be programmed to request that workers audit item inventory when their calculated quantities are low and they are near the storage location. A WMS can also be linked to other IT systems such as MRPII.

Advanced Shipping Notification (ASN)

An advanced shipping notification (ASN) system tracks shipments of customer orders as well as the items making up orders. The identification and tracking is integrated using bar-code scanning of shipments when they leave a supplier's facility and again when a customer receives the shipment and its associated pallets, cartons, and items. Using bar-code scanning technology, an ASN system can identify items within cartons and cartons on pallets by their bar code. This information is immediately sent into a WMS. However, a major prerequisite to an ASN system is that a supplier certification program exists so that items can be received into a WMS without manual inspection. This approach enhances the flow of materials through a supply chain. Table 7.11 also lists several issues commonly associated with ASN systems. These issues are similar to the ones discussed for DRP and WMS. Other issues include late shipments, damaged and missing items, inaccurate data, and a lack of supporting systems such as bar-code scanning and supplier certification. The efficiency of an ASN system is greatly diminished if any of these conditions exist.

Several Lean tools and methods routinely used to prevent these issues include forming continuous improvement teams to identify and eliminate operational problems between customers and suppliers, developing simple and standardized work processes around the IT systems, and mistake-proofing manual operations. Continuous improvement teams are particularly important in bringing suppliers and customers together to discuss the basic rules of how their ASN system will work. Integral to the ASN system is for suppliers to develop internal quality systems to ensure that materials, subcomponents, and finished products arrive at customers' facilities on time and defect free. Otherwise, the advantages of an ASN are lost since automated work tasks become manual. High quality is also directly associated with simple, standardized, and mistake-proofed systems. In these applications,

Table 7.11   Manufacturing: Advanced Shipping Notification (ASN)

Basic Functions	Some Known Issues	Lean Applications	IT Enhancements
• Enables customers and suppliers to know all the items making up an order by their pallet and vehicle using bar-code scanning. A prerequisite to an ASN system is a supplier certification program so items can be received without inspection, the deployment of IT such as bar-code creators and readers, and WMS.	• Shipments arrive late, damaged, missing items, or items are defective. • Incorrect bar coding results in errors throughout transit. • A lack of supporting systems such as supplier certification.	• Form continuous improvement teams to identify and eliminate problems. • Develop simple and standardized work processes around the automation. • Mistake-proof all operations that are not automatically sent from one system to another.	• Prompt shipping and receiving personnel to check scan accuracy against visual measures, such as number of pallets or number of cartons per pallet. • Use automatic weighing and volume measurements to look for possible errors.

Lean has much to offer relative to facilitating the deployment of an ASN system, as well as its supporting subsystems such as bar-code scanning through process simplification, standardization, and similar Lean applications.

IT applications associated with ASN include supporting software systems that increase efficiencies by either prompting employees for information or moving the information associated with receipt of shipments into active inventory locations. ASN systems are also used to track shipments to customers. For example, cartons and pallets can have their bar codes scanned to send information into an ASN system prior to a shipment. This information will then be validated upon receipt of the shipment. In these supporting work activities, it is also important to check bar-code scanning accuracy. In this context, some organizations use verification methods, such as inspection and automatically weighing completed orders, to identify orders having incorrect items or quantities and ensuring the items are not damaged prior to their shipment.

Service Systems

It is obvious that IT systems are important in manufacturing to efficiently integrate its diverse process workflows. In fact, some manufacturing facilities are almost entirely automated with robotic machines manufacturing products. However, service systems also rely heavily on IT systems. This is particularly true in global processes where workers may never meet one another but are responsible for supporting processes. These supporting processes maintain the flow of materials and information through their organization as well as the larger supply chain. The IT systems found in service systems consist of several hierarchal levels designed to collect, analyze, and manage the flow of information across global supply chains. Figure 7.4 shows the hierarchal relationships between the various software systems, which we will discuss each in the next several sections of this chapter. It should be noted that several of these systems may be deployed and used in isolation.

Workflow Management (WM)

Whereas manufacturing systems consist of several well-known and integrated software systems such as MPS, MPRII, WMS, and other software systems, service organizations use several hierarchal levels of workflow management (WM) systems. These systems are used to link work operations and manage the flow of information. Also, more advanced software systems provide offline modeling and simulation of process workflows. Modeling helps to optimize process performance by calculating the relationships between process inputs and outputs. The resultant can be used to set process inputs at levels that will ensure process outputs meet their performance targets.

Table 7.12 describes the basic functions of WM. First, it should be noted that a process workflow consists of one or several operations, which are linked together using rules. These rules describe how operations transform one or more inputs received from one operation into one or more outputs of a subsequent operation using software algorithms. Typical WM rules control the priorities, timing, and formatting, which lower-level work operations or tasks need to pass information within and between other tasks. For example, transformation rules might specify that work task A is completed prior to work task B beginning its work, or that work task A transfers to work task B—a particular output having a specific target and maximum range using a specific format, and sent at a specific time. In addition to these types of transformation activities, process monitoring and control activities also exist in WM.

Workflows also consist of combinations of people, equipment, materials, and information arranged in various physical or electronic (virtual) networks. These networks consist of combinations of serial and parallel work tasks and decision points. Also, process workflows exist in either physical or virtual formats as well as in combination. An important attribute of electronic processes is that, if they are properly

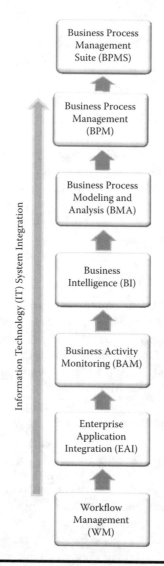

Figure 7.4 Evolution of software in service systems.

designed, then it will be relatively easy to rapidly model and analyze their integrated work tasks to design alternative processes. This enables an optimum process design to be identified and created as needed when process conditions change.

The identification and analysis of process issues or problems depend on a specific system, because there are an almost unlimited number of ways in which a process workflow can fail. However, WM issues can be classified using generalized classification such as time, quality, cost, health, and safety. Examples of timing issues include early or late delivery of materials or information. Quality

Table 7.12   Service: Workflow Management (WM)

Basic Functions	Known Issues	Lean Applications	IT Enhancements
• A process workflow consists of one or more linked operations that transform one or more inputs into one or more outputs using rules. These rules control how lower-level work tasks pass information to one another. • In addition to transformation activities, feedback and control activities exist to monitor, report, and modify workflows. • Workflows also consist of combinations of people, equipment, materials, and information arranged in various physical combinations, such as serial and parallel. • Workflows may be physical or virtual. Physical workflows will be more difficult to analyze and modify than virtual ones. In fact, virtual workflows can rapidly model and analyze a process to create several alternative designs and optimize the best design relative to an organization's goals.	• There are an almost unlimited number of ways in which a process workflow can fail. At a high level, these issues can be classified into the general categories of time, quality, cost, and health and safety. • Examples of time issues include late or early deliveries and long cycle times. Quality issues may include low process yields when a process output is measured against a performance target. Some cost issues include higher expenses, lower revenue, lower cash flow, and low asset utilization ratios.	• There are many types of Lean tools and methods that can be used to improve the performance of a process workflow. Two of the most useful are understanding and mapping customer values to create a quantified value stream map of the process workflow. • Others include balancing the flow of materials and information through a process based on its required takt time and applying simplification, standardization, and mistake-proofing methods to improve the efficiency of the process. After improvements have been made, a process should be continually improved over time.	• The system changes the workflow design based on rules and logic programmed by its users to optimize certain critical outputs. • Optimization algorithms to ensure goal alignment and convergence. • An ability to self-reconfigure, add, delete, and modify workflow elements based on external or internal information.

issues may include low process yields when a process output is measured against its performance target. Cost issues may include unexpected expenses, lower revenues or profit margins, and lower cash. Low cash-flow rates are usually exacerbated by low asset utilization ratios. These issues may also be correlated to each other. As an example, poor quality information will usually increase the cycle time required to complete a job as well as its overall cost.

Although Lean concepts, tools, and methods were developed to analyze and improve process workflows in manufacturing, there are also strong analogies to service systems. For example, Lean methods are useful in identifying and translating customer needs and value expectations into requirements to create a quantified value stream map (VSM). Other applicable Lean methods include balancing the flow of materials and information through a process based on its required takt time and then applying simplification, standardization, and mistake-proofing methods to improve its efficiency. These approaches were discussed in Chapter 5. Finally, a process should be continually improved over time to ensure its value content is maximized and its work tasks map back to customer requirements.

IT enhancements can greatly enhance the quality and speed of the work tasks in service systems. For example, a workflow can be modified based on rules and logic programmed by its users to optimize certain critical outputs relative to one or more process inputs. Optimization algorithms are very useful in these situations to ensure process goal alignment. In fact, more advanced process workflows have the ability to self-reconfigure, add, delete, and modify the sequencing, prioritizing, and arrangement of work tasks to reflect changing internal and external information.

Enterprise Application Integration (EAI)

Enterprise application integration (EAI) systems coordinate purchasing, accounts payables and receivables, inventory warehousing and order management, and similar functions. These are all distinct processes that contain several interrelated subprocesses. In this respect, an EAI system is similar to manufacturing's ERP system. An advantage of an EAI system is that it coordinates several different hardware and software systems using just one interface to coordinate the basic functions described in Table 7.13. Coordination is achieved by using middleware messaging across the various IT platforms to route instructions and other information. EAI issues are the direct result of incompatibilities between lower-level system hardware and software. These incompatibilities inhibit a complete integration of application programming interfaces and their software languages. However, process analysis, simplification, and standardization using a Lean improvement approach will minimize both the extent and magnitude of these incompatibility issues. For example, an application of software and hardware standardization will help to ensure hardware and software integration, at least to a minimum extent.

Table 7.13   Service: Enterprise Application Integration (EAI)

Basic Functions	Known Issues	Lean Applications	IT Enhancements
• Integration of purchasing, accounts payables and receivables, inventory warehousing and order management, and similar functions. • Coordinate several IT interfaces using one interface through software and hardware integration. • Routing of information and instructions, middleware messaging, and control of systems.	• Lower-level software and hardware incompatibilities may inhibit full integration of application programming interfaces. • Different programming languages may be used by different systems.	• Process analysis, simplification, and standardization.	• Application of software and hardware standardization. • Application of integrating software languages.

Business Activity Monitoring (BAM)

Once a basic description of its interrelated work tasks has been created, the application of business activity monitoring (BAM) systems can enhance the performance of a service process. But BAM depends on software availability, sophistication, and compatibility. Also, it is very useful where WM systems are operative. The basic functions of BAM include providing decision rules to monitor the status of a process workflow and control its work activities. BAM also provides a hierarchy of process status notifications to people and systems and describes the required actions based on the notifications of changes of a system's status. Other BAM functions include the extraction, analysis, summarization, and reporting of operational and other business metrics. These functions are described in Table 7.14. This

Table 7.14   Service: Business Activity Monitoring (BAM)

Basic Functions	Known Issues	Lean Applications	IT Enhancements
• Provide decision rules to monitor process status and control work activities. • Provide a hierarchy of process status notifications and determine actions of the persons notified of system status. • Extract operational and other business metrics from various IT systems and their applications. • Enable drill down analysis and reporting of process events.	• Lack of a stable process workflow. • Ambiguous decision rules and process flows. • Alignment between higher- and lower-level metrics may not be clear.	• Design simple and standardized workflow systems. • Create a value stream map and obtain the VOC to focus on important metrics and requirements as well as their relationships. • Develop prioritized lists of metrics including their minimum, target, and maximum levels.	• Automate manual processes related to the monitoring and control of workflow. • The integration of metric status reporting using decision support systems to provide actionable recommendations to users when a system's status changes.

functionality enables business analysts to drill down to increasingly lower levels of process detail to identify the reasons for process changes as seen in the process events and their notifications.

However, there are several known process issues that may adversely impact the implementation of BAM. These issues include a lack of a stable process workflow, ambiguous decision rules and process flows, and the alignment between higher- and lower-level metrics may not be clear. As a result, Lean tools and methods can be advantageous to help deploy BAM systems within process workflows. For example, Lean methods can be used to design simple and standardized workflow systems, create value stream maps using the VOC and VOB to focus on important process requirements. This will enable teams to more easily create their workflow rules. IT enhancements may also be useful in identifying and eliminating BAM issues. For instance, manual work activities can be automated and then software can be used to monitor and control work activities. Processes can also be integrated using decision support systems to provide actionable recommendations to users when the status of a system changes.

Business Intelligence (BI)

Business intelligence (BI) systems are another useful set of software tools and methods. BI enables business analysts to search for and extract relevant information across disparate software systems and databases. This methodology is also called data mining. In today's world, which is characterized as having tremendous amounts of data that are difficult to synthesize and use for practical business applications, BI is very useful. Several key BI functions are described in Table 7.15. Missing and inaccurate data fields or inefficient algorithms are common issues that inhibit the full application of BI.

Two Lean concepts useful in BI applications are developing a better understanding of the VOC and VOB, and deploying multifunctional teams when developing a BI application. An effective VOC and VOB analysis is useful in ensuring that the correct questions are asked in the first place. Multifunctional teams are useful when identifying the best ways to collect and analyze data. In addition to the application of Lean tools and methods, useful IT enhancements could include increases in algorithm efficiency by using statistical methods such as data clustering and classification, the identification of common taxonomies, and less reliance on metatags for the aggregation of data fields. An example would be to search for patterns associated with the information or outcome of interest by extracting key phrases from text.

Business Process Modeling and Analysis (BMA)

Business process modeling and analysis (BMA) is a set of methodologies that specify rules for data capture as well as relationships between system objects to help build process models and analyze their workflows. Table 7.16 describes the basic functions of a BMA system. The first function is an analysis of operational outputs. Examples include operational cycle times as well as overall operational performance of bottlenecks, capacity constrained resources, their throughput rates, operational costs, and service levels. A second BMA function includes an analysis of the impact of changing process inputs, outputs, rules, and conditions. Typical changes include a what-if analysis regarding the elimination of NVA work operations, the addition or reduction of resources, and the impact of other types of process modifications including rules. The goal of a BMA analysis is to identify and then to migrate a process toward its optimum process conditions.

Table 7.15   Service: Business Intelligence (BI)

Basic Functions	Known Issues	Lean Applications	IT Enhancements
• Applies data mining methods to search for relevant information across disparate systems and their databases to provide information that can answer complex questions.	• Missing or inaccurate data fields. • Search algorithms are not efficient.	• Understand the VOC to develop a list of questions that need to be answered by these types of analyses. • Develop multifunctional teams to identify the correct data collection and analysis methods.	• Improve the efficiency of information searches using clustering, classification, and taxonomies. • Less reliance on metatags for the aggregation of data fields by searching for patterns associated with the information or outcome of interest, such as the extraction of key phrases from text.

However, BMA issues will occur if process relationships, their metrics, and functional relationships and rules are not well known. Also, there will be issues if business analysts do not have the necessary education or experience to perform sophisticated analyses or the required data is not available to incorporate into an analytical model. However, Lean tools and methods can help facilitate BMA deployment efforts by first creating an accurate graphical and then quantitative representation of a process workflow. For example, creating a VSM may be useful. Operational linkages and rules can also be superimposed on a VSM to describe resource relationships, prioritizations, and the statistical distributions of key metrics. These metrics might include operational cycle times, resource capacities, and yields.

IT enhancements include the creation of software algorithms that efficiently access and extract data and information to evaluate the operational performance of reconfigured alternative process workflows. Also, leading-edge operations research algorithms, advanced statistical analysis, and similar quantitative methodologies may be available to help a BMA team. In this context, the application of

Table 7.16   Service: Business Process Modeling and Analysis (BMA)

Basic Functions	Known Issues	Lean Applications	IT Enhancements
• Analyze the output of every operation relative to its cycle time and queuing characteristics. • Analyze overall system performance related to bottlenecks, capacity constrained resources, system throughput rates, and operational cost. • Evaluate changes to the process including elimination of NVA operations. • Evaluate the addition of resources and modifications to the remaining VA operations. • Determine optimum solutions relative to the baseline scenario, including all optimized system parameters and their levels. • Document the modified process based on the organization's major quality and other standardization systems such as ISO 9000.	• Process relationships are not known. • Metrics and their functional relationships to one another are not known. • Analysts do not have the necessary education or experience to perform the analyses. • Data is not available to incorporate into the analytical model.	• Create graphical representation of the process. • Specify process rules to model the process flow including its resources; and parameter distributions, levels, and initial states. • Develop baseline cost, time, and quality estimates related to the system's operational cycle times and capacity as well as other specific characteristics, such as yield and uptime. • Specify operational transition-state probabilities for each operation including their frequencies and rates.	• Software and algorithms enable the access and extraction of all required data and information. • Process modeling software facilitates easy reconfiguration of alternative process workflows as necessary. • Leading-edge analytical algorithm related to operations research, advanced statistical analysis, and similar methodologies are available to a BMA team.

quantitative models will dramatically increase the sophistication of a team's analysis. For example, linear programming models are routinely used to reconfigure and manage complex operational systems having thousands of variables and resource constraints. There are also numerous other types of algorithms, which are industry specific, that can help an organization improve the effectiveness and efficiency of its operations.

Business Process Management (BPM)

Business process management (BPM) is a set of software algorithms and methods that structure the management and control of electronic transactions as well as object location and security management. Other basic BPM functions include object management group (OMG) domain specification as well as specifications related to embedded intelligence and security. These functions are described in Table 7.17. The major advantage of BPM technology is that it enables business analysts to reconfigure process workflows without direct IT support. This is a very useful characteristic, because service processes often change and they need to be reconfigured to ensure that software algorithms match actual process conditions. However, although the process couplings used by BPM are relatively loose, reconfigured systems do use approved and standardized software code at lower levels within the various software applications. As a result, BPM facilitates the evolution of process workflow management systems to reflect actual process conditions and requirements as they migrate and as defined by users of a BPM system. This is in contrast to the common practice of forcing users to adapt to a process workflow that does not accurately reflect their process workflow or needs.

Some issues known to be associated with the deployment of BPM are that its process workflows may not be fully understood or standardized, and that business modeling specifications, in the form of business design goals and objectives, are not clearly understood. Typical Lean solutions to these types of issues include accurately obtaining the VOC and VOB; creating process maps to describe the interrelationships between work operations or objects; and simplifying, standardizing, and mistake-proofing activities related to data collection, object location, and time and security management. IT enhancements include building middleware specifications for components, software, telecommunications, and similar subsystems; and developing language mapping and Cobra specifications to control dynamic event scheduling to enable the real-time modeling of a process workflow using metadata specifications.

Business Process Management Suite (BPMS)

A business process management suite (BPMS) system facilitates the exchange of data at several levels within an ERP system to coordinate its supply-chain activities.

Table 7.17 Service: Business Process Management (BPM)

Basic Functions	Known Issues	Lean Applications	IT Enhancements
• Structuring mechanisms for transaction management, data collection and management, time management, object location, and security management. • Object Management Group (OMG) domain specification (operations by industry). • Embedded intelligence specifications. • Security specifications.	• Business modeling specifications (business design goals and objectives) are not available. • The process workflows are not fully understood or standardized.	• Understanding the VOC and VOB. • Creating process maps to describe the relationships between work operations or objects. • Simplifying, standardizing, and mistake-proofing data collection, time management, object location, and security management.	• Middleware specifications (components, software, telecommunications). • Language mapping specifications. • Cobra specifications (dynamic scheduling, real-time modeling). • Modeling and metadata specifications (data warehousing, modeling). • Modernization specifications.

Recall that an ERP's activities are related to the management of demand, supply, and all associated financial and operations functions. BPMS integration is facilitated by the coordination of diverse subcomponents of the ERP system whose functions are described in Table 7.18. Issues with BPMS applications may include software and hardware incompatibility due to a lack of standardization, a lack of process knowledge by developers or users, and poor rules specifying the relationships between systems. Possible Lean solutions may include the creation of process maps that describe the relationships between systems and their work objects. Also, Lean IT teams can be used to investigate any existing compatibility issues between hardware and software. IT enhancements may include creating a high-level software configuration that facilitates the integration and coordination of lower-level software subsystems to view and manage information from diverse IT platforms.

Figure 7.5 attempts to place these diverse software systems in a hierarchal arrangement, which is divided into four levels. Operational or workflow

Table 7.18   Service: Business Process Management Suite (BPMS)

Basic Functions	Known Issues	Lean Applications	IT Enhancements
• Enables the exchange of data and information at several levels within an ERP system to coordinate supply-chain activities. These activities relate to the management of demand, supply, and financial functions.	• Software and hardware incompatibility issues due to a lack of standardization. • A lack of process knowledge and the relationships between system components, including operations or work objects.	• Create process maps of system interrelationships as well as metric linkages. • Use teams to investigate software and hardware compatibility.	• System configurability relative to subsystem integration and coordination enables users to view and manage information from diverse IT systems within the ERP system.

information is at the lowest level. The next higher level contains software applications that use operational, financial, and other information from manufacturing operations and service to manage the flow of materials and information through the larger supply chain. This information can also be accessed at the next level by modeling applications to optimize operational and workflow rules, parameters, and the relationships between systems. At the highest level of Figure 7.5 are online Web-based interfaces. When properly designed and interfaced, these diverse software and hardware platforms can be integrated using BPMS in ways to make them appear as one integral system.

Summary

In this chapter we discussed IT applications that currently exist in manufacturing and service systems. These applications have been used to simplify, standardize, mistake-proof, integrate, monitor, manage, and control process workflows throughout the world and in diverse industries. Lean methods have also been deployed within these diverse production systems, but with mixed results. Recall that the initial applications of Lean methods were in manufacturing systems, which were characterized as having relatively low external-demand

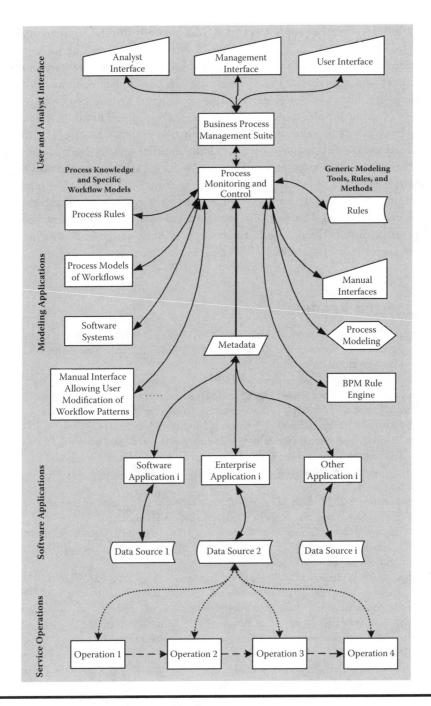

Figure 7.5 Hierarchal relationships between systems.

variation. However, to apply Lean tools and methods in other systems such as high-volume manufacturing and in service systems, there must be some modifications to the original Lean approach. The goals of this chapter were to show that Lean concepts, tools, and methods are directly applicable to any production system, but to varying degrees. This approach takes the key Lean principles of creating simple, standardized, and mistake-proofed production systems to deliver customer value to stakeholders so that system capacity is perfectly matched to external customer demand. From another perspective, as IT project management teams attempt to either deploy new IT systems or modify current ones, Lean methods are always useful to ensure that the project management process itself is streamlined and aligned with customers and stakeholder value requirements. This has been a constant theme throughout this book in that organizations should use Lean concepts to both design and then manage upgrades to their IT systems.

Suggested Reading

Bolstorff, Peter, and Robert Rosenbaum. 2007. *Supply Chain Excellence: A Handbook for Dramatic Improvement Using the SCOR Model*, 2nd ed. New York: American Management Association.

Carroll, Brian J. 2002. *Lean Performance ERP Project Management: Implementing the Virtual Supply Chain*. Boca Raton, FL: St. Lucie Press.

Cavinato, Joseph L., and Ralph G. Kauffman, eds. 2000. *The Purchasing Handbook: A Guide for the Purchasing and Supply Professional*. New York: McGraw-Hill.

Chase, Richard B., F. Robert Jacobs, and Nicholas J. Aquilano. 2006. *Operations Management for Competitive Advantage*, 11th ed. Boston: McGraw-Hill.

Harvard Business Review on Supply Chain Management. 2006. Boston: Harvard Business School Press.

Hobbs, Dennis P. 2004. *Lean Manufacturing Implementation: A Complete Execution Manual for Any Size Manufacturer*. Boca Raton, FL: J. Ross Publishing.

Louis, Raymond S. 1997. *Integrating Kanban with MRPII*. Portland, OR: Productivity Press.

Martin, James William. 2007. *Lean Six Sigma for Supply Chain Management: The 10-Step Solution Process*. New York: McGraw-Hill.

Martin, James William. 2008. *Operational Excellence: Using Lean Six Sigma to Translate Customer Value through Global Supply Chains*. Boca Raton, FL: Auerbach.

Poirier, Charles C., and Michael J. Bauer. 2000. *E-Supply Chain: Using the Internet to Revolutionize Your Business*. San Francisco, CA: Berrett-Koehler.

Reddy, Ram, and Sabine Reddy. 2001. *Supply Chains to Virtual Integration*. New York: McGraw-Hill.

Schragenheim, Eli, and H. William Dettmer. 2001. *Manufacturing at Warp Speed: Optimizing Supply Chain Financial Performance*. Boca Raton, FL: St. Lucie Press.

Suri, Rajan. 1998. *Quick Response Manufacturing: A Companywide Approach to Reducing Lead Times*. Portland, OR: Productivity Press.

Weill, Peter, and Marianne Broadbent. 1998. *Leveraging the New Infrastructure: How Market Leaders Capitalize on Information Technology.* Boston: Harvard Business School Press.

Weill, Peter, and Jeanne W. Ross. 2004. *IT Governance: How Top Performers Manage IT Decisions Rights for Super Results.* Boston: Harvard Business School Press.

Chapter 8

Measuring and Improving Performance

The significant problems we face cannot be solved at the same level of thinking we were at when we created them.

—Albert Einstein

Overview

A major goal of this book is to provide useful information so that Lean practitioners can measure and improve the performance of their information technology (IT) systems to increase organizational productivity. This is an important topic. In fact, a public report, published in May 2002 and available on the National Institute of Standards and Technology's Web site, documents the financial impact of not properly building an IT infrastructure including its measurement and evaluation systems. "The Economic Impacts of Inadequate Infrastructure for Software Testing Final Report" states:

> Based on the software developer and user surveys, the national annual costs of an inadequate infrastructure for software testing is estimated to range from $22.2 to $59.5 billion. Over half of these costs are borne by software users in the form of error avoidance and mitigation activities. The remaining costs are borne by software developers and reflect the additional testing resources that are consumed due to the use of inadequate software testing tools and methods. (p. ES-3)

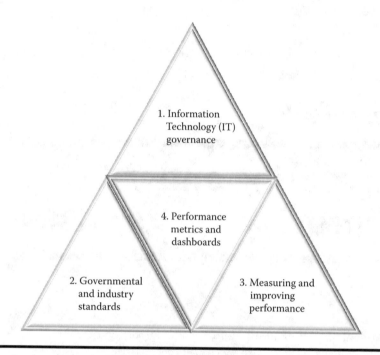

Figure 8.1   Measuring and improving IT performance.

Efficient software design and testing is important. In earlier chapters of this book, it was shown that efficient software testing begins by accurately capturing and translating the voice of the customer (VOC) and key stakeholders into simple standardized and mistake-proofed hardware and software designs that deliver the necessary system features and functions. The measurement of the interrelated project work activities necessary to create these designs as well as the improvements of software design and testing depend on the four key factors shown in Figure 8.1. These factors, which influence the design of software systems, are IT governance, the various governmental and industry standards organizations must adhere to, product and service performance metrics and dashboards, and the measurement and improvement of IT systems.

IT governance is a set of strategies and tactics designed to identify an organization's strategic and tactical IT requirements and ensure that they are integrated into strategic goals and objectives at all organizational levels. Effective IT governance is also necessary to ensure that an organization's IT assets are effectively and efficiently utilized to provide value. In addition to internal governance policies, governmental and industry standards have been created to streamline the design and deployment of software systems across diverse industries and countries. These standards are created by private, governmental, and education institutions around the world. Their purpose is to facilitate the design of hardware and software systems that that they can be easily integrated into higher-level systems. Once standardized frameworks, consisting of rules and best practices, have been created, customers and suppliers can efficiently conduct their requirements translation and design activities. A final outcome of this translation process is the creation of product specifications describing a product's features and functions. Performance metrics and dashboards are also critical in ensuring customer requirements are met day in and day out. We will discuss each of these four factors in detail in the next several sections of this chapter, as well as measuring and improving performance of software and its associated project management activities.

IT Governance

In Figure 8.2, IT governance is broken into its major elements. These elements are the roles and responsibilities of executive leadership, the chief technology officer (CTO) and team, the business unit IT team, and the local IT teams. Executive leadership is responsible for creating the organizational strategies and goals to manage revenue, margin, expenses, investment, and cash flow both now and in the future. Other responsibilities include creating strategies to develop and manage human resources and physical assets. Physical assets include the IT hardware and software, and intellectual capital infrastructure. At an executive level, IT strategies are coordinated to ensure an alignment with an organization's strategic goals and each business unit's execution activities.

The CTO should also be part of an organization's executive leadership team. CTO responsibilities include determining how IT infrastructure will be purchased and positioned within an organization. For example, will the purchase and deployment decisions related to IT resources be made at a CTO level? Or will they be made locally and independently by a business unit's leadership? Alternatively, will there be a hybrid approach to IT deployment and asset management? An organization's CTO works with other key organizational stakeholders to develop these types of IT deployment and management strategies. It should be noted that top-down or bottom-up approaches to the deployment and management of IT infrastructure have advantages and disadvantages. As a result, it is the responsibility of an organization's CTO to help create strategies to acquire, manage, and integrate IT assets and their supporting resources across an organization. Other important CTO functions include the management of IT human resources and physical assets, as well as the management of intellectual property, including copyrights, patents, and proprietary information. In summary, a CTO allocates and manages IT resources to execute organizational strategies.

At a local business-unit level, IT resources are focused on creating or maintaining operational capabilities within a business unit. A business unit is considered to consist of one or more facilities. It is also assumed that a business unit produces similar products or services. Using this definition, a business unit's IT organization

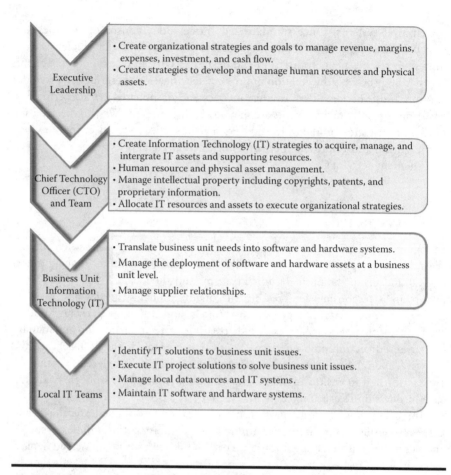

Figure 8.2   Key elements of IT governance.

translates its business requirements into either a modification of currently deployed or new hardware and software systems. Once these systems have been created, modified, or deployed, a local IT organization also manages and maintains them as well as supplier relationships. It should also be noted that whereas a business unit's IT organization helps specify local business unit IT standards and systems, the local IT teams at a facility- or system-application-level help to identify and execute IT project solutions to solve their business unit's issues, manage local data sources, and maintain their local IT software and hardware systems.

Governmental and Industry Standards

Standards help IT teams to efficiently design hardware and software so that other organizations can either directly use or modify them in a standardized manner.

Over the past several decades, several standards organizations have emerged to help manage software design, deployment, and related work activities, such as software and hardware maintenance and disposal. Some standards are controlled by well-recognized organizations such as the International Standards Organization (ISO). The ISO also creates and controls standards on numerous other products and services sold throughout the world. In the software community, there are several specific organizations that create and publish well-accepted standards. Carnegie Mellon University is an excellent example of an organization that has evolved to help standardize software design. IBM®'s Rational Unified Process (RUP) is another standardization approach. Table 8.1 lists several other standards organizations and examples of their standards. Although Table 8.1 is not a complete listing of standards, it does show that there are many national and international organizations as well as professional societies that create and manage hardware and software standards. Their Web sites should be reviewed for additional information for the types of standards they create and manage.

Measuring and Improving Performance

Software measurement systems should also be designed to show how well customer and key stakeholder requirements are satisfied in practice. For example, Figure 8.3 provides additional insight into this concept by breaking down the process of creating a software measurement system into four elements. These four elements are to create stable processes; identify assets having the greatest probability of failure; develop libraries of standardized and proven software algorithms; and create a quality assurance organization to collect and analyze information, and then continuously improve current systems and work methods. It should be noted that different organizations might have different approaches to working through these four elements.

The necessary work activities a team uses to create a stable process have been discussed in several earlier chapters. So the listing shown in Figure 8.3 should be familiar. For example, establishing clear requirements, standardized processes and work methods, increasing a system's availability, formally authorizing users to make changes, and creating formal procedures specifying who can access and change systems are common best practices in software design. To the extent these best practices are followed, the design of a system's measurement system will be easier. The concepts of Agile Project Management (APM) with scrum and Lean are also very applicable in that the concepts of VOC, as well as creating simplified, standardized, and mistake-proofed processes help to create systems that can be more easily measured than complicated and disconnected ones.

The second key element useful in measuring and improving performance is the identification of IT assets having the greatest probability of failure. This is an important concept because IT infrastructure often consists of several supporting

Table 8.1 Common Software Industry Standards

Organization	Key Standards
• IBM • U.S. Department of Defense Software Engineering Institute (SEI) • National Institute of Standards and Technology (NIST) • National Aeronautics and Space Administration (NASA) • ITIL was originally created by the CCTA under the auspices of the British government, and ITIL is a registered trademark of the UK Government's Office of Government Commerce (usually known as the OGC) • International Standards Organization (ISO)	• IBM Rational Unified Process (RUP) • Capability Maturity Model Integration (CMMI)® at Carnegie Mellon University • Software standards related to mathematical algorithms, and statistical and computational sciences. • NMI 2410.10, "NASA Software Management Assurance and Engineering Policy" • NHB 1700.1(V1), "NASA Safety Policy and Requirements Document" • NASA-STD-2201-93, "Software Assurance Standard" • NASA-STD-8719.13A, "Software Safety" • Information Technology Infrastructure Library (ITIL)® • ISO/IEC 20000-1 ITSM Specification for Service Management (Requirements for IT service management); ISO/IEC 20000-2 ITSM Code of Practice for Service Management (Provides guidance to auditors against ISO/IEC 20000-1) • ISO/IEC 15504 is an international standard for process assessment developed under the auspices of the ISO and the International Electrotechnical Commission (ISO/IEC).
• IEEE	• IEEE 1058–Software Project Management Plan (SPMP) • IEEE 830–Software Requirements Specification (SRS) • IEEE 1016–Software Design Description (SDD) • IEEE 1012–Software Validation & Verification Plan (SVVP) • IEEE 829–Software Test Documentation • IEEE 828–Software Configuration Management Plan (SCMP) • IEEE 730–Software Quality Assurance Plan (SQAP)
And many others …	

1. Create stable processes

- Clear requirements.
- Standardized processes and work methods.
- Increase system availability.
- Formally authorize users to make changes.
- Create formal procedures specifying who can access and change systems.

2. Identify assets having the greatest probability of failure

- Analyze failure incidents, repair costs.
- Critical resources.
- Resources impacting other systems.
- Resources impacting major customers or suppliers.

3. Develop libraries of standardized and proven software algorithms.

- Use best-in-class software design principles including the independence of module
- Standardize to the greatest extent possible relative to current software platforms and databases.
- Pull from existing infrastructure rather than create new software unless it is necessary.
- Develop off-line and automated software testing capabilities.
- Integrate these activities with quality assurance to ensure formal approval mechanisms.

4. Create a quality assurance organization to collect and analyze information and then continuously improve current systems and work methods.

- Create metrics to measure the release, day-to-day management, and the improvement of software activities.
- Allocate resources to prevent problems.
- Train people to continually improve the software design and development work activities.

Figure 8.3   Developing software measurement systems.

hardware and software systems. Also, system failure probabilities can be estimated using a design analysis of an IT system or from historical records of failure incidents and repair costs, and similar sources of information. Another consideration is an analysis of critical resources that might impact other systems or major customers and suppliers if they should fail.

A third key element useful in measuring and improving software performance is developing libraries of standardized and proven software algorithms, using best-in-class software design principles including the principle of module independence, standardizing software databases, pulling from an existing IT infrastructure rather than

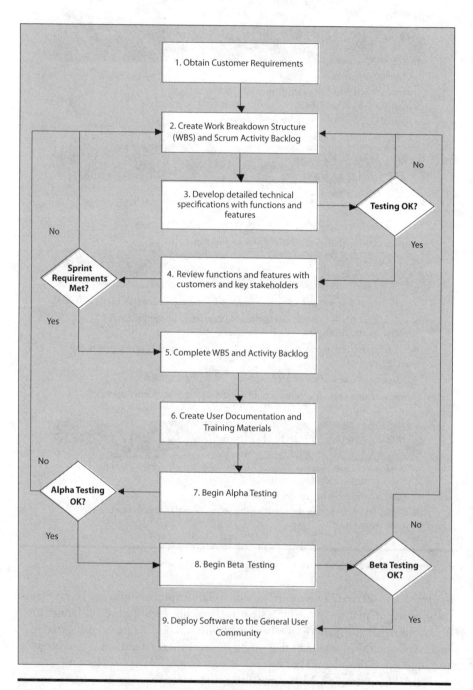

Figure 8.4   Basic steps to create and deploy software.

creating new software (unless it is necessary), and developing offline and automated software testing capabilities. An important activity is the integration, through quality assurance, to create approval systems that are formalized rather than ad hoc.

The fourth key element is continuous improvement of the overall process by creating a strong quality assurance organization to collect and analyze information, and then identify ways to continuously improve current work methods. Important activities in this regard are measuring the release of software, its day-to-day management, and resource allocations to prevent quality problems. Figure 8.4 summarizes the information shown in Figure 8.3 from a different perspective using nine steps.

Performance Metrics and Dashboards

Performance metrics are the basis for process control and improvement. In earlier chapters of this book we presented and discussed the project metrics summarized in Table 1.2 and the metrics summarized in Figure 5.7. In this section we will expand our discussion of metrics to include those listed in Table 8.2. Although these are the most common metrics, the listing is not exhaustive. In fact, several references listed at the end of this chapter discuss the creation and usage of software metrics in greater detail.

Measuring Lean IT Project Teams

The extent of metric usage varies depending on the size and complexity of an IT project team. As an example, project teams assigned the task to build large hardware and software systems may use RUP, which is a highly structured project management methodology. Recall that its structure is necessary to coordinate numerous work teams as they create hardware and software systems across several organizations and functions. An abbreviated listing of the metrics, which are useful for Lean IT project teams, is shown in Figure 8.5. In Chapter 1, we discussed several of these metrics. Notice that Figure 8.5 breaks down these project metrics by cost, time, and quality. It should also be noted that depending on the specific industry, there may be additional classifications such as compliance to procedures or regulations as well as metrics related to health and safety processes. The metrics shown in Figure 8.5 include actual versus budgeted cost, actual versus planned schedule, the average time for problem resolution, the number and percentage of unplanned changes, and the types of quality problems found and documented. These metrics can also be broken down or stratified into lower-level metrics by location, work team, and quality problems or issues.

Measuring Software Creation and Deployment

There are several metrics useful for measuring the work activities associated with the creation and deployment of hardware and software systems. For example,

Table 8.2   Measuring Metrics and Improving Performance

4a. Measuring Lean IT Project Teams[a]	4b. Measuring Software Creation and Deployment	4c. Measuring the Software Testing Process	4d. Measuring the Performance of Lean Systems
• Actual versus budgeted cost • Actual versus planned schedule • Average time for problem resolution • Number and percentage of unplanned changes • Types of problems	• Labor hours per release • Cycle time per release • Errors per 100 releases • Error types and percentages • Cost per configuration item (CI) • Time to resolve CI issues • Number and percentage of CI changes • Number and percentage of failures caused by inaccurate CIs • Design changes without a formal change request • Cost per service issue • Time to resolve a service issue • Actual versus planned service level target by function and feature • Number and percentage of service-related issues • Accuracy of information	• Efficiency • Ease of use • Reliability • Maintainability • Reusability	• Customer satisfaction (Net Promoter Score) • Percentage of value adding to total work time • First time yield (FTY) with no rework and scrap • Concept to market cycle time • Throughput cycle time • Asset utilization efficiency (plant, equipment, and other invested capital) • Cost (measured from a system to transaction level)

Note: Expansion of performance metrics and dashboards from Figure 8.1.

[a] Also see Table 1.2.

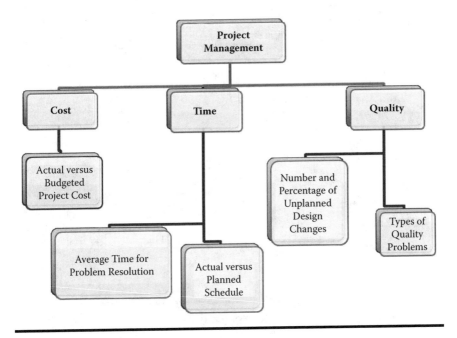

Figure 8.5   Project management metrics.

software deployment activities include the ongoing maintenance, upgrade, and disposal of software.

Common metrics related to these actives are shown in Figures 8.6, 8.7, and 8.8, which also correspond to the metrics shown in Table 8.2. It should also be noted that there are several ways to further stratify the metrics. As an example, the metrics could be stratified by project as well as by software module, feature,

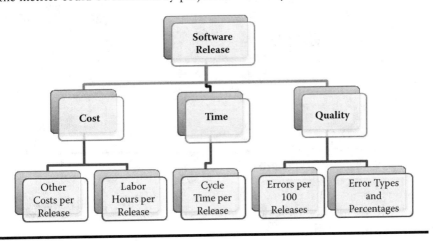

Figure 8.6   Software release metrics.

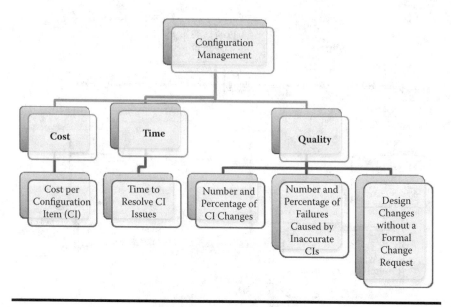

Figure 8.7   Configuration management metrics.

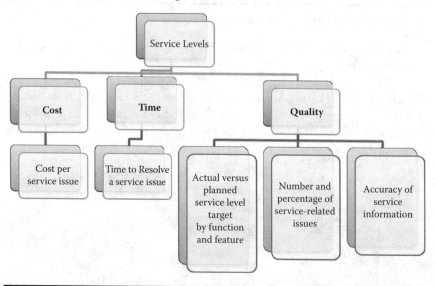

Figure 8.8   Service level metrics.

function, complexity (i.e., lines of software code), and similar project and product attributes. Stratification enables a finer level of management and control of a project's work activities.

Common software release metrics include total labor hours, cycle time per release, and the total number of errors and rework incidents found during a project.

Metrics can also be broken down or stratified into lower-level metrics based on the stratification factors discussed earlier. Configuration metrics measure cost, time, and quality, but from an individual configuration perspective. Because CI metrics actually measure the work activities and outputs associated with the design of software, there is an emphasis on design issues and software changes. Typical examples of metrics used to measure and control the work activities associated with a configuration process are shown in Figure 8.7. These include the cost per configuration item (CI), the time to resolve CI issues, the number and percentage of CI changes, the number and percentage of failures caused by inaccurate CIs, and changes made without having a formal change request. Several common service metrics useful for customer satisfaction or quality problems or similar issues are shown in Figure 8.8. These include the cost per service issue, the time to resolve a service issue, the actual versus planned service level by feature and function, the number and percentage of service-related issues, and the accuracy of the measured service-related information.

Measuring the Software Testing Process

In addition to the metrics just discussed, there are several types of measurements useful for software evaluation. These are shown in Table 8.3 and include efficiency, ease of use, reliability, maintainability, and reusability. Efficiency measures how well algorithms perform relative to time, cost, or quality. One common measure of an algorithm's efficiency is the time it requires to perform its calculations. As an example, a proven principle of good algorithm design is that a minimum number of

Table 8.3 Measuring the Software Testing Process

Testing Goal	Definition
Efficiency	Algorithms using a minimum or optimum number of decision nodes to execute one or more functions or combinations of functions.
Ease of use	Software that can be accessed and understood, and whose commands can be executed and transported without additional work activities that exceed its original design intent.
Reliability	Software available for use at a predetermined probability level.
Maintainability	Software that can be easily modified if necessary with a minimum amount of work activities.
Reusability	Software subcomponents that can be used with little or no modification to build other software systems.

decision steps should be used to execute its functions. Ease of use metrics measure how software is accessed by users and its ability to be clearly understood. Rbeliability metrics measure the conditions required to ensure that software is available for use with a predetermined degree of confidence. Maintainability measures how easy it is to fix or modify software once it has been deployed to users. Reusability measures the degree to which software components, including its features and functions, can be used with little modification to create or modify other software systems.

Measuring the Performance of Lean Systems

Recall from our Chapter 5 discussion that the Lean metrics shown in Table 8.4 are also similar to several metrics used to manage IT projects and software design by APM with scrum teams. For example, customer and key stakeholder satisfaction are routinely measured from several perspectives by project teams regardless of the underlying initiative. Although there may be several ways to measure customer and stakeholder satisfaction, a Net Promoter Score (NPS) metric is considered to be one of the better measures of customer satisfaction because it has been shown to correlate to some degree with repeat customer sales. Frederick F. Reichheld discussed the concept of a NPS metric in his article titled "The One Number You Need to Grow," which was published in the *Harvard Business Review* in 2003. A NPS metric is defined as the percentage of promoters minus the percentage of detractors. Promoters highly recommend a product or service, whereas detractors do not. The percentage of responses classified as neutral is not used in a NPS calculation. The NPS rating scale ranges between 0 and 10 with the levels between 0 and 6 classified as detractors, levels 7 and 8 as neutral, and levels 9 and 10 as promoters. NPS ratings between 10 percent and 20 percent are considered average performance, whereas those exceeding 75 percent are best in class. Customer satisfaction is also measured using several other types of metrics and systems. In these surveys, customers can be asked to rate specific products and services as well as their actual versus expected performance levels. Direct examples include on-time delivery and use of products and services; indirect examples include warranty and returned goods incident rates, lost sales, and complaints.

A second classic Lean metric is the percentage of value adding (VA) to total work time. A VA metric is defined as the ratio of processing time divided by all other time components, including processing time (e.g., setup, inspection, waiting, and transport times) and the time it takes to make up work (i.e., rework and scrap). Recall that the basic concept when evaluating the percentage of VA time in either software design or project management is that features and functions should only be added if they meet the needs and value expectations of external customers. In contrast, non-value-adding (NVA) time components should be reduced and eliminated. Obvious examples of NVA components include time lost due to redoing work or engaging in unnecessary project activities. Measuring the percentage of VA time in IT applications can be viewed from two perspectives. First, a Lean IT project team's

Table 8.4 Measuring the Performance of Lean IT Systems

Lean Metric	Definition
1. Customer satisfaction (Net Promoter Score)	Defined as (% Promoters – % Detractors) with % neutral not used in the calculation. The NPS scale is between 0 and 10 with levels 0 to 6 classified as detractors, levels 7 and 8 as neutral, and 9 and 10 as promoters.[a]
2. Percentage of value adding to total work time	[(Processing Time)/(Setup Time + Inspection Time + Waiting Time + Transport Time + Time to Make Up Work, i.e., Rework and Scrap)] × 100
3. First time yield (FTY) with no rework and scrap	Number of units that meet requirements without having been reworked or made up, that is, if 100 units go into an operation and 10 are scrapped and 5 are reworked then FTY = 85/100 = 0.85.
4. Concept to market cycle time	The time between when a product has been made available for customer purchase versus the start of its design.
5. Throughput cycle time	The time between when a product's components are purchased and the product is sold to a customer, similar to a cash-flow rate.
6. Asset utilization efficiency (plant, equipment, and other invested capital)	Usually measured as "turns." Turns is the average monthly value (cost) of an asset divided into the cost of goods sold (COGS) it supports. If the COGS is $1,200 per year and $100 of inventory is kept on hand to support monthly variation of sales, then the inventory turns is $1,200/$100 = 12 per year.
7. Cost (measured from a system to transaction level)	The standard cost of raw materials, subcomponents, or finished products calculated as materials cost plus variable cost plus fixed costs.

[a] Frederick F. Reichheld, "The One Number You Need to Grow," *Harvard Business Review*, December 2003.

work activities can be analyzed to determine their percentage of VA work. In these analyses, the goal would be to increase the VA content of a team's work activities. Examples may include missed meetings, not obtaining accurate process information, or having to approach customers and stakeholders numerous times for the same information. Second, the VA content of software products and services should also be very high. From this perspective, best-in-class design methods should be employed to ensure that features and functions as well as their specifications are aligned with customer needs and value expectations. It should be noted that the VA content will be higher to the extent that a design is simplified, standardized, and mistake-proofed to ensure it can be easily produced and commercialized.

First time yield (FTY) is an important metric to evaluate quality at both an operational and system level. The concept of FTY is now widely used in practice. However, this was not always the situation. Prior to its wide adoption, it was common for an organization to measure its process yields as a percentage of final production in proportion to original customer orders. In this approach, although rework and scrap rates were also measured, they were not clearly visible. There tended to be a distortion of measurements relative to how well an organization's quality system performed in practice. For example, if 100 units were required to complete an order, but only 85 were produced right the first time, then an additional 15 units would be needed to complete a production order. Making up the work would require either reworking or replacing scrapped production units. Historically, work replacement activities were often done informally, which gave rise to the term *hidden factory*. In a hidden factory, rework and scrap are hidden and final yields (FY) appear higher than FTYs. Hidden factories commonly occur in almost every industry, organization, and work process in both manufacturing and service systems.

If a production system is aligned with customer requirements, and its VA content and FTY are high, then its cycle time should be lower. But, recall the discussion of a system's bottleneck in Chapter 5, which stated the bottleneck operation controls the flow of materials and information through a process. As a result, the VA content and FTY must be high at a system's bottleneck because it constrains the flow of materials and information through a system. Cycle time measurements, such as market cycle time (from product concept to market), can be good indicators of a Lean IT team's schedule performance. Of course, cycle time must also be measured throughout a project from the initial concept through to its commercialization. Recall that a project's critical path, as depicted by its Gantt chart of work activities, provides the best estimate of a project's cycle time. Also, the resources supporting a project can be increased to accelerate the completion of work activities, on a project's critical path, to reduce its current remaining cycle time. However, the concept of market cycle time may be misleading if customers do not immediately pay for their products or services. For this reason, we also introduced in Chapter 5 a throughput metric, which was discussed by Goldratt and Cox in their book *The Goal*. The measurement of a system's throughput rate begins when materials are purchased for production operations and it ends when payment has been received from customers. The concept of cash-flow rate is similar. In other words, it is not how much you produce and place into inventory that improves productivity, but how much you profitably sell to customers.

The term *Lean* implies that a production system meets customers' requirements and produces products and services using a minimum amount of material, labor, equipment, and capital. In other words, a Lean organization should have a relatively higher asset utilization efficiency when compared with competitors or historical baselines within an industry. An example is inventory utilization efficiency as measured by the metric inventory turns. Recall that inventory turns is the average monthly value (standard cost) of an inventory asset divided into the cost of goods sold (COGS) it supports. For example, suppose a product's COGS is $1,200,000 per year and $100,000 of inventory (finished goods inventory in a distribution center) is kept on hand to support its monthly variation of sales. Then it's inventory turns ratio is calculated as $1,200,000/$100,000 = 12 per year. A reasonable goal, to increase asset utilization efficiency, would be to reduce the average inventory investment necessary to support the COGS. If successful, the inventory turns ratio would increase from its initial baseline of 12 turns per year to a higher level.

A cost or expense metric is also an important way to measure how a project's resources are used. As an example, cycle time may be decreased and quality increased by adding additional resources to a project. Or when designing a product, redundant or unnecessary features and functions may be added. Maintaining project and product design cost targets is also important to ensure a balanced approach to the creation or modification of products and services project management. Costs should also be measured at several organizational levels. It should also be noted that in addition to measuring costs, profit margins, revenues, and similar financial metrics are also important.

Mapping Project and Design Metrics

In the last several chapters we have discussed metrics from both project management and software design perspectives. The objective of these discussions was to provide an overview of software design issues for Lean practitioners. But project managers and software designers may be required to use more extensive metric listings. As an example, Table 1.2 provided an extensive listing of project management metrics. Also, the books listed in the Suggested Reading section at the end of this chapter, as well as those listed in Chapter 6, offer more extensive metric listings from a software design perspective.

Figure 8.9 attempts to capture the essential relationships of the major metrics presented in this book. These relationships include metrics required to create, test, and deploy software; the modeling and application of software from a user perspective; and the financial and operational metrics that will be improved if the creation and deployment of software has been effectively and efficiently applied within a Lean system. Several of the metrics summarized in Figure 8.9 were discussed in earlier chapters. For example, the metrics related to IT modeling and software applications were discussed in the figures and tables of Chapter 7 relative to service and manufacturing systems. The service system applications included workflow management (WM), enterprise application integration (EAI), business activity monitoring (BAM), business intelligence (BI), business process modeling and analysis (BMA), and business process management (BPM). Manufacturing applications

Key Financial and Operational Metrics

1. Profit and Loss (PL)
2. Inventory Investment
3. Excess & Inventory Investment
4. Net Operating Profit After Taxes (NOPAT)
5. Equipment Asset Efficiency
6. Fixed Asset Efficiency
7. Receivables Efficiency
8. Gross Profit Margin
9. Return on Assets (ROA)
10. Gross Margin Return on Investment (GMROI)
11. Customer Service Level
12. On-Time Supplier Delivery
13. Overdue Backlogs
14. Inventory Efficiency (Turns)
15. Unplanned Orders
16. Schedule Changes
17. Data Accuracy
18. Material Availability
19. Forecast Accuracy
20. Lead Time

Information Technology (IT) Modeling Applications	Information Technology (IT) Software Applications
I. Workflow Management (WM)	a. Enterprise Resource Planning (ERP)
II. Enterprise Application Integration (EAI)	b. Manufacturing Resource Planning II (MRPII)
III. Business Activity Monitoring (BAM)	c. Material Requirements Planning (MRP)
IV. Business Intelligence (BI)	d. Distribution Requirements Planning (DRP)
V. Business Process Modeling and Analysis (BMA)	e. Master Production Schedule (MPS)
VI. Business Process Management (BPM)	f. Forecasting System
VII. Business Process Management Suite (BPMS)	g. Capacity Requirements Planning (CRP)
	h. Manufacturing Automation Protocol (MAP)
	i. Warehouse Management System (WMS)
	j. Advanced Shipping Notification (ASN)

Manufacturing Systems

Service and Manufacturing Front Office Systems

4a. Measuring Lean IT Project Teams	4b. Measuring Software Creation and Deployment	4c. Measuring the Software Testing Process	4d. Measuring the Performance of Lean Systems
4a1. Actual versus budgeted cost	4b1. Labor hours per release	4c1. Efficiency	4d1. Customer satisfaction (Net Promoter Score)
4a2. Actual versus planned schedule	4b2. Cycle time per release	4c2. Ease of use	4d2. Percentage of value adding to total work time
4a3. Average time for problem resolution	4b3. Errors per 100 releases	4c3. Reliability	4d3. First time yield (FTY) with no rework and scrap
4a4. Number and percentage of unplanned changes	4b4. Error types and percentages	4c4. Maintain ability	4d4. Concept to market cycle time
4a5. Error types and percentages	4b5. Cost per configuration item (CI)	4c5. Reusability	4d5. Throughout cycle time
4a6. Types of problems	4b6. Time to resolve CI issues		4de. Asset utilization efficiency (plant, equipment, and other invested capital)
	4b7. Number and percentage of CI changes		4df. Cost (measured from a system to transaction level)
	4b8. Number and percentage of failures caused by inaccurate CIs		
	4b9. Design changes without a formal change request		
	4b10. Cost per service issue		
	4b11. Time to resolve a service issue		
	Actual versus planned service level target by function and feature		
	4b12. Number and percentage of service related issues		
	4b13. Accuracy of information		

Figure 8.9 Mapping project and design metrics into IT software systems.

included enterprise resource planning (ERP), manufacturing resource planning (MRPII), materials requirements planning (MRP), distribution requirements planning (DRP), master production scheduling (MPS), forecasting systems, capacity requirements planning (CRP), manufacturing automation protocol (MAP), and, at a shop-floor level, manufacturing execution systems, warehouse management systems (WMS), and advanced shipping notification (ASN) systems.

The metrics shown in the first section of Figure 8.9 can help a project team, depending on the industry and application, to create, manage, and improve the software applications shown in the second section of the figure. An extended listing of financial and operational metrics is also shown in the third section of the figure. The first ten metrics are financial and the last ten are operational. A Lean IT project team should understand these 20 metrics because they impact their organization's profitability and productivity. Incidentally, the productivity metric is calculated as an index that measures an organization's year-over-year performance relative to the ratio of sales minus adjustments divided by operating costs minus adjustments.

Relative to the financial metrics, profit and loss (PL) summarizes an organization's revenues minus expenses for a specific time period, such as a month, quarter, or year. Inventory investment is the amount of money spent on inventory that has not been sold. It should be noted that there are several different types of inventory. These include raw material, work in process (WIP), and finished goods. Raw materials are transformed into WIP inventory, which is eventually transformed into finished products that are sold to external customers. Inventory exists because materials and products cannot be produced on demand due to various capacity constraints associated with equipment, materials, labor, energy, or other factors. If inventory cannot be used within the foreseeable future, which is normally multiples of its lead time, then it is classified as excess. If the inventory cannot be used at all, then it becomes obsolete and an organization must write off the cost from its balance sheet. Recall that a balance sheet lists the types and current organizational assets. Assets include inventory as well as plant and facilities, equipment, and other objects that have a monetary value to an organization. Net operating profit after taxes (NOPAT) is calculated by dividing income after taxes by the total revenue. High NOPAT levels are better for an organization. Equipment asset efficiency ratios measure how well equipment is utilized to create sales. Recall that the inventory asset efficiency metric or inventory turns were discussed earlier in this chapter. Fixed asset and receivable asset efficiencies are similarly calculated as sales, or COGS as applicable, divided by the average amount of fixed assets or receivable assets, respectively. Gross profit margin is measured as revenue minus COGS. Return on assets (ROA) is calculated as net profit margin multiplied by asset efficiency. Net profit margin is calculated as net income divided by total revenue, where net income is estimated as total revenue minus all expenses including taxes. ROA estimates the income created from every dollar invested in assets. Gross margin return on investment (GMROI) measures the percentage return (or realized gross margin) for every dollar invested in inventory. As the Lean metrics shown in Figure 8.9 improve, these financial metrics should also improve.

The next ten metrics shown in the third section of Figure 8.9 are operational. Several have already been discussed in earlier chapters from either Lean or project management perspectives. Customer service levels can be measured from different perspectives. Different units can also be used, but at a basic level, they measure operational performance against customer expectations. For example, if we were to make a guarantee that incoming calls would be answered within one minute, a customer service level could measure the percentage of incoming calls answered in one minute or less. On-time delivery is similarly measured in that it is the number of on-time deliveries compared to the number of the total deliveries. Overdue backlogs are orders that have not been produced according to their original production schedule and are late. This metric is different from an order backlog metric, which is a common and planned occurrence in some industries. As an example, military defense contractors typically have order backlogs for military equipment, which they work off over years according to contractual agreements. Inventory efficiency or turns has already been discussed in previous sections of this book. Data accuracy measures the percentage of correct data fields in ERP, MRP, forecasting, and similar manufacturing or service systems. The percentage of incorrect data fields can be calculated by taking a sample of data fields and counting the ones that are in error. Incorrect data fields can cause numerous operational issues. The material availability metric measures the percentage of time materials are not available to support production. If materials are not available for production, then there will be a delay in schedule. Forecasting accuracy measures the differences between actual to forecasted units or dollars. Various forecasting accuracy or error metrics can be calculated depending on analytical assumptions. But a lower forecasting error is always best. The last metric listed in Figure 8.9 is lead time, a critical Lean metric that has already been discussed in previous sections of this book.

Measuring and Improving Performance

Given that there are many different types of metrics an organization uses to measure, manage, and improve its work activities, it is important the organization has a common scale and that quantitative targets are established to show its users when a metric's performance deviates from its target. Figure 8.10 shows this concept. Each of the metrics listed in Figure 8.9 are listed in Figure 8.10, but with a common rating scale ranging between 0 percent and 100 percent to enable them to be aggregated as necessary. These metrics can also be weighted as some are considered to be more important than others. Alternatively, they can be combined in ways that enhance process measurement, management, and improvement. These concepts form the basis of a metric dashboard.

Key Financial and Operational Metrics	Weight	Percentage of Goal									
		10%	20%	30%	40%	50%	60%	70%	80%	90%	100%
1. Profit and Loss (PL)											
2. Inventory Investment											
3. Excess & Inventory Investment											
4. Net Operating Profit After Taxes (NOPAT)											
5. Equipment Asset Efficiency											
6. Fixed Asset Efficiency											
7. Receivables Efficiency											
8. Gross Profit Margin											
9. Return On Assets (ROA)											
10. Gross Margin Return On Investment (GMROI)											
11. Customer Service Level											
12. On-Time Supplier Delivery											
13. Overdue Backlogs											
14. Inventory Efficiency (Turns)											
15. Unplanned Orders											
16. Schedule Changes											
17. Data Accuracy											
18. Material Availability											
19. Forecast Accuracy											
20. Lead Time											

4d. Measuring the Performance of Lean Systems

	Weight										
4d1. Customer satisfaction (Net Promoter Score)											
4d2. Percentage of value adding to total work time											
4d3. First Time Yield (FTY) with no rework and scrap											
4d4. Concept to market cycle time											
4d5. Throughout cycle time											
4de. Asset utilization efficiency											
4df. Cost											

4c. Measuring the Software Testing Process

	Weight										
4c1. Efficiency											
4c2. Ease of use											
4c3. Reliability											
4c4. Maintainability											
4c5. Reusability											

4b. Measuring Software Creation and Deployment

	Weight										
4b1. Labor hours per release											
4b2. Cycle time per release											
4b3. Errors per 100 releases											
4b4. Error types and percentages											
4b5. Cost per Configuration Item (CI)											
4b6. Time to resolve CI issues											
4b7. Number and percentage of CI changes											
4b8. Number and percentage of failures caused by inaccurate CIs											
4b9. Design changes without a formal change request											
4b10. Cost per service issue											
4b11. Time to resolve a service issue											
4b12. Number and percentage of service related issues											
4b13. Accuracy of information											

4a. Measuring Lean IT Project Teams

	Weight										
4a1. Actual versus budgeted cost											
4a2. Actual versus planned schedule											
4a3. Average time for problem resolution											
4a5. Number and percentage of unplanned changes											
4a6. Types of problems											

Figure 8.10   Measuring metric performance using a common scale.

Although there are different types of metrics that can be used to create a metric dashboard, it is important to identify the ones that answer key customer and stakeholder questions. For example, Table 8.5 describes and classifies several customer and stakeholder questions. Using this useful concept, a Lean IT project team should spend sufficient time to ensure that all customer and stakeholder questions have been recorded prior to developing a metric scorecard. Reviewing the questions

Table 8.5 Metric Dashboards Should Answer Basic Questions

Stakeholder Group (Partial Listing)	Typical Questions to Answer
External customers	Does the product or service meet my needs? Do I want to pay for it?
Sales and marketing	Does the product or service help my organization grow its sales and market share? Is it easy to sell to my customers? Will my customers need and value it?
Financial	Is the product or service profitable for my organization? Does it enhance the profitability of other products or at least not deteriorate their profitability?
Operations	Can the product or service be efficiently produced? Can it be produced anywhere? What equipment and skills will be needed to produce it?
Health, safety, and environmental (HS&E)	Can the product or service be safely produced, used, and disposed of throughout its life cycle?

listed in Table 8.5, we see that they make intuitive sense. But, it should be noted that they are a partial listing because the number of relevant questions for any project would be more extensive. Reviewing the external customers stakeholder group, we see that one major concern is that products and services meet their needs. As a result, a team must explore this area in more detail using a more extensive list of questions. As an example, recall that customer requirements were discussed in Chapter 4 and described in Figure 4.1 in the context of Kano needs and values elements. Kano needs were classified as basic, performance, and excitement. Value elements were classified by price, time, utility, function, and relative importance from a customer perspective. As a result, we would expect customer questions to reflect these Kano and value element classification criteria by market segment. This is why the list of external customer questions will be more extensive. Working internally into an organization, the questions that sales and marketing would be interested in answering are related to growing sales and market share as well as creating product and service features and functions customers need and value. Balancing customer, sales, and marketing questions as well as questions posed from several internal stakeholders would be a primary responsibility of a Lean IT team. As an example, finance would want to ensure that new products and services will be profitable. Also, operations would want them designed to enable them to be efficiently produced. The health, safety, and environmental (HS&E) stakeholders would require that new products and services be safely produced and used by customers. Other stakeholders would have their own types of questions.

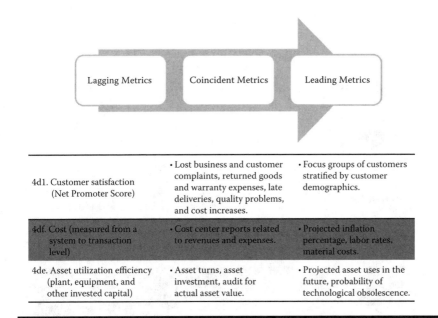

	Lagging Metrics	Coincident Metrics	Leading Metrics
4d1. Customer satisfaction (Net Promoter Score)		• Lost business and customer complaints, returned goods and warranty expenses, late deliveries, quality problems, and cost increases.	• Focus groups of customers stratified by customer demographics.
4df. Cost (measured from a system to transaction level)		• Cost center reports related to revenues and expenses.	• Projected inflation percentage, labor rates, material costs.
4de. Asset utilization efficiency (plant, equipment, and other invested capital)		• Asset turns, asset investment, audit for actual asset value.	• Projected asset uses in the future, probability of technological obsolescence.

Figure 8.11   Some organizational metrics.

Once external customer and key internal stakeholder questions have been identified, metrics must be created to translate them into measurable quantities. Figure 8.11 takes this translation process one step further than previous discussions, by classifying metrics as lagging, coincident, or leading. The concept of lagging, coincident, and leading metrics will be discussed in the context of the organizational, software design, and project metrics shown in Figures 8.11, 8.12, and 8.13. It should be noted that Figure 8.11 presents a few of the higher-level organizational metrics shown in Figure 8.9. Lagging metrics are historical. As an example, lost business, customer complaints, returned goods, and warranty expenses measure past events. Coincident metrics measure current or very recent historical performance. Examples include recent late deliveries, quality problems, and cost increases. In contrast, leading metrics measure future performance and serve as a guide to current controls. An example would be knowledge gained using customer and key stakeholder focus groups. This knowledge may be related to the future gain or loss of major customers, competitive threats, and similar information that may impact future customer satisfaction, cost, and asset utilization efficiencies. In Figure 8.11, an example of a lagging metric is measurement of customer satisfaction using an NPS. Coincident metrics may include costs measured from a system to lower-level transactions using recent cost center reports. Cost center reports measure revenues and expenses and asset utilization efficiencies such as asset turns and investment. Leading metrics would include projected costs, revenues, and asset usages in the future as well as risk analyses related to technological obsolescence.

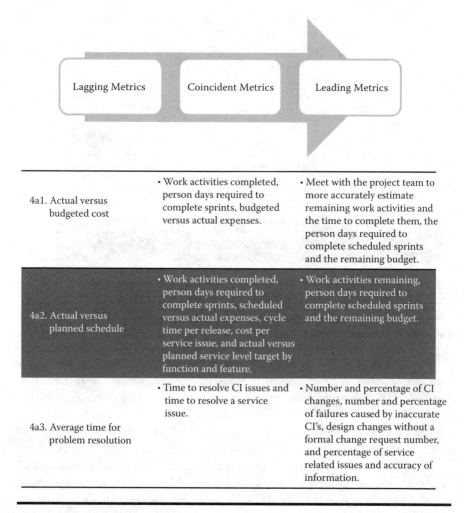

	Lagging Metrics	Coincident Metrics	Leading Metrics
4a1. Actual versus budgeted cost		• Work activities completed, person days required to complete sprints, budgeted versus actual expenses.	• Meet with the project team to more accurately estimate remaining work activities and the time to complete them, the person days required to complete scheduled sprints and the remaining budget.
4a2. Actual versus planned schedule		• Work activities completed, person days required to complete sprints, scheduled versus actual expenses, cycle time per release, cost per service issue, and actual versus planned service level target by function and feature.	• Work activities remaining, person days required to complete scheduled sprints and the remaining budget.
4a3. Average time for problem resolution		• Time to resolve CI issues and time to resolve a service issue.	• Number and percentage of CI changes, number and percentage of failures caused by inaccurate CI's, design changes without a formal change request number, and percentage of service related issues and accuracy of information.

Figure 8.12   Some project metrics.

At the next lower organizational level, we can also discuss the project metrics shown in Figure 8.12 that comprise only a short list relative to the ones discussed in earlier chapters. Lagging project metrics include those reported after their occurrence. Examples include actual versus budgeted cost, actual versus planned schedule attainment, and the average time to resolve a problem. Typical coincident metrics may include total completed work activities that just occurred, person days required to complete scrum sprints, forecast versus actual expenses, the cycle time per software release, the cost per service issue, and the planned versus actual service levels by software feature and function. Examples of a few leading metrics include more accurate estimates of a project's remaining work activities, the time to complete them,

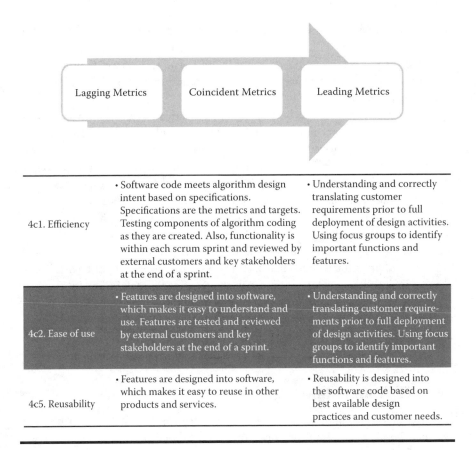

	Lagging Metrics	Coincident Metrics	Leading Metrics
4c1. Efficiency		• Software code meets algorithm design intent based on specifications. Specifications are the metrics and targets. Testing components of algorithm coding as they are created. Also, functionality is within each scrum sprint and reviewed by external customers and key stakeholders at the end of a sprint.	• Understanding and correctly translating customer requirements prior to full deployment of design activities. Using focus groups to identify important functions and features.
4c2. Ease of use		• Features are designed into software, which makes it easy to understand and use. Features are tested and reviewed by external customers and key stakeholders at the end of a sprint.	• Understanding and correctly translating customer requirements prior to full deployment of design activities. Using focus groups to identify important functions and features.
4c5. Reusability		• Features are designed into software, which makes it easy to reuse in other products and services.	• Reusability is designed into the software code based on best available design practices and customer needs.

Figure 8.13   Some software metrics.

the person days required to complete remaining scrum sprints, and the amount of budget remaining. These and similar metrics will enable a project team to modify its work activities to meet goals and objectives.

At a still lower level within a project, several common software design metrics are shown in Figure 8.13. Examples of lagging metrics include efficiency, ease of use, and reusability. These lagging metrics provide information that depends on previous testing. The coincident metrics shown in Figure 8.13 are related to the current testing of the software code to ensure that it meets a system's design intent relative to its features and functions. Coincident metrics are reported both during and at the end of a scrum sprint when software features and functions are reviewed by external customers and key stakeholders. A project team can also create the leading metrics shown in Figure 8.13 by identifying and correctly translating customer requirements prior to full deployment of design activities or by using focus groups to identify important software features and functions. They can also be created using best-in-class design metrics, which are known to increase algorithm efficiency, usability, and reusability. These metrics can also be used to some degree to predict a software system's performance. For instance, the fewer the subcomponents of a system, then the lower its overall cost and cycle time, and the higher its overall quality.

In summary, metrics can be created and evaluated from several perspectives. Remember that an important goal of metric creation and analysis is to answer questions in a manner suggested by Table 8.5. Because questions differ by organization, metric dashboards can take on a wide variety of formats. However, some ideal characteristics of these visual communication tools is that they answer higher-level customer and key stakeholder questions and provide their users with an ability to drill down to the lower-level variables, which drive the variation of the higher-level metrics. Regression models can also be constructed to tie together higher-level metrics (dependent variables) to one or more lower-level metrics (independent variables). There are other characteristics that facilitate the use of metric dashboards. Some of these include using color coding (such as green for normal, yellow for concern, and red for abnormal conditions), and the use of pictures and graphics showing the minimum number of metrics necessary to measure, manage, and improve a system. Figure 8.14 is an example of one of many possible forms of metric dashboards.

Lean IT Applications

A review of various published articles and case studies related to IT within Lean systems shows that significant operational benefits occur when IT methods are effectively and efficiently deployed to increase manufacturing and service system productivity. These benefits often include lower operational transaction costs, lower cycle times, and higher quality levels. However, this may not always be true if a project team must rework software, and other product or service attributes. Estimates of the additional project costs associated with extra rework range up to 30 percent or more of a project's budget. Therefore, a major goal of this book has been to show useful tools and methods that will enable a Lean IT team to avoid many of the problems associated with the project management of IT projects. APM with scrum and Lean methods can help. However, to the extent that a Lean IT project team correctly executes its work activities, then the published literature cites significant business benefits. Relative to enterprise resource planning (ERP) systems these benefits include indirect labor reductions of more than 60 percent, material cost reductions exceeding 40 percent, quality improvements in yield of more than 40 percent, raw material reductions of greater than 30 percent, and logistics cost reductions exceeding 30 percent. Benefits for Manufacturing Automation Protocol (MAP) systems include 50 percent yield improvements,

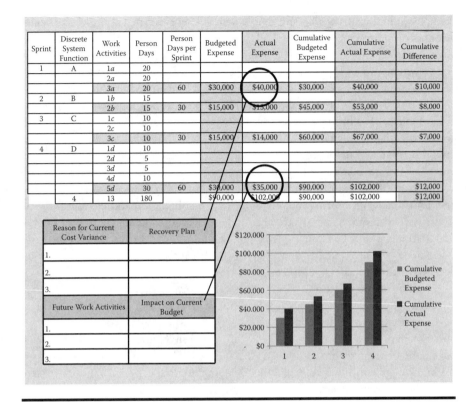

Sprint	Discrete System Function	Work Activities	Person Days	Person Days per Sprint	Budgeted Expense	Actual Expense	Cumulative Budgeted Expense	Cumulative Actual Expense	Cumulative Difference
1	A	1a	20						
		2a	20						
		3a	20	60	$30,000	$40,000	$30,000	$40,000	$10,000
2	B	1b	15						
		2b	15	30	$15,000	$13,000	$45,000	$53,000	$8,000
3	C	1c	10						
		2c	10						
		3c	10	30	$15,000	$14,000	$60,000	$67,000	$7,000
4	D	1d	10						
		2d	5						
		3d	5						
		4d	10						
		5d	30	60	$30,000	$35,000	$90,000	$102,000	$12,000
	4	13	180		$90,000	$102,000	$90,000	$102,000	$12,000

Reason for Current Cost Variance	Recovery Plan
1.	
2.	
3.	

Future Work Activities	Impact on Current Budget
1.	
2.	
3.	

Figure 8.14 Creating a cost dashboard for a project team. (Similar to Figure 5.9.)

50 percent direct labor reductions, 15–25 percent throughput increases, and 40–80 percent cycle time reductions.

Summary

Measuring and improving the performance of Lean IT teams, as well as the systems they create and modify, are important productivity drivers within an organization. The ability of a Lean IT team to successfully complete its product design and project management activities depends on the interdependence of IT governance, various governmental and industry standards, performance metrics and dashboards, and measuring and improving the performance of project work activities and key design attributes. For example, a Lean IT team cannot function in an organizational vacuum. As a result strategic alignment, accurate requirements and supporting resources are critical to its success. There may also be structural barriers that inhibit the ability of a Lean IT team to complete its project activities. As an example, in highly structured and rigidly controlled organizations there may be little opportunity to employ the methods associated with APM with scrum, or Lean. Team communication may also be adversely impacted depending on the organization's approach to its IT governance. In their book *IT Governance*, Weill and Ross describe several common IT governance models. These range from higher-level and highly structured organizational control of IT resources and projects to local control of IT resources at a business-unit level. In fact, in some organizations there may be no control at all (i.e., anarchy). As a result of these realities, IT governance models should be matched to an organization's strategic goals and objectives in a way that maximizes value to an organization. Examples include creating economies of scale, minimizing total organizational cost, process standardization across several business units, sharing information, enabling new technologies, and ensuring digital security. In summary, IT governance models must also match specific organizational strategic and tactical needs. Organizations must continually review their asset management strategies and analyze the advantages of centralization versus decentralization of assets, resources, and knowledge.

Industry standards are also critical to the measurement, management, and improvement of IT systems because creating hardware and software that cannot be integrated with other commercial systems could result in their immediate obsolescence. As an example, a significant amount of industry-specific knowledge is incorporated into an industry's standards. This type of relevant and useful knowledge continues to expand as industry experts, suppliers, and customers update it. Helping to create and then adopt industry standards provides a competitive advantage to participating organizations. Finally, creating metrics to effectively and efficiently manage a Lean IT project team and capture customer and key stakeholder requirements will help an organization to measure, manage, and improve its operational performance. When metrics are incorporated into metric dashboards and linked to their underlying data structures, then monitoring, controlling, and improving process performance is easier and more sustainable.

Suggested Reading

Behr, Kevin, Gene Kim, and George Spafford. 2007. *The Visible OPS Handbook*, rev. 1st ed. Eugene, OR: IT Process Institute, Inc.

Dunn, Robert H., and Richard S. Ullman 1994. *TQM for Computer Software*, 2nd ed. New York: McGraw-Hill.

Goldratt, Eliyahu M., and Jeff Cox. 1992. *The Goal: A Process of Ongoing Improvement*, 2nd rev. ed. Great Barrington, MA: North River Press.

Martin, James William. 2007. *Lean Six Sigma for Supply Chain Management: The 10-Step Solution Process*. New York: McGraw-Hill.

Martin, James William. 2008. *Operational Excellence: Using Lean Six Sigma to Translate Customer Value through Global Supply Chains*. Boca Raton, FL: Auerbach.

Martin, James William. 2009. *Lean Six Sigma for the Office*. Boca Raton, FL: CRC Press.

Steinberg, Rodney A. 2006. *Measuring ITIL®: Measuring, Reporting and Modeling the IT Service Management Metrics That Matter Most to IT Senior Executives*. Victoria, British Columbia: Trafford Publishing.

Weill, Peter, and Jeanne W. Ross. 2004. *IT Governance: How Top Performers Manage IT Decisions Rights for Super Results*. Boston: Harvard Business School Press.

Conclusion

Vision is the art of seeing the invisible.

—Jonathan Swift

When my editor, the late Raymond O'Connell, asked me to write this book, he mentioned that there was a gap regarding the use of information technology (IT) in Lean systems. As I planned to write the book, I looked at this gap from two perspectives. First, given that an IT project was deployed in a Lean environment, how should it be managed? Second, if Lean practitioners were asked to join these IT teams, what basic information would they need to be useful team members? In other words, how could their Lean expertise be useful to their team? As I did research for this book, it became immediately apparent that IT professionals have been working for several decades to create unique project management tools and methods to accelerate software creation and deployment. Although I already knew that such methods existed, I did not know their origin or extent of usage. This became apparent through research for this book. For example, I had the privilege to work with several Agile Project Management (APM) and scrum experts at C.C. Pace Systems in Fairfax, Virginia. These people included Tiran Dagan, who is currently the east coast director for NBC Universal's Strategic Initiatives and Analysis, as well as Arlen Bankston and Sanjiv Augustine, now partners in Lithe Speed, LLC.

With these thoughts in mind, this book was written to provide Lean practitioners with an introduction to the basic concepts, tools, and methods IT practitioners have developed to manage their projects and develop software systems. This subject is important because production systems rely to an increasing degree on IT systems. Everyone knows this, but my point is that IT within Lean systems could be more efficiently deployed using tools and methods from both approaches. This has been true for manufacturing systems for a long time, but it is especially true for service systems. Because Lean practitioners will invariably participate in IT projects to automate their processes, it is important that they understand the similarities as well as differences between IT and Lean project management and software design as they impact Lean operations. This information is also important

221

from the perspective that process workflows have become increasingly global in nature. As a result, it is important to understand how to create, measure, and improve process workflows using leading-edge methods. In the absence of effective measurement baselines, as mentioned in earlier chapters, process improvements are difficult to initiate and sustain over time.

It was also shown that IT applications can make Lean systems more flexible and easy to reconfigure. This enables them to more closely match customer needs and value expectations when they change. In this context, it was shown that IT systems can greatly enhance the performance of Lean systems. For instance, in Chapter 7, the deployment of hybrid MRPII and Quick Response Manufacturing (QRM) were shown to facilitate the control of manufacturing schedules by local work teams. Lean principles can also greatly accelerate the completion of IT projects by creating simple, standardized, and mistake-proofed software systems. Several examples of APM with scrum were discussed in the context of IT project management. Recall that APM and scrum events had much in common with Lean's kaizen events. At its most basic level, this book attempts to provide practical advice on the concepts, tools, and methods that have been shown to reduce process waste, to manage software projects as well as promote the design of more efficient software code with a view toward process improvements within Lean systems.

In process improvement it is important to differentiate between the two concepts of effectiveness and efficiency. Effectiveness is defined as doing the right work, and efficiency is doing the right work the right way. Effectiveness implies that we understand customers' needs and value expectations, and translate these into product and service specifications. Efficiency implies that we are using the best-in-class tools and methods to execute these translation activities. In my opinion, the application of IT to Lean systems is still in its infancy because current global supply chains differ greatly relative to their degree of effectiveness and efficiency. In this spirit, this book attempts to link the concepts, tools, and methods of project management, the efficient development of software code, and the application of both to improve the effectiveness and efficiency of Lean systems using IT. For example, IT systems should automate manual work tasks in a way that increases their flexibility to respond to external demand or variations in the availability of resources. Ideally, software should also be easy to reconfigure as product and service requirements change. APM with scrum was shown to be particularly useful in facilitating the design of software using APM with scrum sprints, as well as in creating simple and standardized approaches to IT project management with customers and stakeholders. It's an exciting concept that modifications to existing IT systems can be used to increase the productivity of Lean systems. This is particularly true in manufacturing systems having a heavy investment in IT infrastructure or a large number of diverse products.

In Chapter 1, we discussed the fact that IT project management methods have evolved to use combinations of several project management methodologies. This book focuses on two critical management approaches: IBM®'s Rational Unified

Process (RUP), which is designed to manage large and complicated projects, and APM with scrum to manage smaller projects including modifications to existing IT infrastructure using scrum sprints. Several important project management tools and methods were also discussed, including a requirements analysis, a work breakdown structure (WBS), Gantt charts, team facilitation tools, and scrum sprint activity backlogs. It was shown in Chapter 2 that an essential element of APM during each scrum sprint was creating products and services having simple, standardized, and mistake-proofed characteristics. Chapter 3 discussed several effective change-management tools and methods, which included project charters, clarification of team authority, an analysis of stakeholder resistance, organizational structures, and project risks and issues. In Chapter 4, the discussion focused on the accurate translation of customer requirements to design products and services. It was shown that these translation activities begin by classifying customers into market segments and then identifying their Kano needs and value expectations. This information was further translated into customer requirements and finally into product or service specifications for prioritization by an APM with scrum team using an activity backlog. Requirements were then prioritized and organized into scrum sprints to design and deliver discrete functions and features. Prioritization tools, such as the analytical hierarchy process (AHP) and Pugh matrix, were also discussed in the context of quality function deployment (QFD). In Chapter 5, the discussion focused on basic Lean tools and methods using an activity backlog and scrum sprints. In Chapter 6, several important principles of software design were discussed from a Lean practitioner perspective to show similarities between the efficient design of software and Lean concepts, tools, and methods. For example, it was shown that the basic concepts of accurate translation of customer and stakeholder requirements and the design of simple, standardized, and mistake-proofed systems had direct applications to IT systems. Major IT applications were discussed in Chapter 7. Chapter 8 discussed measuring and improving the management of Lean IT teams as well as hardware and software systems to increase organizational productivity. This discussion focused on IT governance, and governmental and industry standards. Metric dashboards were shown to be useful in creating integrated metrics to help an organization to measure and improve its performance.

In conclusion, I have found that there is often little synergy between an organization's IT systems and deployment of Lean operations. In other words, Lean systems are often unplugged from IT systems. However, a more useful operational strategy is to intelligently deploy IT to simplify, standardize, and integrate the hardware and software components of disparate IT and Lean systems to enable dynamic responses to changes in customer requirements and capacity constraints to increase the value-adding (VA) content of process workflows.

Glossary

5S techniques: Lean techniques that encourage local work teams to sort, set in order, shine, standardize, and sustain their workplace.

Activation: Using a resource only when it is needed.

Activity backlog: Project activities that need to be completed by a scrum team.

Actual versus planned service level target: A comparison between the actual percentages of time that a feature or function will perform under expected use conditions (availability).

Advanced shipping notification (ASN): An integrated system that allows customers and suppliers to know all the items making up an order by their pallet and vehicle using bar-code scanning. A prerequisite is a supplier certification program.

Agile Project Management (APM): A project management system based on Lean concepts and used to develop software products.

All-pairs testing: Inputs are tested pairwise in combination for their effect on an algorithm and the defects created by the combination.

Alpha testing: Testing focused on evaluation of software by a few users.

Analysis of collected data: The process of applying analytical tools to understand data relationships to obtain information.

Application programming interface (API): The software used to transfer data between different manufacturing systems.

As-is map: A graphical depiction of a process, which is usually quantified and created by "walking the process."

Assessment: A methodology for evaluating process performance.

Asset efficiency: Asset efficiency (or turnover) is calculated by dividing the total sales revenue (or COGS) by the total asset investment necessary to obtain these sales for the time under analysis. Asset efficiency is an important metric to measure the degree of supply chain "leanness." Lean supply chains have high asset efficiencies relative to their competitors.

Asset utilization efficiency (plant, equipment, and other invested capital): Usually measured as "turns." Turns is the average monthly value (cost) of an asset divided by the cost of goods sold (COGS).

Availability: Availability = Reliability + Maintainability

Balance sheet: A financial statement that records assets and liabilities.

Basic need: One of the three types of Kano needs. Customers expect a basic need to be met by all suppliers.

Batch and queue system: A system in which production is moved using discrete lots.

Benchmarking: A system of tools, methods, and techniques that compare the performance attributes of one system to another.

Beta testing: Beta testing expands the user evaluation population to gain higher confidence that software will function as expected under a larger set of actual usage conditions.

Black-box testing: Occurs when software is tested without an understanding of its internal functioning.

Bottleneck management: The process of ensuring a system bottleneck is utilized to meet the takt time without disruption.

Boundary value analysis: Tests of algorithms where the inputs are near (either at or outside) their minimum and maximum levels.

Budget variance: A difference between a budgeted amount and actual.

Business Activity Monitoring (BAM): Decision rules applied to a system to monitor its status and notify users when it is not performing up to standards. Integral to BAM is the establishment of a stable process workflow and metrics.

Business intelligence (BI): Tools and methods used to collect and analyze data across disparate sources with an emphasis of identifying patterns.

Business metrics: A measure of performance used to provide information to manage or improve a process. These metrics can be aggregated across an organization.

Business process management suite (BPMS): Integrates several information technology systems to improve supply-chain coordination within an enterprise resource planning environment.

Business process modeling and analysis (BMA): Tools and methods that create a graphical representation of a process workflow and that layer process rules and specifications to estimate system metrics related to time, cost, and quality to determine an optimum system configuration.

Business value added (BVA): Operations not valued by the external customer but necessary to meet their requirements.

Capability Maturity Model Integration (CMMI)®: Consists of five information technology (IT) maturity levels: initial, repeatable, defined, managed, and optimized.

Capacity: The amount of material or information that can be put through a system in a unit amount of time.

Capacity constrained resource: A resource that can become a bottleneck if process conditions change.

Capacity requirements planning (CRP): A system which uses MRPII information related to open and current manufacturing orders as well as routings and time standards to estimate required labor and machine time across facilities.

Cash flow statement: A financial statement that estimates the amount of free or available cash by time period.

Cash to cash cycle: The cycle time between paying for material, labor, and other expenses, and receipt of payment from the customer.

Champion: A person who removes project barriers.

Concept to market cycle time: The time difference between when a product is made available for customer purchase and the start of its design.

Configuration management planning: Management of specifications including features and attributes, revision control, and the roles and responsibilities of team members; and conducts audits.

Continuous flow system: A process workflow where there are no discrete units, such as oil refining.

Continuous improvement: Process improvement activities deployed over an extended time.

Control strategies: Combining various control tools to ensure process improvements are sustained over time.

Corrective maintenance: Maintenance applied after equipment has failed.

Cost avoidance: A potential cost to an organization that will occur if not prevented.

Cost per configuration item (CI): The total configuration cost divided by the number of CIs to create an average of the total cost recorded for each type of CI.

Cost per service issue: The monetary amount required to record, analyze, and fully resolve an issue related to software features and functions. The cost may consist of direct labor and materials as well as overhead expenses.

Cultural change: A situation in which an organization begins to practice one or more new behaviors.

Cultural survey: A method that asks employees their opinion of their organization's strengths, weaknesses, external threats, and opportunities.

Current map: A graphical representation of a process as it currently exists.

Customer service target: Service-level targets that can be defined from several perspectives, such as on-time delivery.

Customer value: Cost, time, function, utility, and importance of a product or service as perceived by a customer.

Data analysis: Various tools and methods designed to create information to answer questions from data.

Data collection: The process of bringing people and systems together to obtain information from a process.

Defect waste: Work that does not meet requirements and must be redone, wasting time and money, and in some situations reducing customer satisfaction.

Demand pull: The scheduling process in which actual customer demand is used to schedule upstream work operations.

Demand push: The scheduling process in which forecasted demand is used to schedule work operations.

Dependent demand: Demand related to independent demand through a bill of material (BOM).

Design failure mode and effects analysis (DFMEA): A tool and related methods used to identify how a design can fail to meet requirements and the causes of this failure.

Design standards: Information used to ensure designs meet minimum accepted standards related to fit, form, and function.

Direct labor: An expense component on the profit and loss statement representing the cost of hourly labor.

Disaggregating: The process of breaking a larger workflow system into components for insourcing or outsourcing.

Distribution requirements planning (DRP): A system that replenishes inventory at branch locations throughout a distribution network using a time-phased order point for every item and location to translate planned orders via MRPII to suppliers.

Diverse team: A group of people brought together to work a project and having diverse viewpoints, skills, or demographics.

Ease of use: Software that can be accessed and understood, and whose commands can be executed without additional work activities that exceed its original design intent.

Economic value added (EVA): The income shareholders receive for their investment in an organization.

Effectiveness: A situation in which the right things are being done.

Efficiency: A situation in which the right things are being done in the best way.

Electronic data interchange (EDI): An electronic system that enables IT systems to exchange information between organizations.

Enterprise application integration (EAI): A system that integrates several supply-chain functions and their IT interfaces using just one interface through intelligent routing of data.

Enterprise information system (EIS): Separate software systems that manage specific protons of a supply chain.

Enterprise resource planning (ERP): A more sophisticated version of an MRPII system that includes accounting-related information, as well as the resources needed to plan, manufacture, and ship customer orders.

Equivalence partitioning: Using the minimum number of tests to evaluate an algorithm by dividing the range of an input so that invalid and valid levels are chosen for testing.

Excitement need: One of the three types of Kano needs.

Failure modes and effects analysis (FMEA): An analytical tool that shows the relationship of failure modes to causes, and evaluates their risk levels.

Fault injection: The intentional introduction of known coding errors (faults) to test software code. An important application is testing algorithms under conditions that are not typical.

Financial justification: The process of developing financial estimates of project benefits.

Financial metric: A project metric that shows cost savings, revenue increases, or cash flow increases if successful.

First time yield (FTY): Production that meets requirements without having been reworked or made up, that is, if 100 units go into an operation and 10 are scrapped and 5 are reworked, then FTY = 85/100 = 0.85.

Fixed asset efficiency: Fixed Asset Efficiency (Turns) = Sales/(Average Property + Plant + Equipment).

Force-field analysis: A method used to analyze barriers to the countermeasures that are necessary to eliminate root causes of process breakdowns.

Forecast accuracy: Poor forecasting accuracy results in too much or too little inventory. There are many reasons for poor accuracy.

Forecasting system: A system that uses historical demand to create forecasting models to predict future demand.

Forming stage: The first stage in a team maturation process.

Functional interface: The handoff between organization functions.

Functional process map: A detailed process map showing all process operations by their function and sequence.

Functional silos: Different departments or work areas within an organization having different responsibilities and work tasks.

Functionality: How a product or service performs.

Fuzz testing: Simulated data representing the full input specification range of an application is run through an algorithm to detect defects.

Gantt chart: A chart that shows the start and finish times of work tasks in a project.

Gross margin: The profit before taxes calculated by subtracting cost of goods sold (COGS) from revenue minus adjustments.

Gross Margin Return on Investment (GMROI): Gross Margin/Average Inventory Investment at Cost.

Group think: A situation in which team members consistently agree with one another even if their decisions are incorrect.

High-performance work team: A diverse team that has been through all four maturation stages and consistently achieves its objectives.

IBM® Rational Unified Process (RUP): A highly structured project management method consisting of inception, elaboration, construction, and transition phases.

Income statement: A financial statement that records income and expenses by time period.

Independent demand: Direct external customer demand for products or services.

Indirect labor: Labor not used to produce a product or provide a service.

Information technology (IT) governance: A set of strategies and tactics designed to identify an organization's IT requirements and ensure that these requirements are integrated into its strategic goals and objectives at all organizational levels.

Inventory efficiency (turns): The number of times that an inventory "turns over" during a year is calculated as the ratio of annualized cost of goods sold (COGS) divided by monthly average inventory investment.

Inventory investment: The amount of money invested in inventory.

Just-in-time (JIT): A Lean system in which material or information arrives when needed and in the required quantity.

Kano needs: A system that classifies customer needs into basic, performance, and excitement needs.

L-shaped work cell: A work-cell layout arranged as an L.

Labor hours per release: The number of hours required to create or modify a software system or to deliver a discrete number of features and functions.

Lead time: The time required to perform a single operation or series of operations in a network.

Lead-time analysis: The process of decomposing lead time into its time elements.

Lead-time elements: Lead time can be broken into transportation, setup, waiting, processing, inspection, idle time, and other time elements.

Lead-time reduction: The process of reducing non-value-adding time within a process.

Lean: A system designed to create simple, standardized, and mistake-proof processes based on customer value.

Lean enterprise: An organization that exhibits Lean principles.

Lean performance measurements: A series of operational and financial metrics that can be used to evaluate the effectiveness of a Lean system.

Lean supply chain: A supply chain that uses a minimum amount of resources to satisfy customer requirements.

Lean tenets: Stable demand, operational stability, and continuous improvement.

Library control: Software code creation and revision control.

Maintainability: Maintainability = Preventive Maintenance + Corrective Maintenance.

Manufacturing Automation Protocol (MAP): A system based on International Standards Organization (ISO), which enables communication between systems from different organizations. It depends on ISO's Open Systems Interconnection (OSI) standards.

Manufacturing resource planning II (MRPII): A system that integrates functions related to sales and operations planning, master production plans, material requirements planning, and capacity planning.

Master production schedule (MPS): A system that uses the sales forecast and order book demand, gross capacity, and on-hand inventory manufacturing planning to develop a "netted" manufacturing schedule.

Material availability: Material that can be used for production.

Metric: A measure of performance.

Metric dashboard: A graphical tool used to collect information on several metrics to provide integrated information for a process.

Metric dashboards: A series of visual and graphical displays that link lower- to higher-level metrics based on known relationships between them.

Mistake-proofing: A system of tools and methods that prevents or detects errors and their defects.

Mixed-model scheduling: A scheduling system that allows more frequent scheduling of products or services using lower-cost setups.

Model-based testing: Developing functional tests based on abstractions of an application model.

Mutation testing: Making small modifications to source code to mimic known user errors.

National Institute of Standards (NIS): United States Government agency that creates and manages standards.

Net Operating Profit After Taxes (NOPAT): Net operating profit after taxes is calculated by dividing income after taxes by total revenue.

Net Promoter Score (NPS): Defined as (% Promoters – % Detractors) with % neutral not used in the calculation.

Number and percentage of configuration item changes: A record of the counts related to a request to change a feature or function. When volume is adjusted, a percentage can be created.

Number and percentage of failures caused by inaccurate configuration items: A count of inaccurate errors caused by configuration requests. The assumption is that configuration items have been formally recorded prior to making a change. When these failures have been volume adjusted, percentages can be calculated.

Object Management Group (OMG): An organization that develops standardized criteria for software evaluation to enable industry participants to interact in a fact-based manner.

On-time supplier delivery: A supplier's on-time delivery performance is calculated based on an agreed upon versus actual delivery time. There could be several variations of the metric.

Operation: A combination of several work tasks that provides similar work within a process workflow.

Operational balancing: Every operation in a system is modified to contribute material or information at a rate necessary to maintain the system's takt time.

Operational efficiency: How well a system functions relative to a target of 100 percent.

Operational excellence: An umbrella initiative including Lean, Six Sigma, and Total Productive Maintenance (TPM).

Operational linkage: Ensuring an operational metric is consistent across functional boundaries.

Operational metrics: Metrics other than financial that indicate process status relative to time, performance, or quality.

Optimum map: A process map containing only value-adding operational work tasks.

Overdue backlogs: Products or services that have been promised to customers, but not delivered on schedule.

Overproduction waste: Materials or information produced in advance of requirements that are not needed.

Percentage of value adding to total work time: [(Processing Time)/(Setup Time + Inspection Time + Waiting Time + Transport Time + Time to Make Up Work, i.e., Rework and Scrap)] × 100.

Performance gap: The difference between target and actual performance.

Performance metrics: Measures related to time, cost, quality, or other categories used to monitor, control, and improve processes.

Performance need: A Kano need that differentiates one supplier from another.

Performing stage: The fourth stage in a team maturation process in which a team works for common goals and objectives.

Pilot of solution: A test of a proposed process change under controlled conditions.

Preventive maintenance: A system of tools, methods, and concepts designed to ensure equipment is available for use.

Problem statement: A verbal description of the operational problem that must be solved by the project.

Process mapping: A method used to show the movement of materials and information through a system.

Process workflow: A set of operational work activities coordinated to produce products or services.

Product life cycle: The demand phases that a product moves through over time, including its introduction, growth, maturity, and decline.

Productivity: A year-over-year measure of outputs divided by inputs.

Profit and loss statement (PL): Summarizes an organization's revenues and expenses for a specific time period. Expenses on the PL are costs incurred in the course of business operations.

Profit margin: Profit Margin = Gross Profit/Sales.

Profitability index: The ratio of present value of cash inflow to present value of cash outflow.

Project activity: A group of project work tasks that have starting and ending dates and consume resources.

Project charter: A document that describes and authorizes a project.

Project evaluation and review technique (PERT): A project management tool that shows work activity relationships, their expected completion times with probabilities, and the network's critical path.

Project identification: A process of identifying projects to increase organizational productivity, customer and stakeholder satisfaction, or other business objectives.

Project management: A set of tools and techniques used to manage a project's resources to meet schedule, cost, and performance objectives.

Project metric: A metric used to measure project success, and correlates to financial and business metrics.

Project milestone: A major set of project activities used to monitor project schedule completion.

Project objective: A section of a project charter that states the specific purpose and benefits of the project.

Project plan: A combination of work tasks and resources brought together to achieve a project's schedule, cost, and performance objectives.

Project resources: Materials, labor, money, and information necessary to complete the project.

Project selection: The process of identifying work to benefit a business and customers.

Prototype phase: A phase in product development in which samples or prototypes are created for test and evaluation.

Pugh matrix: A tool that enables several design alternatives to be compared against a baseline design.

Pull scheduling: A scheduling system in which the system produces according to external customer demand.

Push scheduling: A scheduling system that uses a forecast through the master production schedule to schedule orders.

Quality control plan: Documentation describing important product features which must be controlled when designing or producing a product or service.

Quality Function Deployment (QFD): A system of tools and methods used to translate the VOC and VOB into internal specifications.

Receivables efficiency: Receivables Efficiency (Turns) = Net Credit Sales/Average Accounts Receivables.

Reliability: A system available for use at a predetermined probability level.

Return on assets (ROA): Return on Assets = Net Profit Margin × Asset Efficiency.

Return on investment (ROI): Net income divided by the assets used to create the income.

Reusability: Software subcomponents that can be used with little or no modification to build other software systems.

Rework: A situation occurring when something must be done more than once due to defects.

S-shaped work cell: A work-cell layout arranged as an S.

Schedule changes: Schedule changes are the result of unplanned orders, process changes, or unforeseen circumstances that impact a production schedule.

Scrum sprint: A set of project activities that create discrete features and functions at frequent intervals, which an Agile Project Management (APM) team, customers, and key stakeholders review.

Seven forms of process waste: Overproduction, waiting, transportation, inventory, unnecessary processing, unnecessary motion, and defect waste.

Should be map: Graphical depictions of a process without its non-value-adding (NVA) work operations.

Standard operating procedure (SOP): Procedures that are the best way to do a job.

Storming stage: The second stage of the team maturation process in which a team disagrees on a project's goals and objectives due in part to the team's diversity.

Strategic flowdown: A method used to ensure alignment of strategic goals and objectives throughout an organization.

Strategic project selection: The processes of ensuring projects are selected to align with senior management's goals and objectives.

SWOT analysis: Strengths, weaknesses, opportunities, and threats to an organization.

Takt time: The time in which one unit must be produced to meet a production schedule tied to external customer demand.

Target costing: Determining the price at which a product or service will sell and then subtracting its required profit margin.

Throughput: The cycle time between paying for materials, labor, and other production expenses, and receipt of payment from a customer.

Time to resolve a configuration issue: A record of how long it takes to receive, investigate, and fully resolve a CI issue.

Time to resolve a service issue: A record of how long it takes to receive, investigate, and fully resolve a service issue.

Traceability matrix: Using a two-way matrix to map one set of requirements into a second set.

Transfer batch: A system that moves a unit of production immediately to the next downstream operation.

Transportation waste: Information or materials unnecessarily moved through several operations.

U-shaped work cell: A work-cell layout arranged as a U.

Unnecessary motion waste: Using a higher number of work elements than the best method requires.

Unnecessary processing waste: Adding nonessential design or service features to a product or service, or work operations that are non-value adding (NVA).

Use case actors: The functions and objects making up a use case.

Use cases: A simple and easy to understand description of what a system will provide to its users. Use cases consist of a combination of graphical representations of a system with higher-level requirements, and functions and objects.

Value-adding operations (VA): Operations a customer needs and values in a product or service.

Value elements: These consist of time, price, utility, function, and relative importance to a customer.

Value stream mapping (VSM): A process of mapping material and information flow through a process and classifying work operations into three categories of non-value adding (NVA), value adding (VA), and business value adding (BVA).

Visual controls: A control system using graphical and electronic displays to show the status of a process.

Visual displays: Graphics used to convey system status.

Visual workplace: A workplace in which system status can be immediately seen by looking at visual metric displays.

Voice of the business (VOB): Key stakeholder requirements.

Voice of the customer (VOC): Customer requirements.

Waiting waste: Work operations that are unnecessarily idle.

Warehouse management system (WMS): A system that dynamically manages received materials and components, and assigns an inventory storage location. More advanced versions of these systems enable efficient order fulfillment and cycle counting activities.

White-box testing: Software is tested with knowledge of its algorithms, software, code and data structures.

Work breakdown structure (WBS): A method used to breakdown project activities into discrete work activities and tasks.

Work element: A component of a work task consisting of a single action such as picking up a form, adding information to its data fields, or sending it to a subsequent operation.

Work task: A combination of work elements that are organized to provide a single unit of work, such as completing a form, answering a request for information, providing a report, and similar tasks.

Workflow management (WM): Tools and methods that enable process workflows to be analyzed to create alternative process designs.

Appendix: List of Figures and Tables

Introduction

Chapter 1

Chapter 2

Chapter 3

Chapter 4

Chapter 5

Chapter 6

Chapter 7

Chapter 8

Index